YOUR FINANCIAL GUIDE

▶ *Advice*
for Every
Stage
of Your
Life

▶ **RAY MARTIN**

**& THE FINANCIAL PLANNERS
OF THE AYCO COMPANY**

MACMILLAN SPECTRUM
AN IMPRINT OF
MACMILLAN • USA

MACMILLAN
A Simon & Schuster Macmillan Company
1633 Broadway
New York, NY 10019

Library of Congress Cataloging Card Number: 96–068549

ISBN: 0-02-861114-4

Interpretation of the printing code: the rightmost number of the first series of numbers is the year of the book's printing; the rightmost number of the second series of numbers is the number of the book's printing. For example, a printing code of 96-1 shows that the first printing occurred in 1996.

Book design by A & D Howell

Printed in the United States of America
9 8 7 6 5 4 3 2 1

Publisher's Note: Every care has been taken in the preparation of the test to ensure its clarity and accuracy. Readers are cautioned, however, that this book is sold with the understanding that the Publisher is not engaged in rendering legal, accounting, or other professional service. Readers with specific financial problems are urged to seek the professional advice of an accountant or lawyer.

CONTENTS

▼

INTRODUCTION

▼

ALL ABOUT THE AYCO COMPANY, L.P.

Chances are that you've never heard of The Ayco Company. That's understandable; Ayco doesn't advertise, so it's not exactly a household name. But corporate America has heard: Ayco has more than 6,000 financial counseling clients—including CEOs, chairwomen and men, and top-level executives—at about 200 corporations, most of them Fortune 100 and Fortune 500 firms.

And Ayco provides financial planning advice to literally hundreds of thousands of corporate employees and their families each year through its broad-based seminar, education and counseling programs such as *Money in Motion,® RetireRight,™* and the *SurvivorSupport®* Financial Counseling Service.

Why does corporate America hire Ayco to guide its employees? Because Ayco is the nation's oldest and largest fee-based financial planning firm, with more than 400 employees, including a professional planning staff of more than 100 attorneys, CPAs, and MBAs.

How did Ayco get so big and successful? Founded in 1940 by Bill Aydelotte as a private planning practice, and incorporated by him and Jim Conway in 1971 (Aydelotte and Conway provided the "Ay" and "Co" of the company's name), The Ayco Company's beginnings were modest: a handful of professionals working long hours in rented offices that never quite managed to keep up with the company's growth. The idea of objective, fee-based financial planning was one whose time had come: People were finding that their finances were becoming more and more complex while their free time was becoming more and more scarce. Too often, clients were in the frustrating situation of earning good salaries but having relatively little financial security to show for it. Ayco, which had the answers to these kinds of problems, grew and grew.

In more recent years, under the leadership of co-presidents John Breyo and Barry Hamerling, Ayco has achieved phenomenal success based on its two underlying strengths: unparalleled financial expertise and single-minded dedication to its clients' needs. Ayco's large and well-qualified technical groups (tax and estate experts, employee benefits consultants, investment planners, and financial analysts) produce a steady stream of information and interpretation on complex and fluid issues of law and practice. This output then becomes the basis for objective, unbiased advice, giving Ayco an edge its competitors can't match. Ayco's financial counsel is not tied to commissions on sales of products such as insurance, stocks, or bonds; and most of its financial counselors are attorneys, whose training emphasizes devotion to clients' interests above all else.

"So how can I put these people to work for me?" you're probably thinking. The answer is in your hand. This book makes Ayco's expertise available to the general public—not just the lucky people whose employers provide Ayco's services—for the first time. In effect, Ray Martin has put Ayco—and the accumulated value of more than 25 years of cutting-edge planning experience—at your fingertips.

How did this book come to be written? The story is instructive. Ayco has been a source of authoritative planning information for the media for years, and in September 1994 the *Wall Street Journal* interviewed Ray, a financial counselor and vice president at Ayco, on the topic of how people can get more bang for their bucks. A producer at NBC's *Today* read the article and was impressed. She called the day the article appeared and asked whether Ray could appear on the show to answer some questions from Bryant Gumbel. The rest, as they say, is history.

But although Ray presents Ayco's most public face to millions of morning TV viewers, he'd be the first to tell you that he's only a part of the Ayco story. The Ayco Company is a major force in financial planning, and it's also the sum of the accumulated knowledge, dedication, and integrity of hundreds of professionals with one simple mission: "To help people make decisions and take actions that improve their financial well-being."

Why is it important for people to make decisions and take actions to improve their finances? Because when it comes to our money, all too often we experience what the psychologists call "regret." We miss an opportunity, we fail to plan for contingencies, we slip into debt so deep that we can't easily get out, we get caught short by a life event that turns into a financial disaster. Preventing such disasters—and taking full advantage of opportunities available to the average person to build financial security—is the main goal of this book.

MORE ABOUT AYCO

Ayco offers a wide array of financial planning, along with employee and management benefits services—nationwide. Its headquarters are in Albany, NY, and there are seven fully staffed regional offices: in Atlanta, GA; Dallas, TX; Clifton Park, NY; Florham Park, NJ; Irvine, CA; Lake Forest, IL; and Pittsburgh, PA. The main business units are the following:

FINANCIAL RELATED SERVICES (FRS)

This group provides a full range of company-paid and voluntary education and counseling programs for corporate employees at all levels, at some of America's largest and best-known companies. Its seminar programs include *FastTrack,* which provides financial education and counseling for middle-level managers, and *Investing in Your Future,* based on a comprehensive planning guidebook.

FRS' *Money in Motion*® financial education program includes a range of components: seminars, the toll-free *Ayco AnswerLine,*™ the *Updates* planning newsletter, *RoadMap*® interactive retirement-planning software and nine guidebooks. FRS also publishes *Your Quick-Start Money Guide—Financial Planning for Those Who'd Rather Be Doing Something Else* and *Don't Lose Out! Your Company Savings Plan Is the Key to a Secure Retirement.*

And it offers two other counseling programs:

1. The *SurvivorSupport® Financial Counseling Service,* a uniquely valuable corporate benefit that provides comprehensive and objective financial counseling to survivors of deceased or terminally ill corporate employees, and

2. *RetireRight,*™ a toll-free advisory service that helps employees near retirement make the right pension and benefits decisions at this crucial life juncture.

MANAGEMENT BENEFIT SERVICES (MBS)

This group designs and installs compensation and benefit plans for senior management at hundreds of major corporations. It also provides consulting services. Its Estate Enhancement Program for top executives converts deferred compensation accumulations into tax-free benefits for survivors, at no cost to the sponsoring corporation.

FINANCIAL COUNSELING

This business unit provides comprehensive financial planning and counseling assistance to corporate executives and to high-net-worth individuals such as corporate CEOs and chairmen and women, entrepreneurs, professional athletes, and entertainers.

AYCO ASSET MANAGEMENT

This group manages core stock and bond portfolios, primarily for Ayco clients. It currently has more than $400 million under management.

FOR MORE INFO

If you would like further information about The Ayco Company, L.P., call the Client Relations Department at (800) 437-6382, or write to

The Ayco Company, L.P.
P.O. Box 15073
Albany, NY 12212-5073

FOREWORD

▼

When was the last time you asked for financial advice, searched out financial information, or needed an answer to a financial issue you had to act upon at a particular moment in your life? If you're like most people, you'll remember that there was an event that triggered the need for financial decisions—*a life event.*

Over the last two years, during which I've done more than 30 segments on NBC's *Today,* given hundreds of seminars, and advised thousands of individuals, it has become crystal clear to me that most people are faced with important—even crucial—financial decisions when a life event such as those outlined in this book occurs. And most people react to these events by asking for specific financial answers to the issues they perceive to be most urgent. But while some of these issues jump right out at us, some other very important things are more subtle and are often overlooked. Many of us tend to seek the short answer to our financial needs and move on with our lives instead of taking the time to plan through an event—or consider other important aspects of our personal finances.

It's one of those funny facts of life. By and large, most people would rather read yesterday's newspaper than read a financial planning book or spend a few hours a month learning about and planning their personal finances. *But if you don't do your own financial planning—who will?* There are many excuses, and I've heard them all: "I don't have the time," "I don't have enough money to plan with," "I'll never get ahead, so it doesn't matter," and "It's boring, and yes, I do find yesterday's newspaper more exciting." But today it's more important than ever to get involved with your personal finances.

Here are just a few reasons why:

▶ Companies no longer promise lifetime employment.

▶ Pension plans that promise lifelong retirement pay (defined benefit plans) are declining in number and quality.

▶ Health care choices (HMOs, PPOs, indemnity plans, self-insured plans, and long-term care insurance) are more complex.

▶ There are flexible spending accounts, 401(k)s, 403 (b)s, mutual funds, annuities, and income and estate taxes to deal with.

Not to mention the fact that you're bombarded with financial information from mass-market magazines that are willing to give you and their other million readers the same "personal" investment advice.

It's been my experience that 90 percent of what you need to do can and should be addressed during a life event. In the past, it was quite possible that you could live a lifetime without having to make any special financial plans or without needing to consult a financial planner. But today, it's much more likely that you will need help. And when you're touched by a life event that calls for special plans, this book can offer the specific and practical advice you'll need.

So let this book guide you during those times of excitement, uncertainty, or sorrow. When a life event occurs, this book will offer specific recommendations about what you should do and when you should do it. And remember, this is a reference guide: Each chapter focuses on a specific life event that you may have been through or are going through right now. And each chapter will explain your options, offer advice, and suggest an action plan to help you make those important decisions.

This is a book for all generations and all stages of life—from young graduates fresh out of college, to newlyweds, to parents with newborns, to executives changing jobs, to retirees, and so on. Your personal finances are a part of your life, so there is no separating the two. No matter how old you are, you've got more life events coming at you—more twists and turns. And the more you live life, the more valuable this book will be to you.

How Can You Get the Most Benefit from This Valuable Reference Guide?

Take a look at the life events highlighted in each chapter. Read the ones that apply; you don't have to read the whole book at once. This book is meant to be used a guide for you and your family, so pass it around—or better yet, give a copy to someone who is going through one of life events covered inside. Armed with the right information and sound recommendations, you, your family, and your friends should be able to handle most financial concerns and issues as they arise.

And remember . . . it's your life and your money—nobody cares more about them than you. **If you don't do your own financial planning . . . who will?**

GRADUATING FROM COLLEGE

For college graduates and their parents

Graduating from college is a milestone for both the graduates and their parents: they all begin a new phase of their lives.

If you're the graduating student, you now have new responsibilities. You probably have accumulated thousands of dollars in loans and other debts. So you're full of knowledge related to higher education but what have you learned about personal finance? What do you need to know? Are you aware of the difference between saving and investing? How much money will you need for your retirement? What's the difference between a CD and a Treasury bond? How much debt is too much, and how should you pay it off? In today's world of personal finance, you'll need to know the answers to all these questions and more. If you assume or have been taught that it's all right to be in debt, sorry! Nothing could be further from the truth. Your status in the eyes of the world has changed from being an extension of your parents to being self-sufficient, at least financially speaking. You're no longer a dependent. (But that doesn't mean *all* your ties to your parents are cut.)

If you're a parent, you should recognize that even though your kids are now independent, you will need to provide guidance in dealing with some pressing issues. Parents should also take a moment to consider their role in helping shape their children's views on personal finance. You can help your kids build some fundamental skills; later in this chapter, you'll read about some steps you can take. First, let's look at the issues that college graduates must face.

GRADUATES

After graduating, you face several key concerns:

▶ **Establishing credit in your name.** You're on your own and you want to establish and build a credit history so you can qualify for a loan to buy a car or get an apartment.

▶ **Repayment of student loans.** That's right. It's a bummer, but your loans will no longer be deferred (unless you begin graduate studies) and the banks are going to ask *you* for the loan payments.

▶ **Health insurance.** The day you walk across the stage and you're handed your diploma, you're no longer covered under most insurance plans. Most plans specify that dependent coverage ceases "upon graduation" or when the dependent reaches age 24.

For most of you, getting a job will be your immediate priority. Once you've done that, you'll be in a better position to start dealing with these issues.

EMPLOYEE BENEFITS

Let's suppose that you've found a job. Congratulations! But you shouldn't assume that someone will explain all the details of your benefit package to you. The old days of employers saying "We'll take care of you for life" are gone. You have to get used to the benefits world of the twenty-first century, where you may have to ask several different people, several times to find out what benefits you'll receive. Chances are that you're entitled to health coverage, and your employer may even help you repay your loans, provide tuition assistance for graduate school, or offer a retirement savings plan. You have to ask about these benefits. You may feel intimidated at first, but by starting now, you'll develop great financial habits in the long run.

Here's a guide to taking advantage of the most common employee benefits:

Health Insurance

Fortunately, most companies still provide some form of health coverage for their employees. If you don't have any major health problems, you should take the option with the lowest cost, which is probably a health maintenance organization (HMO). However, if you require a special type of treatment or regularly take certain prescription medicine, then you should ask a benefits counselor to explain each type of coverage in detail, to find out which plan best suits your needs.

If your employer doesn't provide health insurance, you may be able to get individual coverage on your own, at a cost of roughly several hundred dollars monthly. You also may be able to get coverage through a trade association in your industry. Contact your state insurance commissioner's office for a list of insurers in your area who will cover you. If your parents have covered you under their employer's group policy, they should review this coverage. If you're no longer eligible for coverage under this group plan, your parents should notify their employer within 60 days of your graduation that they intend to enroll you in Consolidated Omnibus Reconciliation Act (COBRA) continuation coverage.

COBRA is a government-mandated program that lets employees extend their own or dependent coverage under the group plan for usually up to 18 months, and in some cases for up to 36 months as long as the employees pay the premium. After this 18-month period, the COBRA coverage stops and the dependent must get his or her own insurance.

Savings Plans

If your employer offers a savings or thrift plan, you should start contributing immediately. Parents reading this should encourage their children to contribute at least enough to get a company match and more, if possible, even if the kids are screaming that they can barely live from paycheck to paycheck.

There are several types of company savings plans: 401(k) plans for most corporations, 403(b) plans for nonprofits, and section 457 plans for state and government workers. They all work roughly the same way. You contribute pre-tax dollars (up to a specific amount), and in many cases, your employer matches these contributions (up to 100 percent). You should contribute the minimum required to get the company to match your contribution. The following example illustrates why all new employees should begin taking advantage of these plans immediately.

Suppose that a 25-year-old (Employee A) contributes $1,000 a year ($83.33 per month) to an employer savings plan and the money earns a modest 10 percent a year. After 10 years, his or her account would total $17,070. Even if Employee A stopped making contributions at that point (though I don't recommend doing so), the $17,070 would increase to $338,633 by the time he or she reached age 65. And this figure doesn't take into account any company contributions, which would make the sum even higher!

Employee B, on the other hand, doesn't contribute to the savings plan for the first 10 years and then begins to make $1,000 annual contributions. How many years will this worker have to spend contributing before he or she accumulates as much or more than Employee A? Unfortunately, Employee B can never catch up!

Table 1-1: Impact of Time on Savings

Age	Year	Employee A (started at age 25 and stopped at age 35)		Employee B (waited 10 years and started at age 35)	
		Total Contribution	Balance at 10%	Total Contribution	Balance at 10%
26	1	$1,000	$1,047	$0	$0
35	10	1,000	17,070	0	0
36	11	10,000	18,858	1,000	1,047
65	40	10,000	338,633	30,000	188,374

On a rational level, you probably understand why contributing to a company savings plan is a smart move, but wait a minute, you don't have enough money to start contributing now. After all, you've got loans to repay, your rent, a car payment, and day-to-day living expenses. You also know that you'll have to pay taxes and penalites on any money you take out of the account.

Wait a second, you're getting way ahead of yourself. Why do you care about taxes right now? You can't afford not to contribute. Especially if your employer matches your contributions, it's like getting a free gift. For example, if you put in $100, your employer may match your contribution by 50 percent and in some instances, a full 100 percent. Even if you had to cash out—you'd pay a 10 percent penalty and if you're in the 28 percent tax bracket, you'd pay 28 percent income taxes—you lose just 33 percent to 40 percent of your distribution. Assuming a 50 percent match, you're still getting a 29 percent after-tax return on your money without any risk. Where else can you get this type of return? You can't afford not to get started—and you've got to start saving for retirement someday.

Take a look again at the differences between Employee A and Employee B in the preceding table. Remember, you can start small, contributing less than $20 a week—about the cost of dining out just once.

It's true that your paycheck will be reduced by the after-tax amount you contribute to your company plan. This itself provides you with an invaluable lesson:

 CAUTION   Learn to spend your net pay—what you take home after paying taxes and contributing to your savings plan—not your gross pay.

Most people can spend their gross pay. That's why so many people spend more than they make. Assuming that you can spend your gross pay is a big mistake that will inevitably cause you money worries in the future.

ESTABLISHING YOUR FINANCIAL IDENTITY

Paying off debt should be one of your key financial objectives. But should you pay off your student loans before other loans? First, find out the interest rate on your student loans. Chances are that you'll have to dig out your loan documents or call your bank. You should start repaying your college loans. If you have any credit cards, however, you should look at the interest rates on these cards. Even my wife (who's very bright) made the mistake of starting to make additional payments on graduate school loans before paying off her credit card debt. She felt a sense of urgency to repay the government. Not knowing what interest rate she was paying on the loans, she called the toll-free customer service number listed in her payment book and found out the interest rate was 8.75 percent. The interest rate on her credit card was 18 percent. You do the math—which debt would you repay first? So my wife made the minimum payments on her loan and started to reduce her credit card balances.

Building up debt on credit cards is terrible financial hygiene—like forgetting to brush your teeth. Eventually, you will regret it. While it's tempting to buy things on credit—especially after you've lived so frugally in school—it's the worst thing you can do. The best investment you can make is to pay down on your credit card debt in the first year after you graduate. Look at it this way: Instead of paying 18 percent interest rates to credit card issuers, you're giving yourself an 18 percent after-tax return by paying off the debt.

Sit down and work out a plan to reduce your credit card debt. If necessary, consult a credit counselor or use the Debt Zapper (a service available from the nonprofit Bankcard

Holders of America (540) 389-5445, which will walk you through different repayment scenarios based on the amount of debt you have and your income).

If you're one of the fortunate few who hasn't accumulated wildly high credit card debts, good for you. But that doesn't mean you shouldn't work on your credit. Having no credit record can be worse than having a bad credit record when it comes time to borrow to buy a house or car. For your first credit card, try getting an American Express card. You have to pay off your balance in full every month, so you can't go overboard on your charging. Or get a gasoline card. You can charge only small amounts, and after all, gas is a necessity. After you've paid off this card for several months, you should apply for a widely accepted credit card as a way to build up your financial identity. Remember, though, don't abuse your credit cards. Accumulating credit card debt is a sure way to sabotage your finances for the future.

REPAYING YOUR STUDENT LOANS

You, the student, will be primarily liable for making the payments on your student loans. These loans include the following federal loans:

▶ Stafford (formerly Guaranteed Student Loan Program)

▶ Perkins (formerly National Direct Student Loans)

▶ PLUS (Parent Loans for Undergraduate Students)

▶ SLS (Supplemental Loans for Students)

You can defer repayment under specific conditions, such as the following:

▶ You're studying at a post-secondary school.

▶ You're enrolled in a school run by the federal government.

▶ You're in the Peace Corps.

▶ You are enrolled in specific eligible graduate fellowship programs.

▶ You are temporarily but totally disabled.

▶ Continued repayment would cause undue hardship.

To find out whether you're eligible to defer repayment of your student loan, request the Student Guide from the U.S. Department of Education.

Federal Student Financial Aid Programs
Public Documents, Distribution Center
31451 United Avenue
Pueblo, CO 81009-8109
(202) 708-8391 or (800) 621-3115

Don't assume that you can voluntarily cancel your loan for other reasons, such as bankruptcy. Student loans are generally not dischargeable in bankrupty. If you're thinking of trying to skip out on your loans, you're making a big mistake. Not only will you hurt your chances of building credit, but the government is cracking down on deadbeat borrowers. Defaulters who work for the federal government are subject to partial witholding of their salary until they repay the loan. Even if you work for a private corporation, the U.S. Department of Education can require your employer to deduct 10 percent of your take-home pay. In addition, in the case of either Stafford or Perkins loans, the IRS can withhold income-tax refunds from defaulters for two consecutive years.

RENTING AN APARTMENT OR HOUSE

If you've lived away from home during school, you've learned the basics of getting and keeping your own apartment or house. To rent an apartment, you've got to have money coming in as well as savings. Most landlords want you to be working as assurance that you'll be able to pay the rent. If your name is going on the lease, you'll also need from one to three months' worth of rent as security and deposit. Try to find an apartment near your job, if you live within 10 miles of your job, you may get a deduction on your car insurance.

Before you sign your lease, be sure you understand your rights and obligations as a tenant. Remember that a lease is a binding contract. The laws and regulations governing leases vary from state to state and even from municipality to municipality. If necessary, speak to a real estate lawyer before signing your lease. Make sure you get answers to the following questions *before* you sign a lease:

- ▶ Does the lease have a maximum or minimum term?

- ▶ What is the penalty, if any, if I move out before the end of the lease term?

- ▶ Can I sublet to another tenant?

- ▶ Is a security deposit required? How much? When will I get it back? Will the deposited amount return interest?

► Who pays for which utilities—the landlord or the tenant?

► Is the property "rent-controlled"? That is, is there a legally mandated ceiling on rent charges and periodic increases?

► Can children and pets live in the apartment?

► When can I move in?

► Does the landlord have to paint the apartment before I move in? Most states require this!

► Can I redecorate?

► Do I have to pay to park my car(s)?

► Is the neighborhood safe? Are the premises secure? Is there an alarm system?

► Do I even have to sign a lease? Some landlords don't require a written lease. Generally, a contract still exists without one! Be sure to weigh the freedom of not having a written lease agreement against the protections provided by it: Remember that the lease binds you and the landlord.

You should also consider getting renter's insurance, especially if you have expensive stereo and computer equipment. Renter's policies are relatively inexpensive and protect your belongings against fire and theft. Some policies include personal liability coverage for injuries to others. Call a national property and casualty insurance company or your local insurance broker for quotes on this coverage.

 Your auto insurance company may also provide this coverage or refer you to a company that does.

PARENTS

Parents should be aware that if they cosigned the student loans, they are also considered in default when payments are not made. The bank or government agency that issued the loan will notify credit bureaus of the name and address of both parents and former students. After you finish screaming at your kids and working out a plan for them to repay you, you have to take some steps to protect your own credit rating. You should do the following:

1. Work out repayment terms with your bank.

2. Tell your bank to notify the credit bureau that you've worked out a repayment term. Sign a letter explaining your position and your commitment to repay the loan on time.

GIFTS TO YOUR CHILDREN

There's no reason not to help your kids establish their financial independence, if you can afford to do so. You don't have to provide them with a lot of money; in fact, it's more important that you help them understand the value of money. You should explain that savings and investments are two separate issues.

Savings

Your children should understand that savings is three to six months' worth of living expenses kept on hand as emergency money. You might want to give your children this money and stress that they can use it only if they crash their car or lose their job, not to go on a vacation or buy a new wardrobe. Ask your kids to promise that they'll keep the money in a savings or checking account as a kind of get-out-of-jail pass.

Investments

You can start an investment account with as little as $500 and add to it on a monthly basis. In fact, the money can be deducted automatically from a checking account at a minimum of $25 a month. Tell your children that you'll provide the $500 needed to open the account. If you can afford to, you may also want to match every dollar—for, say, six months—that your child puts into the mutal fund account.

Explain that the money is for long-term goals such as the down payment for a house, or even longer-term goals such as retirement or paying for your kids' kids' college education. Let's say that you put $500 a year into a growth mutual fund for 40 years. If the fund matched the historic rate of the return for the S&P 500, then by the time your 21-year-old reached age 61, he or she would have a nest egg of more than $221,000! That's not a bad return on an investment of $500.

EMERGENCY SOURCES OF CASH

Your kids may need a quick infusion of cash—perhaps if they're traveling or looking for work in another city. If you're able and want to help them out, here are some ways to get them funds quickly:

▶ Western Union credit card transfer (MasterCard and VISA only). You can send up to $2,000 in the U.S. or in 25 other countries. Telephone: (800) 225-5227

▶ American Express MoneyGram. You can send up to $1,000 in the U.S. or 60 other countries. Telephone: (800) 926-9400

▶ ATM transfers, if you share a bank account with your child

▶ Bank wires of money

▶ U.S. Postal Money Order

Your Action Plan

For Parents

▶ Make certain your son or daughter has health coverage when he or she graduates.

▶ Help your child establish a budget that includes a repayment schedule for school loans or credit card debts.

▶ Explain to your children the difference between saving and investing, and help them get started on both.

▶ Encourage your children to make contributions to their company-sponsored savings plans, if available. If not, help them set up and contribute to an IRA.

For Graduates

▶ Start a debt repayment plan.

▶ Establish your own credit now so that you'll have it in the future when you really need it.

▶ Make sure you have health coverage, or make plans to get health insurance.

▶ Learn to live off your net pay, setting aside something from every paycheck.

▶ Enroll and start contributing to any company savings plans. Try to contribute the maximum amount you can.

▶ Establish an emergency savings account and build towards a goal of three to six months' worth of living expenses.

▼

BUYING A CAR

For anyone who is buying a new or used car

Almost everyone has to buy a car at some point. How much do you really know about the process. After all, how hard is it to go into a showroom, kick some tires, and start negotiating with the dealer? In fact, the decision to buy a car is much more complicated. Buying a car is the most expensive purchase you'll make, next to buying a home or financing a college education. And car-related expenses—gas, maintenance, and insurance—can take a big bite out of your wallet.

HOW MUCH CAN YOU AFFORD?

Americans have had a love affair with the automobile for a long time. You probably have vivid memories of your first car or your parents' favorite model. Sorry to disappoint you, but it's time for you to fall out of love with your car and view it as a purchase of something that will be worth 10 to 20 percent less the day you drive it off the lot.

Before you even begin looking for a new car, you must understand two key issues:

1. **Know your limits and what you should be spending.** You may be inclined to take whatever money you have after paying your rent and bills and use this to buy a car. That's not a sound approach. You shouldn't spend more than 10 percent of

11

your gross income on car expenses; this includes the cost of the car along with insurance, gas, and maintenance. For example, if you make $40,000, your car allowance shouldn't be more than $4,000. If your insurance is $600 annually, you can afford to make $3,400 in car payments a year. This would work out to a car loan of $15,000 at 8 percent over five years. You could buy an average-priced car or a great used model. Obviously, if you earn $100,000 or more, you can afford to spend more on your car, but it just doesn't make sense.

2. **Realize that everything is negotiable,** not just the price of the car, but the extras—from the floor mats to the interest rate on your loan to lease payments.

CHOOSING THE RIGHT TYPE OF CAR

Once you know how much you can afford to pay for a car, you have to do some serious thinking about what type of car to buy and what features are important to you. For example, you should know which options you'll really use. If you live in New England, you'll need a back-window defroster. If you park in a city at night, you may not want a fancy CD player that could easily be stolen.

You want to buy a car that you really *need,* not one you simply *want,* and you should evaluate those needs and wants *before* you go to a dealer. Otherwise, a highly trained salesperson may persuade you to buy a car that's not right for you, featurewise or pricewise. Before going to the dealer, you should:

▶ **Look at consumer magazines, such as *Consumer Reports*.** They explain what models are rated best for reliability, maintenance costs, safety, fuel economy, and insurance rates.

▶ **See whether your credit union offers Autofax.** This service provides information on prices, safety records, mileage, and so forth.

▶ **Make a preliminary choice.** Decide on the type and style of car that best suits your needs—and your pocketbook.

▶ **Narrow the field.** Choose specific makes and models in your current price range.

▶ **Decide on the equipment.** What kind of standard equipment and what kind of extras do you want in your new car?

It is also important to get a sense of how much your current car is worth so that you can consider a trade-in offer. There are several ways to find this information:

▶ **Use a used-car price service.** Auto Price Line, (900) 999-2277, is a hotline that gives prices on used cars and trucks in your state. The cost is $1.75 for the first minute plus 75¢ for each additional minute. *Consumer Reports'* Used Car Service, (900) 446-0500 available from 7 A.M. to 2 A.M. EST, seven days a week, charges $1.75 a minute (a typical calls last five minutes) and provides regional resale prices for any 1985 to 1993 vehicle.

▶ **Consult the latest copy of the National Automobile Dealers Association (NADA) monthly** *Official Used Car Guide.* Also known as the Blue Book, it is available at many banks, credit unions, car dealers, and libraries.

▶ **Review** *Edmund's Used Car Guide.* It costs about $5, is published quarterly, and is available on newsstands or by mail from Edmund's, 515 Hempstead Tpk., West Hempstead, NY 11552.

▶ **Check local classifieds.** Look at the advertised prices of similar car models. Remember, though, that you'll have to spend some time and effort if you choose to sell your car privately.

STRATEGIES AT THE DEALER

There was a great *Cosby Show* episode in which Dr. Huxtable was trying to teach his son the best way to buy a car. He told Theo to go to the showroom, kick some tires, and slip the dealer a piece of paper with the price he was prepared to pay. The dealer would then slip him back a piece of paper, and this would go on for a few minutes. The end result, however, was that Dr. Huxtable bought a car at a high price because he was taken in by the salesman's smooth talking.

Now *you're* ready to go to the dealer, and you should know the psychology of salespeople because they certainly know yours. The best thing you can do is show the dealer that you're prepared. Say, "I know what I want to spend, and I want a car with the following options. Let's work out something." If the dealer starts to talk about something else, you should simply say, "You'll need to work within my limits—or I'll have to look elsewhere." Good salespeople will respect and stick with you. If they try to uproot you from your decision, they probably have another agenda. They may be more concerned with getting a bonus or a higher commission for selling you a more expensive car or a leasing arrangement.

Never walk into a car dealer and volunteer what you're able to afford. Once you tell the salesperson a dollar figure, you're far more likely to drive away with a car in the upper range of your budget, whether or not you could have gotten something for less.

Don't make snap decisions, regardless of what the salespeople say about special one-time offers. You're making a significant purchase, and you should definitely wait a minium of 24 hours, although waiting two or three days is even better. There's no deal that's so good you can't wait it out to deliberate.

After you've been to one dealer, you should visit or call several others to get information and compare prices. After all, the price of a car can vary by hundreds of dollars from one dealer to another.

When you call other dealers, pressure them to give you specifics on the phone before you agree to come in. Always ask for the name of the person you talk to, and write down any prices that he or she tells you. And even if you're interested in trading in your current car, *never* commit over the phone to a trade-in deal.

Here are the most important strategies to use at the dealer:

▶ **Find out how much the dealer is paying for models you're interested in.** You can get this information from an industry publication such as the *Kelley Blue Book* and *Automobile Invoice Service,* usually available at local libraries. Or use Prodigy, the on-line service that provides manufacturers' suggested list prices for most cars. Prodigy will also help you calculate monthly purchase or lease payments, find the location of your nearest dealers, and let you order additional information.

As a general rule, the dealer expects to make a profit of 5 or 6 percent over invoice. If you drive a hard bargain, you should be able to get a new car for 3 percent over invoice. You should be bargaining up from the dealer's cost, not down from the sticker price on the car.

▶ **Find out about any incentives or rebates that might lower your cost.** Read the "Incentive Watch" column in the weekly trade publication *Automotive News,* available at libraries and credit unions.

► **Watch out for dealer add-ons.** "Protection packages," "conveyance fees," and "dealer prep" are just a few. Make sure these items are *included* in the negotiated price. Don't fall for dealers who insist that you need features such as rustproofing and fabric conditioning.

► **Ask about last year's models.** Are any still available—at reduced prices?

► **Anticipate your insurance costs.** Consider spending extra for safety features such as an airbag. Some insurance companies will reduce rates in most states by 25 percent for cars with a driver's airbag. Other companies offer similar discounts for passive restraints. Another safety feature worth considering is an anti-lock brake system (ABS).

► **Select the best deal *in your price range.*** You may find that the first couple of choices are priced higher than you can afford, even after you subtract trade-in, rebates, and discounts, so be ready with backup choices. The car you finally select may be your second or third choice, but it may save you hundreds of dollars, even when you include all the equipment you want.

► **Shop near the end of the month.** Before Christmas, or after June are also a good times to look. During the weeks before Christmas, business is usually slow, so you should be able to negotiate a lower price. Also good are January and February and the end of any month, when dealers are often struggling to reach sales quotas. The worst time to buy is from March through June, when people begin planning summer vacations.

► **Take the cash rebate.** If your car dealer offers you a choice between a cash rebate and a low-interest-rate loan, you usually are better off taking the cash rebate. You'll have to check the numbers, but if you apply the rebate to the down payment and get your own loan, you're borrowing less, which could save you hundreds of dollars in interest payments.

► **Ask how long the dealer has been in the same location.** The ideal dealer is one who has been in the same location for at least five or six years. You don't want to buy a car from a fly-by-night operation.

► **Keep all your transactions separate.** Trading in or selling your old car, financing the new car, and negotiating the new car's price are separate decisions. Each should be conducted independently.

▶ **Keep the deal simple.** Don't discuss trade-ins or financing until you have a firm price.

▶ **Be prepared to walk away.** If you don't get the deal you want, don't be afraid to walk away.

Nontraditional Buying Options

Instead of going to a dealer, you can use a car-buying service, of which there are several. Most work the same way: You tell them the exact model and color you want and pay a fee of $150 to $8,000. The service offered through the American Automobile Association (AAA) requires that you be a member (annual fees range from $18 to $65 per year); it collects its $75-per-car fee directly from dealers.

How to Pay for Your Car

Paying for your car with cash is your best move. Chances are, however, that you'll have to take out some type of financing. You have several options:

▶ **Home equity loan.** With a home equity loan, you are borrowing against the value of your home. Not only are interest rates lower than those for auto dealer loans, but the interest on home equity loans is tax deductible. Remember, though, that if you're unable to repay the home equity loan, you're putting your home at risk. You still want your total debt to be no more than 30 percent of your income, so if you're already up to your eyeballs in debt, then you should postpone buying the car in the first place rather than putting your home at risk.

▶ **Private bank loan.** You should shop at your local hometown bank for a car loan. The interest rate will still be lower—possibly as much as one percentage point—than the loan rate available at the car dealer. That's because the bank is holding onto your loan; a dealer will have to hire a financing agency to handle your loan.

▶ **Car dealership.** Borrowing from the dealer where you're buying a car is convenient, and, especially if you're buying your first car, it may be the only way you can borrow money. Generally, car dealers have less restrictive credit requirements than banks do. However, be wary of cut-rate financing deals that dealers frequently push. These attractive 3 percent interest rates may apply only to certain models or short-term loans of up to 12 months.

TERM OF LOAN

Generally, car loans feature terms of two, five, or seven years. The type of loan you choose is determined by how much you can afford to pay per month. The lower the monthly payment, the longer the term of the loan. You also have to consider how long you expect your car to last. If you maintain and provide good upkeep, your car should last for four to five years. Generally, you shouldn't take out a car loan for more than five years, because your car could be falling apart while you're still making payments.

LEASING

Despite all the publicity that car leasing has received lately, leasing is not for everyone. Remember that although you're making payments, you're not buying a car. When you take out a car loan to buy a car, you will, after the term of the loan, probably have your car for several more years, during which you will make no payments. When you lease a car, however, you're always making payments.

But there are some reasons why leasing may be a better option for you. For example, if you use your car for business, you're eligible for certain tax benefits (talk to a tax professional or read IRS publication 917 on leasing autos for business use). And, on occasion, manufacturers offer such attractive lease payments that you may want to consider them.

The key question you should ask before deciding whether to lease is whether you're leasing to drive a car that you otherwise couldn't afford to buy. If you answer "yes," then you probably should not take the lease.

If you can afford the luxury of leasing, however, then you should consider it. After all, it has some advantages:

▶ Minimal down payment and low monthly payments

▶ Convenient maintenance programs

▶ Return of the car at the end of the lease period, with no resale responsibility

▶ Tax savings, because you pay sales tax only on the lease portion, not on the purchase price of the car

The best way to decide whether a lease is a good option is to compare the total cost of each transaction. Make sure you read the fine print of your lease agreement. For example, an otherwise attractive lease may require purchasing expensive insurance from the lessor, or the lessor may add a nonrefundable charge called "capitalized cost reduction" to cover part of the depreciation during the lease term.

There are two types of leases:

1. **Open-end lease.** This gives you the option of buying the car at the end of the lease period for a set price. But if the car is not worth the set price at that time, the open-end lease holds *you* responsible for the difference. If the car is worth more than the set price, the open-end lease may allow you to share in the profit.

2. **Closed-end lease.** With this type of lease, you simple return the car at the end of the lease period. Typically, *closed-end leases are preferable* because they shift the responsibility for the value of the car to the lessor at the end of the lease term. But you have to watch out for additional charges that may be assessed for early terminations. You could get hit with an early-termination charge equal to several months' lease payments, plus "disposition" fees and other charges—even more if the leasing company can't sell the car at its estimated residual value). Plus, you may be assessed for "excessive wear and tear," body damage, or mileage driven above a set limit (usually 15,000 miles per year).

The details of both types of lease may vary considerably. Some companies couple them with a "vehicle-purchase option," also known as a lease with the option to buy. In this situation, the company guarantees to sell you the car at a set price at the end of the lease period. This price is known as the "residual value." If, at the end of the lease period, the car is worth *more* than the predetermined price, you may want to buy it. If it's worth less, you can turn it in.

Leasing a car usually costs more than buying or financing a car. However, if the benefit of the lower monthly payments outweighs the overall added costs, consider the following when shopping for a car you plan to lease:

▶ Know what you want.

    Tell the lessor how you want the car equipped.

    Don't accept options you don't need.

    Decide in advance how long you will keep the car.

▶ Find out how much you are required to pay at delivery.

> Most leases require one month's down payment. Others require a security deposit, registration fees, and other "hidden" costs.

> Make sure price quotes include taxes—sales tax, personal property tax, monthly use tax, or gross receipt tax.

▶ Know the annual mileage limit.

> Most standard contracts allow 15,000 to 18,000 miles per year. Don't accept a contract with a limit lower than you'll need. If you use less than the allowance one year, you may exceed it the next. Find out much you'll be charged for exceeding the mileage limit.

▶ Understand whether you have a "capitalized-cost reduction" or an "equity" lease.

> These leases give you a low monthly payment but defeat the objective of leasing by requiring a higher down payment. By paying more initially, you lose the opportunity to use this money for other purposes such as investing.

▶ Read the terms of the lease carefully.

> Check, for instance, whether you can take the car out of the country without paying extra charges.

> Find out what the financial penalties are for terminating the lease early.

> Ask the dealer exactly what you would owe at the end of each year if you wanted to end the lease before its stated term. Will you be required to buy the car when the lease ends?

> Remember: If your car is stolen, the lease usually will be terminated.

▶ Avoid maintenance contracts.

> Getting work done privately is cheaper in the long run.

> A new car comes with a standard warranty, whether leased or bought.

▶ Arrange for your own insurance, which usually will be less expensive.

▶ Find out in advance about service charges, ranging from $100 to $250, at the end of the lease. You may be able to negotiate these down or out of the lease.

▶ Keep your option to buy the car at the end of the lease at a preset price. Make sure the preset price equals the residual value, which is the car's value after the lease ends. Lease prices generally are based on the manufacturer's suggested retail price, less the preset residual value. The best values are cars with a relatively high expected residual value as a percentage of cost.

To protect themselves, lessors *often underestimate residual value,* so make sure the estimate of the residual value is reasonable. Consult the *Automotive Lease Guide—New Vehicle Edition* or the *ALG Residual Percentage Guide* (published by First National Lease Systems; (805) 563-0777).

▶ Check the lease's terms by shopping with an *independent* leasing company. Look in the Yellow Pages under "Automobile Renting and Leasing."

The "Gap" Trap

Don't buy "gap" insurance, which covers the difference between what your auto insurer would pay if your car were "totaled" and what you would owe the leasing firm. It's just too expensive, and this risk is no different than that faced by a car purchaser who would find that the loan amount on a car might exceed the value of an insurance settlement.

Remember, insurance is best used for a "catastrophic" loss, and many people will conclude that this is a loss they could accept.

The Bottom Line on Leasing

▶ The shrewd consumer often will do better buying a car because he or she usually can negotiate a lower price.

▶ Don't use a lease to drive away more car than you can truly afford.

▶ Don't base your decision on the *monthly payment amount* instead of the total cost—this is always a mistake.

▶ Negotiate the lease terms just as hard as if you were paying cash. If you're not sure about the deal, forget the lease and *pay cash or borrow* instead.

The following simplified example illustrates the difference between leasing and purchasing a car. The worksheet uses certain assumptions, such as the car's purchase price. Leasing firms call this the "capitalized cost." This refers to the price or residual value applied to the car at the end of the lease period.

Worksheet 2A: Leasing or Buying a Car: Which Is Better?

	Lease			Buy	
	Example	Your situation		Example*	Your situation
Security deposit: ($270) Add upfront payment*	Refunded + $1,200	$ _____ + _____	Down payment	$ 3,000	$ _____
Add payments: ($270 x 48 months)†	+ 12,960	_____ + _____ _____	Add payments: ($304 x 48 months)	+ 14,590	+ _____
Subtract alternative investment of down payment: ($3,000 earning 6% x 4 years)	– 720	– _____			
Add purchase cost ("residual value"): (48 months)	+ 4,500	+ _____			
Total cost to lease:	$17,940	$ _____	Total cost to buy:	$17,590	$ _____

* Some lessors may require an upfront, nonrefundable payment. Sometimes this can include a sales tax (or use tax) for the entire purchase price of a car.
† Add here the "capitalized cost reduction," sales taxes or other nonrefundable costs if they apply.

The preceding example assumes a 10 percent financing rate with a 6 percent *after-tax* return on investment funds. If you can borrow against your home through a home-equity line of credit, your after-tax borrowing cost could be 7 percent or lower instead of 10 percent, which would make purchasing a more attractive option than leasing.

YOUR ACTION PLAN

► Figure out how much you can afford to pay for your car.

► Decide what model and what options you want in your car before you start shopping.

► Find out car prices before going to a dealer.

► Decide whether leasing or purchasing is a better option.

► When you go to a dealer, be prepared to negotiate.

► Carefully review any type of financing arrangement to make sure you're not exceeding a safe amount of outstanding debt.

► If you can't afford to buy a new car comfortably, buy a used car or consider keeping your old car.

▼

GETTING MARRIED

*For about-to-be's, newlyweds, and people marrying
for a second time*

MARRIAGE MEANS PARTNERSHIP

There's no question that marriage is a significant life event, not just for you and your spouse but for your family and friends. Planning the big event can be exciting but also extraordinarily stressful, so you may postpone discussing money with your intended. Or you may not even think you have to. But if you don't talk about it before the wedding, you're making a critical mistake.

Why? Because when you get married, you're joining your finances with those of your spouse to create a new entity. Creating this entity impacts your investments, savings, property, and your relationship with the IRS.

Furthermore, arguments about money are one of the leading, if not the foremost, causes of marital difficulties, so it's essential that you and your future spouse begin an honest and open dialogue about money before the wedding. There are two key reasons for doing this:

1. **Your current finances should determine the type of wedding you have.** This is especially true if you, rather than your parents, are paying for it. If one or both of

you already have large credit card debts, you may opt for a less costly reception. You should incur as little new debt on your wedding as possible. If you do have to run up some bills, you want to be able to repay them within six months after the wedding.

2.   **It's better to be prepared.** You don't want to find out after the fact that you married the world's biggest tightwad or a super shopaholic. Remember *The Odd Couple*? Waiting until after the honeymoon to talk about your finances may be too late.

BEFORE THE WEDDING

To get your finances off to a sound footing, do the following before your wedding:

Talk About Money Issues

While this may not sound romantic, you need to sit down and compare your net-worth statements (this is a list of your assets and liabilities). Talk about what each of you *owns* and what each of you *owes*. Getting married doesn't necessarily mean that you're taking on someone else's debts for better or worse. But if your spouse is in debt, it's likely that you'll end up assisting your partner in paying off his or her debts.

▶ Compare what each of you earns in a year so that you can apportion household bills accordingly.

▶ Decide whether you will invest separately or together.

▶ Will you have one checking account or two?

▶ Has either of you ever filed for bankruptcy?

▶ After the marriage, will one spouse quit working outside the home?

▶ If you're planning to have children, consider what arrangements you'll make after the baby is born. Will both of you continue to work outside the home? If one of you already has a child, what financial contributions for that child will be made by the non-parent spouse? (When determining financial aid eligibility, college financial aid personnel take into account the applicant's stepparent's finances.)

▶ Will one person pay the bills each month, or will you share this job?

▶ What are your attitudes toward money? For example, are you a spender or a saver? Are you an impulse buyer or a thoughtful consumer? Do you want to buy "things," or would you rather spend money on travel?

THE PRIORITY GAME

You may have difficulty addressing these issues, but understanding your partner's attitudes about and outlook on finances is important. You may want to focus on key money priorities. Write down your answers to these questions and then discuss them with your partner:

1. Name the top five items you'd like to spend money on in the next three years.

2. Do you feel that investing for retirement is something you should start doing *today*?

3. How much of your family's financial resources should be for children (if you're planning on having any), for you alone, and for the two of you as a couple?

Talk About Insurance

Do you each need life insurance? If so, how much will you need? Remember, the aim of insurance is to replace lost income. If you're both working and can afford to pay your fixed expenses such as rent or mortgage, loans, utilities, and so forth, then you may not need insurance. On the other hand, if you want to make sure your surviving spouse will have money to pay off debts, and if you have children, then you will need insurance. Getting coverage through your employer is a good option, although you will have to replace it if you lose your job. You should also review your homeowner's, auto, and liability coverages. If you received expensive engagement presents, you may want to add on a valuables rider to your homeowner's policy.

Talk About Health Insurance

Will you maintain separate coverage or use only one of your policies? With insurers now "coordinating benefits," there's no reason for you to carry duplicate health insurance, especially if you pay a portion of the premium. You should compare the cost and the benefits of each of your employers' plans to see which is best. One plan may offer a better prescription plan, while the other may provide a broader choice of doctors. It may be less expensive for one spouse to drop his or her employer-provided coverage and be covered as a dependent under the other spouse's employer's plan. If an employer has a flexible cafeteria plan, this could free up "benefit dollars" for some other option.

Talk About Savings

As a general rule, you should strive to save at least 10 percent of your before-tax combined income. If you don't have children, you should try to live on just one spouse's earnings and save or invest the rest. Use an automatic payroll deduction if your company provides it. Funding 401(k) and IRA plans can be the best way for a young couple just starting out to save for retirement, especially when a company matches a portion of your contributions. You should each have a retirement account in your own name, separate from your spouse's. This allows you to have a retirement plan in place in case you divorce or your spouse dies. If you are self-employed, start a SEP or Keogh plan (for more information on these plans, see Chapter 9). If your employer doesn't offer a savings or retirement benefit, open your own automatic investment plan through a mutual fund, brokerage firm, or bank.

Talk About Houses

If each of you owns a home, will you sell them and buy a new home together or will you be moving into one of your homes? If you and your future spouse had two separate gains from the sales of homes that had been your separate main homes before your marriage, you can postpone the tax on both gains. You must purchase a new replacement home jointly, and one-half the amount of the cost of the new home must be at least as much as the adjusted selling price of each of your old homes. See Table 3-1.

Table 3-1: Can you postpone capital gains on home sales?		
Dave and Jane are getting married. Dave owns a condo, and Jane has a house.		
	Dave's condo	**Jane's house**
Selling price	$120,000	$ 80,000
Less: Selling expenses	(9,000)	(5,000)
Less: Fixing-up expenses	(1,000)	NONE
Adjusted selling price	$110,000	$ 75,000
Basis	(100,000)	(55,000)
Gain	$ 10,000	$ 20,000

If the couple from Table 3-1 buys a $120,000 replacement home, neither will be able to postpone any gain. If they buy a $150,000 replacement home, Jane will be able to postpone all of her gain, but Dave will not. If they buy a $220,000 replacement home, they both will be able to postpone their gains.

 CAUTION Don't let the tax tail wag the dog. Don't buy more house than you can reasonably afford just because you may get additional benefits.

Capital gains considerations may be more complex with second marriages. For example, Jim and Anne are on their second marriage, and they each have owned their homes for many years. Both are 55 years old. The issues they should consider are different from those in Table 3-1.

Each of them gets a once-in-a-lifetime exclusion of up to $125,000 in gain from the sale of a residence. To obtain this exclusion, you must:

▶ be age 55 or older,

▶ never have used or been a joint filer with someone who has used his or her exclusion since July 26, 1978; and

▶ have owned and lived in your home three out of the last five years.

Let's assume that Jim has $160,000 of gain and Anne has $50,000 of gain.

If neither one has used his or her exclusion (nor been a joint filer with someone else who has used the exclusion), then *before they get married* Jim can exclude $125,000 and Anne can exclude $50,000. Total gain excluded is $175,000.

If they get married without taking their exclusions, they will be limited to a joint exclusion of $125,000. What if they claim "married filing separate"? Then each will receive an exclusion of up to $62,500.

Jim never used his exclusion, but Anne's former husband, Tom, claimed the exclusion previously when Anne was 51 years old. If Jim and Anne first marry and then claim the exclusion on a joint return when they sell their home in the future, they cannot use the exclusion. Anne is barred because she was a joint filer with someone who used the exclusion. Jim is barred because his wife, Anne, has, by law, used her exclusion. When a couple files a joint return and one has used the exclusion, the other is barred. However, Jim could file a *separate return* and claim up to half his exclusion or $62,500. The better solution would have been for Jim to claim his entire $125,000 exclusion before getting married.

For more information on the sale of a home, review IRS Publication 523, "Buying and Selling a Home."

Talk About Prenuptial Agreements

The concept of a prenuptial agreement may offend you. After all, if you're marrying someone, presumably you trust that person. In fact, prenuptials are increasingly common among professionals who have accumulated valuable assets that they want to protect in the event the marriage fails. Some situations in which a prenuptial agreement may be appropriate are the following:

► Both parties want to protect substantial income and assets.

► One party wishes to preserve one particular asset, such as a family home.

► One or both wishes to preserve property for the children of a previous marriage.

► One or both parties has a closely held business that they want to retain in the event of a divorce. In some cases, business partners may require that a partner have a prenuptial agreement to prevent an ex-spouse from gaining control of the business.

If you decide to prepare prenuptial agreements, each of you should have your own attorney. Once you create a prenuptial agreement, a court will be hard-pressed to break it.

CAUTION You cannot waive rights to employee benefits. A recent federal court case ruled that pension rights cannot be waived in a prenuptial agreement. The law allows *spouses* to waive such rights, but not grooms or brides-to-be.

Keep property acquired before the marriage separate from assets held with your new spouse. In many states, "jointly held property," or property acquired during the marriage, will be split upon divorce. On the other hand, property acquired by gift or inheritance will usually not be split unless the spouse "mingled" that money, or earnings from that money, with assets held with the other spouse.

AFTER THE WEDDING

Update Beneficiary Designations

Review your beneficiary designations on your life insurance, pension plans, annuities, living trusts, IRA, SEPs, and Keoghs. This is especially important because beneficiaries can receive the proceeds if you die, without having to go to probate. (A beneficiary designation supersedes any designations you make in your will assuming the beneficiary is a person and not an estate.)

Update Your Will

You may put off updating or even writing a will because you find it too depressing. Writing your will, however, is really about protecting your loved ones and specifying how you want your assets divided according to your wishes. If you die without a will, most states have an intestacy statute that provides a benefit for your spouse. However, your spouse will not get anything until after the will goes through probate, which can take both time and money. Many states also provide for a minimum benefit to a spouse if a will leaves nothing to him or her, whether this was done accidentally or intentionally. To avoid these problems, make sure that you include your spouse in your will. If you have children from a prior marriage, you may want to ask your lawyer about a Q-TIP trust. A Q-TIP trust provides income to your spouse for life, starting at your death. But when your spouse dies, the trust property will pass to beneficiaries, usually including the children from the prior marriage.

Changing Names

Traditionally, women have taken the name of their husbands. However, it is becoming more and more accepted and convenient for a woman to maintain, either in a hyphenated form or on its own, her maiden name. This is especially true for professional women who have worked a number of years under one name. If you do make a change, notify Social Security, the Department of Motor Vehicles (for driver's license, titles, and registrations), your insurance companies (life, property, and casualty), banks, brokers, mutual funds, all of your creditors, and anyone else with whom you do business.

Joint Ownership

You should maintain a joint checking account to pay for household expenses. Usually, the marital residence should also be titled jointly, with a right of survivorship. Whether other property should be held in joint or separate accounts is your own decision. You may find it useful to have a joint account for all your assets.

"Separate property" is a legal term. It means property you owned before the marriage or received as a gift or inheritance after the marriage and which you have not transferred into a marital asset. Generally, you shouldn't mingle property that you would want to keep in the event of a divorce. You can transfer property into marital property by changing the deed or title to joint ownership or by maintaining the property with marital funds. For example, if one spouse owned a piece of real estate before the marriage but uses money from a joint checking account to pay for the taxes and upkeep, this real estate now may be marital property even if the deed is still in the original spouse's name.

Durable General Powers of Attorney

Especially if you have substantial assets, each of you may want to give your spouse a durable power of attorney. This legally empowers your spouse to make decisions—such as choosing an investment or selling your house—if you're unable to make these decisions yourself (for example, if you're ill).

Review Your Taxes

If you work, you should notify your employer of your change in marital status and amend the number of dependents on your withholding form. Although most couples file a "married filing jointly" return, you may want to file "married filing singly," depending on your income or other circumstances. Consult an accountant or tax planner if you think one option will save you money.

Joint Responsibility

When you take out a loan or make a purchase on credit with your spouse, you both are equally responsible for repaying this debt. If you have a joint credit card and your spouse charges up a storm and then disappears, you're still responsible for the bills. Likewise, if you cosign a mortgage, you're legally bound to repay it if your spouse leaves you or dies. On the other hand, debts that you incurred when you were single, such as your student loans, don't become the responsibility of your spouse.

Set Up Financial Housekeeping

There's no right or wrong way to run your household finances. You want to find a system that works for you and allows you to keep your finances organized and on track so that you'll reach your goals. Keep track of your spending, saving, and investing. Clarify each of your roles in your family's personal finances. Decide whether you will merge all your expenses and income and whether you'll maintain separate accounts. If one of you prefers to pay the bills and balance the checkbook, that's fine, provided the arrangement works. Remember, though, that you're partners in love and finance, so you should be able to reverse your roles in case of an emergency.

YOUR ACTION PLAN

Before the Wedding

▶ Talk about finances, including your income, expenses, debts.

▶ Decide where to live and whether you should rent or sell any property that one of you owns.

▶ Draw up a prenuptial agreement, if appropriate.

After the Wedding

▶ Review your beneficiary designations on your insurance policies and investments.

▶ Review your health coverage and select the employer insurance that best meets your medical needs.

▶ Start a savings plan and strive to save 10 percent of your income.

▶ Contribute as much as you can, if you're not already doing so, to your 401(k) or other retirement plans. Make sure you're taking advantage of the matching contributions from your employer.

▶ Draft a will.

▼

WELCOMING A BABY TO THE FAMILY

For expectant parents, new parents, and anyone thinking about becoming a parent

Congratulations! Whether you've been planning for the blessed event or you're surprised by the news that you're expecting, you're ready for the spectacular happening that will undoubtedly have the biggest impact on your life.

Planning for parenthood is more than just deciding when to have children. While your first concern is naturally for the health of the mother and child, you also must determine how to take care of your family's financial needs once the baby arrives. To do this, you'll need to take a financial inventory. If you're about to have, or recently have had, a baby, you'll need to evaluate your spending habits, beef up your savings, and review your estate, among other concerns. Here's a rundown of the major issues you should consider before pregnancy, during pregnancy, and after the baby is born.

BEFORE THE PREGNANCY

CHECK YOUR MEDICAL INSURANCE

If you have coverage, you'll want to know your out-of-pocket maximum. If you don't have medical insurance and want to get it before starting a family, check all potential policies to see whether they require that you buy the policy three months or more before pregnancy begins; otherwise, you could find yourself with a policy that doesn't cover pregnancy or the birth of your baby.

REVIEW YOUR DISABILITY POLICY

You may be entitled to receive pay while on maternity leave, and disability payments plus vacation pay may provide you with sufficient income to take several months off.

START BUDGETING

Whatever expenses for your child you've planned for, you're sure to underestimate them! The first year of a child's life is especially expensive. Insurance will probably cover about two-thirds of the cost of routine hospital and delivery fees. Normal medical care, including visits to the pediatrician every month for the first year, usually costs $400 or more. You'll also need clothing, diapers, a crib, a carriage, and so forth. The money you once spent on romantic dinners or nights at the theater will probably go toward baby gear!

GET LIFE INSURANCE

Once you have a child, it's essential that at least one of the parents have life insurance coverage. If one works and the other stays at home to care for the child, the working spouse should have life insurance. Although there is no loss of income if the stay-at-home spouse dies, the working spouse would have to hire a full-time nanny or secure day care. What would it cost to replace the services performed by the stay-at-home spouse? A full-time nanny can cost more than $1,200 a month. Assuming a modest 3 percent increase over an 18-year period, the working spouse would need approximately $200,000 worth of life insurance to cover that risk for a newborn.

Which kind of life insurance is best? Level term is guaranteed renewable and non-cancellable. It's flexible, simple, and cheap.

DURING PREGNANCY

TALK TO YOUR EMPLOYER

Some women work right up until the day of delivery, and some come back to work within a few weeks after delivery. Talk to your supervisor or the human resources department. Find out about the company maternity policy. Ask about a modified work schedule if your condition warrants one. If your employer needs to make arrangements during your leave and for your return, be as frank as you can about your plans. Obviously, you may change your mind after the birth, but you should try to be fair to your employer. Perhaps your employer will consider a part-time schedule or a job-sharing arrangement. Also, benefits don't always apply only to mothers. Would-be fathers should see whether their employers offer any paid or unpaid leave.

UPDATE OR WRITE YOUR WILL

As unpleasant as the process of thinking about your own mortality and drafting plans for you heirs is, the alternative—doing nothing—is worse. If you and your spouse do not already have wills—and two-thirds of all Americans don't—the state in which you reside will decide not only how to dispose of your property but also *who will be the guardian of your minor children, if both of you perish.*

If only one spouse dies, the surviving spouse will automatically have custody of their children and no special provision in a will is necessary. Having a will, however, enables parents to decide who will care for their offspring if both parents pass away.

NAME A GUARDIAN

Naming a guardian—the person who will be responsible for raising your children in the event that you cannot—is a difficult decision. Your first inclination is probably to name one of your parents. But think about whether your parents will be healthy and able to care for a child for the next 20 years or so. An alternative often recommended by lawyers is to choose one of your siblings. If, however, you really want to choose your parents or parents-in-law, you should name one or two successors, just in case. Remember, the person you name as guardian can always refuse the job. If he or she does, the court is then responsible for finding and appointing a substitute. To avoid this situation, make sure you discuss the prospect with your first choice and also with any backup guardian whom you name in your will.

Ideally, you should choose a couple rather than a single person so that your child will be raised in a household with adults of both sexes. However, lawyers advise that you make only one spouse the legal guardian, in case the couple you choose decides to divorce.

Guardians often have a dual role: They handle the child's day-to-day upbringing and take charge of his or her finances. The parents can appoint different guardians for each set of responsibilities. If the "guardian of the person" makes a great parent but isn't experienced in managing money, you can choose someone else to manage your child's inheritance. This person is the "guardian of the property."

The guardian of the property must submit an annual accounting to the court of how he or she is investing and spending the money. Typically, he or she must also get permission from the court to spend large amounts of money—for example, to buy a car.

A letter to the guardian attached to your will lets you explain your wishes for your children. To ensure that this "honor" does not become a financial drain on your child's new family, you should carry sufficient term life insurance to cover the added expense.

If your children are minors, you should leave the proceeds and other assets from your estate in trust for your children. You can set up a *testamentary trust* (in your will), with provisions that will take effect after you die. This document spells out how you want the money in the trust to be spent and names a *trustee* —a financially savvy friend, relative, or professional—to be responsible for managing the cash on behalf of the *beneficiary*, your child.

Tour the Delivery Facilities at Your Hospital

Will you use a hospital or a separate birthing center? A stay in a birthing center often costs half as much as a stay in a hospital maternity ward.

 CAUTION Most birthing centers, however, do not have the high-tech operating rooms or intensive-care facilities that hospitals have.

If something goes wrong at a birthing center, you may have a long ride to the hospital.

If you're leaning toward a hospital, find out whether it has a package plan that includes comfortable birthing rooms, prenatal exercise classes, and any other amenities. Find out what the usual stay is for a normal delivery. Comparison-shop if you have a choice of hospitals.

AFTER THE BIRTH

NOTIFY YOUR HEALTH PLAN

Many employer health plans don't cover a child automatically at birth. You must notify your insurer within a certain time period, typically 30 days. If the mother is going to quit work and the family is covered by her company's group health insurance, she can continue the coverage under the federal COBRA law, which applies to employers with at least 20 employees.

Under COBRA, a departing employee can maintain his or her group health-care plan for up to 18 months following his or her departure. However, he or she must pay the full premium, which usually ranges from $400 to $500 a month for full family coverage. If you want to maintain health coverage, you must notify your employer within 60 days of leaving your job.

CHECK YOUR BENEFICIARY DESIGNATIONS

After the baby arrives, check your designations of *contingent,* or secondary, beneficiaries. You probably have named your spouse as primary beneficiary and parents or other children as secondary beneficiaries. You may want to update your list of contingent beneficiaries to include your new child. You'll need to review a variety of documents, including your life insurance; employer savings/thrift plans; deferred-compensation plans, including IRAs, and employee stock-ownership plans; commercial annuities and so on.

START SAVING FOR COLLEGE

You can't start too soon! An automatic, regular savings plan—no matter how modest—should be started immediately! An education fund is a great gift from a grandparent or other relative. Most financial institutions, including banks, mutual funds, brokerage firms, and insurance companies, will allow you to set up a custodial account for the child. Custodial accounts make sense for those who want to earmark funds for a child's education and at the same time save on income taxes. That's because the first $1,400 of investment income is taxed at the child's rate for children under age 14.

There is, however, one major drawback: Gifts to a custodial account are irrevocable and become the legal property of your child at ages 18 to 21, depending on your state's law. Although your intent may have been to provide funds for education, your child, by the age of majority, may have other ideas on how to spend the money. For more on college financing, read Chapter 5 on planning for a child's education.

DAY CARE

Working parents may spend 15 to 25 percent of their income for day care. Here are your day-care choices, ranked by cost:

▶ **Full-time housekeeper or nanny.** A "live-in" nanny costs about $1,200 a month. In addition to paying salary, you should plan on paying for health insurance, half the Social Security tax, unemployment taxes, workers' compensation (in some states), and a paid vacation.

▶ **Day-care centers.** The cost of group day care at centers for infants under age two averages $300 to $500 a month, according to the Department of Health and Human Services.

▶ **Family day care.** These day-care homes are usually run by neighborhood residents who take care of two to six children. They generally cost $400 to $600 a month.

▶ **After-school care for older children.** You should expect to pay no more than half the cost of full-time day care in these situations.

▶ **Grandma/Grandpa.** If grandparents are able and willing to serve as caretakers, you'll save a great deal of money. And, of course, the advantage of a bond between grandparent and grandchild can't be measured in dollars. But, remember, even grandparents need a break. A combination of grandparents and day care may be the ideal solution.

What to Look for in a Day-Care Facility

▶ A state license, if one is required

▶ A stable workforce without frequent employee turnover

▶ Cleanliness

▶ Open visitation policy, which means that you are allowed to visit when you wish

▶ The ability to view the day-care facility without being observed by your child or the care providers

▶ A staff-child ratio of at least one adult for every four infants and one adult for every six toddlers

▶ A doctor or nurse on call at the facility

▶ Procedures for medical emergencies

▶ Organized games, crafts, activities, and so on

In addition, you should always ask for references and call these parents. Ask them very specific questions about how the facility is run, how their children are treated, and any other concerns you have.

Taxes and Day Care

Uncle Sam helps defray day-care expenses with a tax credit. For example, if your family income is $28,000 or higher, you can get a 20 percent credit on your yearly child-care expenses, up to $2,400 for one dependent. That can yield a tax reduction of as much as $480 a year.

As an alternative, your company may offer a dependent-care reimbursement account. These accounts allow you to put a portion, up to $5,000, of your before-tax salary, into a special account, from which you can reimburse yourself for the cost of a nanny, group day care, family day care, or even a babysitter. If you use a reimbursement account, however, you may not write off reimbursed expenses on your taxes. Generally, the flexible spending account offers more savings if you have a higher income. You can do the calculations yourself by checking a tax guide, but if you're not certain which option makes the most sense for you, talk to an accountant or tax planner.

YOUR ACTION PLAN

Before the Baby

▶ Review your health insurance coverage.

▶ Get life and disability coverage.

▶ Find out about your employer's maternity policy.

▶ Choose a physician and hospital for the delivery.

▶ Revamp your budget to accommodate expenses for your child.

▶ Write a will.

▶ Name a primary and secondary guardian for your child.

After the Baby

▶ Change beneficiary designations on insurance, investment, and other accounts.

▶ Notify your health insurer of your baby's birth.

▶ Get a social security number for your child by taking the birth certificate to the local social security office.

▶ Secure your own or dependent health coverage if you stop working.

▶ Contribute to a flexible-care spending account through your employer, if it is available.

▶ Start saving for your kid's college education.

▶ Look into child-care arrangements.

▶ Decide whether to contribute to a flexible spending account or take a tax credit to help defray the cost of child care.

▶ Create a trust, if necessary.

▼

SAVING FOR COLLEGE

For parents and for kids—this is a good chapter to read as a family

Failing to plan properly for a child's education could jeopardize *your* financial well-being as well as your child's. Let's play *jeopardy*—"education" category:

Answer: $408,720

Question: What is the average additional income earned by a college graduate *versus* a high school graduate during a 30-year career?[*]

Answer: $37,140

Question: What is the average four-year cost for a resident student entering a public four-year college for the 1995–96 school year?[†]

---

[*] *Source:* Don't Miss Out 94/95 *by Robert Leider and Anna Leider*

[†] *Source: The College Board*

Obviously, despite its high cost, college is still an excellent investment, and as a parent, you probably want to take advantage of it to open as many doors as possible for your children. You may even be willing to put off saving for retirement in order to save for your children's college tuition. After all, you may not have had the opportunity to go to college, and you may think that although your life won't get any better, you can make your children's lives better than yours. Wrong. You *do* have a life, and when your kids graduate from college, chances are that they will start earning more than you did. Suppose that you scrimp and save and spend your life savings to pay their college bills and they get out and get a job with a starting salary of $80,000. Are you going to ask them to repay you? Probably not. Therefore, your children should *partner* with you to cover education expenses. Don't confuse footing the bill for college with love for your children. Love doesn't cost you anything. College does. Be a good parent and do what you reasonably can to pay for their college expenses. But don't put your financial plans on hold; make sure you continue to put away 20 percent of your income for retirement.

Remember, you don't have to come up with a huge lump sum to pay the entire bill. If you have a newborn, you have 18 years, plus the four years of college, to accumulate some of the money you'll need. If you take out loans, you'll have more time. Instead of thinking of saving for college as the 3Rs, think of it as the 3Ss—start early, save often, and seek resources. You should:

▶ Start early so that your money will compound and grow over time.

▶ Build up a reserve.

▶ Look for ways to cut down expenses. Research good, lower-cost schools and encourage your kids to pursue athletic and academic scholarships.

▶ Investigate all possible sources of financial aid.

▶ Ask your kids to take on some of the burden for financing their education. Having children help pay for their own education also prepares them for the real world.

In this chapter, you'll learn how to:

1. "Prefund" a child's future education

2. Take advantage of the financial-aid system

3. Manage any shortfalls that result

Keep in mind that government rules and regulations regarding financial aid and loans change regularly, usually coinciding with the upcoming school year. The rules discussed here apply generally to the 1995–96 school year. The rules are not expected to change for the 1996–97 year, but loan interest rates and limits are reset annually.

INVESTING MONTHLY TO MEET COLLEGE COSTS

With today's college education costs ranging from several hundred dollars to $25,000 plus per year, you may find yourself paralyzed by the sheer magnitude of the potential expense. Use Table 5-1 to determine how much you need to set aside a month for *each* child. You might want to set up a separate investment account and have money transferred to it automatically at the beginning of the month.

Table 5-1: Monthly education calculator

How much will you need to invest each month to afford the college of your choice?

Annual four-year college cost in today's dollars

Age	Expected after-tax rate of return	$6,000	$8,000	$10,000	$12,000	$14,000	$16,000	$18,000	$20,000	$22,000
Newborn	8.0%	$135	$180	$220	$265	$310	$355	$400	$445	$490
1	7.8	140	185	235	280	325	375	420	465	510
2	7.6	150	195	245	295	345	390	440	490	540
3	7.5	155	210	260	310	360	415	465	515	570
4	7.3	165	220	270	330	380	435	490	545	600
5	7.1	170	230	290	345	400	460	520	575	630
6	6.9	180	245	305	365	425	485	545	610	670
7	6.7	195	260	320	385	450	515	580	645	710
8	6.5	205	275	340	410	480	545	615	680	750
9	6.3	220	290	360	435	510	580	650	725	800
10	6.0	230	310	385	465	540	620	695	770	850

(continued)

Table 5-1: (continued)

Annual four-year college cost in today's dollars

Age	Expected after-tax rate of return	$6,000	$8,000	$10,000	$12,000	$14,000	$16,000	$18,000	$20,000	$22,000
11	5.9	250	330	415	500	580	660	745	830	910
12	5.6	270	360	445	535	625	715	805	890	980
13	5.3	290	390	485	580	680	775	870	970	1,065
14	5.1	320	425	530	640	745	850	955	1,060	1,170
15	4.9	355	470	590	710	825	945	1,060	1,180	1,300
16	4.4	400	535	665	800	935	1,065	1,200	1,335	1,465

Table 5-1 is based on three important assumptions:

▶ Expected average annual after-tax rate of return on your investment is higher the younger your child is because you can invest more aggressively

▶ Six percent inflation rate for college expenses

▶ Payments required until the child is 22

Let's be practical. Putting aside money may be difficult, especially if you're trying to cope with other financial commitments at the same time, such as buying a home, a car, or simply paying for everything else kids need. This chart shows you what you should aim to save. Instead of focusing on the negative and saying, "We *can't* afford to save $180 per month for our child's education" (that would be the amount necessary to fund a $6,000 per year education for one child who's presently six years old), you should carefully examine your living expenses to determine how much you can realistically save. Then put aside the most you *can* each month and increase it later if possible. Partial prefunding of this expense is better than none at all. Also, these figures for monthly contributions are a *worst-case* scenario. You need to raise this kind of money if you end up financing your child's *entire* college education. Bear in mind that you don't have to save the entire cost of your kid's college education. Assume that you'll be able to pay for it with a combination of your savings, loans, and scholarships.

The key is to start early and save what you can afford to, increasing this amount later if possible. Join the 1 percent club: Start with something you can afford, and each year try to increase what you set aside by 1 percent. If you put aside $100 a month this year, then aim to set aside $110 a year next year. Look at it this way: If you get a 4 percent salary increase, if you put aside just 1 percent more of your earnings, you'd still have that other 3 percent.

Put your plan on "automatic pilot." Most of you will find it easier to save money if it happens automatically—through payroll deduction or a similar method. If automatic investments are available from your bank account to a mutual fund, begin by designating the amount each pay period that will go toward your family's education fund. Don't worry if it's a modest amount at first; $50 saved regularly over time adds up!

 Average college costs

$9,300 per year   State

$19,800 per year   Independent

$31,500 per year   Ivy League

If you have already started to save for your kid's education, use Worksheet 5A to calculate how much your present savings will reduce your monthly deposits.

Worksheet 5A: Adjusting for previously accumulated savings

		Example	Your Situation
1.	Amount saved	$ 5,000	$ _____
2.	Current four-year cost	$24,000*	$ _____
3.	Divide Line 1 by Line 2	.2083	_____
4.	Amount from **Table 5-1** at child's current age	$ 180†	$ _____
5.	Multiply Line 3 by Line 4 and subtract total from Line 4	− 37	_____
6.	Adjusted monthly savings needed	$ 143	$ _____

* $6,000 per year x 4
† Age 6

Determining Your Family's Annual Contribution

Rather than looking at the anticipated annual expense as your savings target, you should focus on the "expected annual family contribution." This is the calculation used by financial-aid officers to determine what portion of a child's education a parent will be expected to pay. *Federal Worksheet A* will give you an estimate of how much most *public* colleges will expect your family to contribute toward the cost of a child's education each year. The rest of the money would then come from loans and/or grants.

Although most *private* schools also follow this methodology, some will count assets that public colleges might not count, such as the value of your home, company retirement accounts, and the cash value of life insurance and annuities.

According to this estimate, a family of four, with parents making $40,000 and assets of $40,000, would be expected to contribute $3,709 per year, or a total of $14,836, for one child attending college for four years. The same family of four, with two children in college at the same time, would be expected to contribute $2,307 per child, per year, or a total of $18,456. If their children went to schools with a cost of $4,500 per year ($36,000 total for both children), they might be able to cut their college costs in half.

The following table shows only the expected contribution for parents *with one child in college and one parent working*. The figures also assume that the child attending college has earned income of $2,000 per year and assets equal to 2 percent of the parent's assets.

Here's what most schools will expect you to pay each year toward one child's college education.*

Table 5-2: Your expected annual contribution as a parent

Assets†	Number of children‡	$30,000	$40,000	$50,000	$60,000	$70,000	$80,000	$100,000
$ 40,000	1	$2,273	$4,682	$7,943	$11,006	$14,146	$17,321	$23,671
	2	1,616	3,709	6,533	9,756	12,896	16,071	22,421
	3	999	2,937	5,313	8,591	11,731	14,906	21,255
	4	618	2,196	4,169	7,227	10,401	13,575	19,925
$ 60,000	1	$3,266	$5,755	$9,211	$12,274	$15,414	$18,589	$24,939
	2	2,539	4,623	7,801	11,024	14,164	17,339	23,689
	3	1,922	3,731	6,483	9,859	12,998	16,174	22,523
	4	1,228	2,888	5,151	8,495	11,669	14,843	21,193
$ 80,000	1	$4,090	$6,978	$10,479	$13,542	$16,682	$19,857	$26,207
	2	3,259	5,661	9,069	12,292	15,432	18,607	24,957
	3	2,590	4,625	7,751	11,127	14,267	17,442	23,791
	4	1,954	3,652	6,268	9,763	12,937	16,111	22,461
$100,000	1	$5,022	$8,246	$11,747	$14,810	$17,950	$21,125	$27,475
	2	4,061	6,843	10,337	13,560	16,700	19,875	26,225
	3	3,298	5,639	9,019	12,395	15,535	18,710	25,059
	4	2,564	4,509	7,536	11,031	14,205	17,379	23,729

* Once assets exceed $100,000, the "expected family contribution" usually increases by 5.6 percent. Beginning in 1993, families with adjusted gross income of less than $50,000 no longer needed to report parental assets to determine eligibility for entitlement programs such as the Stafford loan. However, the asset may be considered in making other awards, including the college's own funds.

† See *Parents' assets* in Federal Worksheet A: Calculating your annual expected family contribution.

‡ Total number of children in your family.

Federal Worksheet A

1995-96 EFC FORMULA A : DEPENDENT STUDENT

REGULAR WORKSHEET Page 1	A

Please note: All tables related to *Worksheet A* (*i.e.,* Tables 5-1 – 5-8) will be sequenced in relation to it rather than to the other tables in this guidebook.

PARENTS' INCOME IN 1994

1. Parents' Adjusted Gross Income (FAFSA/SAR #66)

2. a. Father's income earned from work (FAFSA/SAR #68) _____

   b. Mother's income earned from work (FAFSA/SAR #69) + _____

   Total parents' income earned from work = 2.

3. Parents' Taxable income
   (If tax filers, enter the amount from line 1 above
   If non-tax filers, enter the amount from line 2)*

4. Untaxed income and benefits:

   • Social Security benefits (FAFSA/SAR #70) + _____

   • AFDC/ADC (FAFSA/SAR #71) + _____

   • Child support received (FAFSA/SAR #72) + _____

   • Other untaxed income (FAFSA/SAR #73) + _____

   Total untaxed income and benefits = 4.

5. Taxable and untaxed income (sum of line 3 and line 4)

6. Exclusions (FAFSA/SAR #74) –

7. **TOTAL INCOME**
   (line 5 minus line 6) If negative, enter zero. =

ALLOWANCES AGAINST PARENTS' INCOME

8. 1994 U.S. income tax paid (FAFSA/SAR #67)
   (tax filers only); if negative, enter zero.

9. State and other tax allowance (Table A1) +

10. Father's Social Security tax (Table A2) +

11. Mother's Social Security tax (Table A2) +

12. Income protection allowance (Table A3) +

13. Employment expense allowance:

    • Two working parents: 35% of the lesser of the
      earned incomes, or $2,500, whichever is less.

    • One-parent families: 35% of earned income,
      or $2,500, whichever is less. +

14. **TOTAL ALLOWANCES** =

AVAILABLE INCOME

Total Income (from line 7)

Total allowances (from line 14) –

15. **AVAILABLE INCOME (AI)**
    May be a negative number. = *

PARENTS' CONTRIBUTION FROM ASSETS

16. Cash, savings, & checking (FAFSA/SAR #83)

17. Other estate/investments value** (FAFSA/SAR #84) _____

    Other estate/investments debt** (FAFSA/SAR #85) – _____

    Net worth of real estate/investments
    If negative, enter zero = 17.

18. Business value** (FAFSA/SAR #86)

    Business debt** (FAFSA/SAR #87) –

    Net worth of business
    If negative, enter zero = 18.

19. Farm value** (FAFSA/SAR #88)

    Farm debt** (FAFSA/SAR #89) –

    Net worth of farm. If negative,
    enter zero. If the family resides on
    the farm, enter zero. = 19.

20. Net worth of business/farm
    (sum of lines 18 and 19)

21. Adjusted net worth of business/farm
    (Calculate, using Table A4.) +

22. New worth (sum of lines 16, 17, and 21) =

23. Education savings and asset
    protection allowance (Table A5) –

24. Discretionary net worth
    (line 22 minus line 23) =

25. Asset conversion to income rate X .12

26. **CONTRIBUTION FROM ASSETS**
    If negative, enter zero. =

PARENTS' CONTRIBUTION

Available income (AI) (from line 15)

Contribution from assets (from line 26) +

27. Adjusted available income (AAI)
    May be a negative number. =

28. Total parents' contribution from AAI
    (Calculate, using Table A6; if negative, enter zero.)

29. Number in college in 1995-96
    (FAFSA/SAR #52) +

30. **PARENTS' CONTRIBUTION** (standard
    contribution for 9-month enrollment)

* STOP HERE if both of the following are true: line 3 is $12,000 or less, *and* the parents are eligible
  to file a 1994 IRS Form 1040A or 1040EZ (they are not required to file a 1994 Form 1040, or they
  are not required to file any income tax return) — the student's EFC is zero.

** Do not include the family's home.

Federal Worksheet A (continued)

REGULAR WORKSHEET
Page 2

STUDENT'S INCOME IN 1994		
31. Adjusted Gross Income (FAFSA/SAR #55)		
32. Income earned from work (FAFSA/SAR #57)		
33. Taxable Income (If tax filer, enter the amount from line 31 above. If non-tax filer, enter the amount from line 32.)		
34. Untaxed income and benefits:		
• Social Security benefits (FAFSA/SAR #59)		
• Other untaxed income (FAFSA/SAR #62)	+	
Total untaxed income and benefits	= 34.	
35. Taxable and untaxed income (sum of line 33 and line 34)		
36. Exclusions (FAFSA/SAR #63)	−	
37. **TOTAL INCOME** (line 35 minus line 36) If negative, enter zero.	=	

ALLOWANCES AGAINST STUDENT INCOME		
38. 1994 U.S. income tax paid (FAFSA/SAR #56) (tax filers only); if negative, enter zero.		
39. State and other tax allowance (Table A7)	+	
40. Social Security tax allowance (Table A2)	+	
41. Income protection allowance	+	1,750
42. **TOTAL ALLOWANCES**	=	

STUDENT CONTRIBUTION FROM INCOME		
Total income (from line 37)		
Total allowances (from line 42)	−	
43. Available income (AI) If negative, enter zero.	=	
44. Assessment of AI	X	
45. **STUDENT CONTRIBUTION FROM AI**	=	.50

STUDENT CONTRIBUTION FROM ASSETS		
46. Cash, savings & checking (FAFSA/SAR #75)		
47. Other real estate/investment value* (FAFSA/SAR #76)	_____	
Other real estate/investment debt* (FAFSA/SAR #77)	− _____	
Net worth of real estate/investments If negative, enter zero.	= 47.	
48. Business value* (FAFSA/SAR #78)	_____	
Business debt* (FAFSA/SAR #79)	− _____	
Net worth of business If negative, enter zero.	= 48.	
49. Farm value* (FAFSA/SAR #80)	_____	
Farm debt* (FAFSA/SAR #81)	− _____	
Net worth of farm If negative, enter zero. If the family resides on the farm, enter zero.	= 49.	
50. Net worth (sum of lines 46 through 49)	=	
51. Assessment rate	X	.35
52. **CONTRIBUTION FROM ASSETS** If negative, enter zero.	=	

EXPECTED FAMILY CONTRIBUTION		
PARENTS' CONTRIBUTION (from line 30)		
STUDENT CONTRIBUTION FROM AI (from line 45)	+	
STUDENT CONTRIBUTION FROM ASSETS (from line 52)	+	
53. **EXPECTED FAMILY CONTRIBUTION**	=	

*Do not include the student's home.

Table 5-3: State and other tax allowance for Worksheet A (parents only)

State	Percent of total income $0-14,999	$15,000+	State	Percent of total income $0-14,999	$15,000+
Alabama	5%	4%	Missouri	6%	5%
Alaska	3%	2%	Montana	8%	7%
American Samoa	4%	3%	Nebraska	8%	7%
Arizona	6%	5%	Nevada	3%	2%
Arkansas	6%	5%	New Hampshire	7%	6%
California	8%	7%	New Jersey	8%	7%
Canada	4%	3%	New Mexico	6%	5%
Colorado	7%	6%	New York	11%	10%
Connecticut	6%	5%	North Carolina	8%	7%
Delaware	8%	7%	North Dakota	6%	5%
District of Columbia	10%	9%	Northern Mariana Islands	4%	3%
Federated States of Micronesia	4%	3%	Ohio	8%	7%
Florida	4%	3%	Oklahoma	6%	5%
Georgia	7%	6%	Oregon	10%	9%
Guam	4%	3%	Palau	4%	3%
Hawaii	8%	7%	Pennsylvania	7%	6%
Idaho	7%	6%	Puerto Rico	4%	3%
Illinois	6%	5%	Rhode Island	9%	8%
Indiana	6%	5%	South Carolina	8%	7%
Iowa	8%	7%	South Dakota	4%	3%
Kansas	7%	6%	Tennessee	3%	2%
Kentucky	7%	6%	Texas	3%	2%
Louisiana	4%	3%	Utah	8%	7%
Maine	9%	8%	Vermont	8%	7%
Marshall Islands	4%	3%	Virgin Islands	4%	3%
Maryland	9%	8%	Virginia	8%	7%
Massachusetts	9%	8%	Washington	4%	3%
Mexico	4%	3%	West Virginia	6%	5%
Michigan	9%	8%	Wisconsin	10%	9%
Minnesota	9%	8%	Wyoming	3%	2%
Mississippi	5%	4%	Blank or invalid state	4%	3%
			OTHER	4%	3%

Multiply parents' total income (from Worksheet A, line 7) by the appropriate rate from the table above to get the "state and other tax allowance." Use the parents' STATE OF LEGAL RESIDENCE (FAFSA/SAR #49). If this item is blank or invalid, use the student's STATE OF LEGAL RESIDENCE (FAFSA/SAR #11). If both items are blank or invalid, use the STATE in the student's mailing address (FAFSA/SAR #6). If all three items are blank or invalid, use the rate for a blank or invalid state above.

Table 5-4: Social Security tax

Calculate separately the Social Security tax of father, mother and student.

Income earned from work*	Social Security tax
$0 – $60,600	7.65% of income
$60,601 or greater	$4,635.90 + 1.45% of amount over $60,600

* Father's income earned from work is FAFSA/SAR #68. Mother's income earned from work is FAFSA/SAR #69. Student's income earned from work is FAFSA/SAR #57. Social Security tax will never be less than zero.

Table 5-5: Income Protection Allowance

Number in parents' household including student (FAFSA/SAR #51)	Number of college students in household (FAFSA/SAR #52)				
	1	2	3	4	5
2	$11,150	$ 9,240	–	–	–
3	13,890	11,990	$10,080	–	–
4	17,150	15,240	13,350	$11,440	–
5	20,240	18,330	16,430	14,520	$12,620
6	23,670	21,760	19,860	17,960	16,060

Note: For each additional family member, add $2,670.

For each additional college student, subtract $1,900.

Table 5-6: Business/farm net worth adjustment for Worksheet A (parents only)

If the net worth of a business or farm is:	Then the adjusted net worth is:
Less than $1	$0
$1 to $80,000	40% of net worth
$80,001 to $240,000	$32,000 + 50% of net worth over $80,000
$240,001 to $400,000	$112,000 + 60% of net worth over $240,000
$400,001 or more	$208,000 +100% of net worth over $400,000

Table 5-7: Contribution from AAI (Adjusted Available Income)

If AAI is:	Then the contribution from AAI is:
Less than −$3,409	−$750
−$3,409 to $10,000	22% of AAI
$10,001 to $12,500	$2,200 + 25% of AAI over $10,000
$12,501 to $15,100	$2,825 + 29% of AAI over $12,500
$15,101 to $17,600	$3,579 + 34% of AAI over $15,100
$17,601 to $20,100	$4,429 + 40% of AAI over $17,600
$20,101 or more	$5,429 + 47% of AAI over $20,100

Table 5-8: State and other tax allowance for Worksheet A (student only)

Age of older parent*	Allowance if two parents	Allowance if only one parent	Age of older parent*	Allowance if two parents	Allowance if only one paren
25 or less	0	0	45	38,900	26,900
26	2,300	1,600	46	39,900	27,600
27	4,600	3,200	47	40,900	28,300
28	6,900	4,900	48	42,000	29,000
29	9,100	6,500	49	43,000	29,500
30	11,400	8,100	50	44,100	30,200
31	13,700	9,700	51	45,500	30,900
32	16,000	11,300	52	46,700	31,700
33	18,300	13,000	53	48,100	32,500
34	20,600	14,600	54	49,700	33,400
35	22,900	16,200	55	50,900	34,200
36	25,200	17,800	56	52,500	35,000
37	27,400	19,400	57	54,100	36,000
38	29,700	21,100	58	55,700	37,100
39	32,000	22,700	59	57,700	37,900
40	34,300	24,300	60	59,500	39,000
41	35,200	24,700	61	61,600	40,100
42	36,100	25,300	62	63,400	41,300
43	37,000	25,800	63	65,600	42,400
44	38,000	26,500	64	67,900	43,600
			65 or more	70,200	45,100

AGE OF OLDER PARENT is FAFSA/SAR #82, if blank, use age 45 on the table.

Table 5-9: State and other tax allowance for Worksheet A (student only)

Alabama	3%	Kentucky	5%	Ohio	5%
Alaska	0%	Louisiana	2%	Oklahoma	4%
American Samoa	2%	Maine	5%	Oregon	6%
Arizona	3%	Marshall Islands	2%	Palau	2%
Arkansas	4%	Maryland	6%	Pennsylvania	3%
California	5%	Massachusetts	5%	Puerto Rico	2%
Canada	2%	Mexico	2%	Rhode Island	4%
Colorado	4%	Michigan	4%	South Carolina	5%
Connecticut	2%	Minnesota	6%	South Dakota	0%
Delaware	5%	Mississippi	3%	Tennessee	0%
District of Columbia	7%	Missouri	3%	Texas	0%
Federated States of Micronesia	2%	Montana	5%	Utah	5%
		Nebraska	4%	Vermont	4%
Florida	1%	Nevada	0%	Virgin Islands	2%
Georgia	4%	New Hampshire	1%	Virginia	4%
Guam	2%	New Jersey	3%	Washington	0%
Hawaii	6%	New Mexico	4%	West Virginia	4%
Idaho	5%	New York	7%	Wisconsin	5%
Illinois	2%	North Carolina	5%	Wyoming	0%
Indiana	4%	North Dakota	2%	Blank or invalid state	2%
Iowa	5%	Northern Mariana Islands	2%	OTHER	2%
Kansas	4%				

Multiply the total income of student (from Worksheet A, line 37) by the appropriate rate from the table above to get the "state and other tax allowance." Use the students' STATE OF LEGAL RESIDENCE (FAFSA/SAR #11). If this item is blank or invalid, use the STATE in student's mailing address (FAFSA/SAR #6). If both items are blank or invalid, use the parent's STATE OF LEGAL RESIDENCE (FAFSA/SAR #49). If all three items are blank or invalid, use the rate for a blank or invalid state above.

By doing these calculations, you should feel more confident that you're on track with your college savings program. You can also try these other strategies:

SAVE IN YOUR NAME

If you expect to qualify for need-based financial aid, you should save and/or accumulate these funds in *your name*, not the child's (or a custodial account for the child). That's because 35 percent of a student's assets are included in the expected family contribution, but only 5.6 percent of the parents' assets are included. (Also included in the calculation is 50 percent of a student's after-tax income less $1,750 income protection allowance.)

UNCLE SAM'S HELP

Take advantage of the tax rules on children's earnings. The *Tax Reform Act of 1986* (TRA '86) significantly changed long-term planning for children's education. The "kiddie tax" limits every child under the age of 14 to a maximum of $1,300 in *unearned* income. All unearned income—from dividends, interest, and capital gains—in excess of that first $1,300 is taxed at the parents' rate. Children 14 and older pay tax on 100 percent of their taxable income, earned or unearned. Therefore, it may make sense to put enough assets in a child's name to generate up to $1,300 in income each year.

If, for example, a child under 14 had $1,000 in interest income in 1995, the child would pay a federal income tax of $52.50 on that amount ($1,000 – $650 standard deduction = $350 × 15% = $52.50). Yet that same $1,000 in the parents' tax bracket would cost $280 in taxes at the 28 percent rate; $310 at the 31 percent rate. So a family could save $227.50 (at 28 percent) or $257.50 (at 31 percent)—even more in the higher brackets—using this technique! It's not a fortune, but it is a significant "small advantage," especially if you could save that much each year and add it to your college-funding account.

Just remember that you must file a tax return for a dependent child who had more than $650 of gross income, if any portion of that income was generated by investments. If the child had more than $1,300 of investment income, use *Form 8615* to calculate the child's tax.

CUSTODIAL ACCOUNTS

These are established either under your state's *Uniform Gift to Minors Act* (*UGMA*) or the *Uniform Transfer to Minors Act* (*UTMA*) because minors usually cannot buy and sell property *directly*, but an adult custodian can on their behalf. You open either type of custodial account with a bank, mutual fund, or brokerage house. You list yourself as the owner of the account and as custodian under your state's *Uniform Gift to Minors Act*. But keep in mind that the transfer of funds into a custodial account is *irrevocable*. The account becomes the property of the child when he or she reaches the age of 18 to 21, depending on state law. Before the child reaches legal age, the custodian can withdraw funds from the account *only* if they will be used for the child's benefit.

 UTMA accounts

Generally, a *Uniform Transfer to Minors Act* account (*UTMA*) allows you to defer distributions from the account until the child reaches age 21.

The child also will be taxed on all income from the custodial account (subject to "kiddie tax" rules) unless the income is used to fulfill child-support obligations. In New Jersey and California, some judges have ruled that a college education is an "obligation of support." If these rulings are upheld in nondivorce situations, you could lose tax benefits if you use custodial-account funds to pay college expenses. Ask your attorney what laws apply in your state.

Custodial accounts make sense for most people who need the discipline of earmarking funds for their children's college education. At the same time, the income-tax savings give an added boost to your educational funds.

Shift Taxes through a Gift of Appreciated Stock

Suppose you purchased stock more than a year ago for $20 per share and it's now worth $45 per share. If you sell the stock to pay for college expenses, you'll have a $25 *capital gain that will be taxable*. On the other hand, if you give the stock to your child and let the child sell the stock, your child will owe income taxes at the rate for his or her lower tax bracket. If you're in the 28 percent tax bracket and your child is in the 15 percent bracket, you'll save about $3 per share by using this tactic.

Investing for College Expenses

As parents, you'll be deluged by offers and information about investments geared specifically for college savings. Don't be fooled by an especially enticing offer. Remember, your priority is to accumulate as much money as you can in the years until your child reaches college age. If you've been a hesitant investor, you have to change your perspective. Since college costs are rising some 6 to 8 percent a year, you can't afford not to take risks. You need your money to earn more than the rate at which college costs are increasing.

MATCHING YOUR INVESTMENTS TO YOUR TIME HORIZON

You should choose investments with a risk level that matches your tolerance for risk or fluctuation in the market. What's important is to diversify and achieve a reasonable risk-return ratio.

The younger your child, the more aggressive your portfolio should be. Then, as your child approaches college age, you should reallocate your money into fixed-income securities such as short-term bond funds or money market funds.

If your child isn't starting college for at least five years, it's generally a good idea to set aside no more than one-third of your college funds in fixed-income investments. You should keep the remaining two-thirds in growth-oriented investments like stock mutual funds.

USE MUTUAL FUNDS TO PREFUND

If your child won't be attending college for ten or more years, you should invest your college funds in mutual funds. Consider investing in several no-load funds. Most allow you to transfer money automatically each month from your checking account to the fund, *without writing a check.* It's like a payroll deduction. And if you agree to the automatic transfers, many no-load funds will let you open accounts with no (or only a small) initial investment.

If your children are under age 14—and especially if they're under age 10—invest for growth through stock mutual funds. Some parents may be reluctant to do this because investing in stocks can be risky. The value of your stock mutual fund can and *will* fluctuate over time, but stocks consistently have done better than other types of investments such as CDs or money market instruments or bonds. In fact, there hasn't been a 10-year period since 1926 when stocks have lost money and when their average annual return hasn't been higher than that of most other investments.

CONVERT TO FIXED-INCOME SECURITIES BEFORE YOU START TO PAY TUITION

If you're doing your own investing in mutual funds or other vehicles, you need to be more cautious as you get closer to your child's first year in college. Move your money gradually out of stocks and into fixed-income securities, giving yourself plenty of lead time. For example, when the child is age 14 or 15, convert to money market funds, CDs, or short-term, high-quality bond funds enough money to meet the fall freshman term commitment. Six months later, convert enough for the spring freshman term, and so on. Just as you dollar-cost averaged your way into this stock position, you should dollar-cost average out, hoping for a good average sale price.

 Be a good record-keeper!

With all of this buying and selling of stock mutual fund shares, you'll need to keep accurate records of your basis. The basis is the cost and the reinvested dividend or income and any reinvested capital gains. This means that you should keep the year-end summary statements from your mutual funds showing the year's purchases and reinvestments. To simplify your taxes, it's usually best to sell all your shares of a particular mutual fund at one time.

Your basis, compared with how much you sell the investment for, determines your gain or loss. For mutual funds, you can elect to use an average-cost-basis method for determining your gain or loss, or a first-in, first-out (first-bought, first-sold) method. In either case, remember that your basis includes the amount of your original investment *plus* the income or gains that you reinvested while in the fund.

Each year at tax time update your basis records for all investments.

As tuition payments come due, have in place a system that makes the needed dollars available automatically. Depending on the school, this might be in August for the fall term and in January for the spring term.

Alternative Sources of College Money

CollegeSure CD

One response to escalating college expenses is a program offered by The College Savings Bank of Princeton, New Jersey. The *CollegeSure CD* is designed to pay (upon maturity) the average cost of a year's tuition, general fees, and room and board at a four-year private college in the U.S.

The *CollegeSure CD* is a certificate of deposit that pays a variable interest rate which is tied to the annual increase in college costs; investors with deposits of $10,000 or more receive a return 1 percent less than the college inflation rate, while other investors receive 1.5 percent less than the college inflation rate. So it allows you not only to save money for anticipated college expenses but also to hedge against future increases. To receive this inflation hedge, you'll pay an up-front "premium" that will reduce your yield by approximately 2 percent.

The minimum investment is $1,000, although additional purchases are available for as little as $250. And, like any other investment option, there are restrictions (penalties for premature withdrawals) and tax implications (interest is taxable each year as it accrues, although the interest is not paid until the CD matures). For more information, call (800) 888-2723.

To accumulate the amount of money needed to fund educational expenses, most people will need more growth than the *CollegeSure CD* offers.

Zero-Coupon Bonds

Since zero-coupon bonds are sold at a deep discount to their face value, they're affordable for most parents. Both the accrued interest and the bond's face value are received when the bond matures. Bear in mind that you'll be responsible for paying taxes each year on the unpaid interest. If you choose these bonds, time the maturities to coincide with the dates when you'll need the funds.

Baccalaureate/College Savings Bonds

These are **general obligation** zero-coupon bonds. Unlike other municipal bonds, they're usually **noncallable** and tax-exempt. And they typically offer special features that may make them more attractive than most municipal bonds. For more information, you'll need to contact a stockbroker or your bank.

Series EE Savings Bonds

The interest rates for bonds purchased after May 1995 are announced semiannually on May 1 and November 1 in two categories—a "short-term rate" for bonds less than five years old and a "long-term rate" for bonds more than five years old. The short-term rate is 85 percent of the average interest rate on six-month Treasury bills over the three months before each semiannual payment. The long-term rate is 85 percent of the average five-year Treasury note. For the current interest rate, call (800) 4US-BOND—(800) 487-2663.

With Series EE bonds, you can choose when to pay tax on the interest. You can elect either to defer taxes until the bonds are redeemed (sold or gifted) or to have the interest taxed annually as it accrues. If you defer the tax (which is usually appropriate for a parent or child once the child's taxable income exceeds $1,300 per year), no action is required until redemption.

But if you plan to declare the income each year on these bonds, you'll need a copy of the current table—published monthly by the IRS—that shows the bond's value, maturity date, and current interest due. Contact your bank or the IRS for the latest copy.

You should buy a Series EE bond in your child's name that will mature after his or her 14th birthday. That way, it will be taxed at the child's tax rate. By using this strategy, you avoid having to pay the "kiddie tax" on unearned income for children under age 14.

You may be entitled to take advantage of a special EE bond benefit if you meet certain qualifications. Parents who are at least 24 years old may purchase Series EE savings bonds without paying federal income tax on the accrued interest, *if the bonds are used to pay for college expenses* (tuition, but not room and board). This tax break is available only for bonds issued after December 31, 1989.

In addition, the parents' modified adjusted gross income (MAGI) at the time of redemption must be less than $65,250 ($43,500 for single parents), including the interest from the bonds. That deduction is phased out as you earn more. If you're single and your MAGI falls between $43,500 and $58,500, or if you're married and your MAGI is $65,250 to $95,250, only some of the interest is tax-free. These are the 1996 figures; they are indexed for inflation annually.

To determine your exclusion and to compute your MAGI, use IRS *Form 8815,* "Exclusion of Interest from U.S. Savings Bonds Issued After 1989." To keep a written record of the post-1989 Series EE education bonds that you redeem, use *Form 8818*, "Optional Form to Record Redemption of College Savings Bonds."

 Buy savings bonds at the end of the month, and you'll still receive interest for that entire month.

Redeem bonds purchased after May 1, 1995, in the month that interest is paid. Partial interest will not be paid on bonds that are redeemed between scheduled interest payment dates, May 1 and November 1.

YOUR INVESTING REPORT CARD

Since you're investing for your child's education, you should aim for the highest "grades" you can. Here's a quick summary:

C   You deserve a C if you're doing something, even if you're using a life insurance policy to start saving.

B   You get a B if you've put your money into a CD or are using automatic payroll deductions to buy Series EE savings bonds.

A   You deserve an A if you start early and use stock mutual funds, which will get you the highest return over time.

A+ You get the best grade if you're increasing your contributions every year, even by a few dollars.

STATES THAT OFFER BACCALAUREATE OR COLLEGE SAVINGS BONDS

Alabama	Connecticut	Ohio	Vermont
Alaska	Iowa	Oregon	Washington
California	New Hampshire	Texas	

 Put your investment program on "automatic pilot." Some mutual funds will allow you to invest as little as $50 a month with no money down. Setting up an automatic investment plan is an excellent way to reduce risk through dollar-cost averaging and save for your child's education in a disciplined way.

UNDERSTANDING THE AID SYSTEM

Nearly $50 billion in student aid was awarded this past school year. College expenses, however, can be as much as two and one half times the amount of aid. Government-sponsored financial aid comes in two main types—grants and loans. A grant is an outright gift of funds to be used toward education and related expenses, and a loan . . . alas, a loan must be repaid. Both are available on the basis of "need," which means the family's or student's ability to meet the educational expense.

Schools award aid based on a complex formula that takes into account several factors. One major factor you should be aware of is how much of your income you're expected to use for college expenses.

Table 5-10: Income Protection Allowance (Parents)

Your expected contribution is high because the Income Protection Allowance is so low.

Number of family members, including student	Allowance for one student
2	$11,150
3	$13,890
4	$17,150
5	$20,240
6	$23,670
Each additional	$2,670

Your need is determined by a complex series of formulas that have been developed by Congress, aptly known as "Congressional Methodology." If you're interested in the reasoning behind the formula, get the "College Cost Book," available from the College Board. What's important is that you get all the necessary financial-aid forms you may use, and keep careful track of the dates you must submit them. Remember that the basic financial form, "Fee Application for Federal Student Aid" (FAFSA) is due on January 1.

 If you purposely give false or misleading information on your form, you may be subject to a fine of $10,000, receive a prison sentence, or both.

The timing of the application for admission and for financial aid doesn't match. Your child may be accepted to the school of his or her dreams but may not know what aid will be available until the summer preceding the fall semester.

SCHOLARSHIPS AND GRANTS

Your search for financial assistance should begin here. Scholarships and grants are considered gift aid, and need not be repaid.

MERIT AID SCHOLARSHIPS

Merit aid is based on a student's scholastic achievements or particular talents. Colleges and universities are turning more to scholarships based on merit rather than financial need—to recruit the best students.

Private colleges generally have a great deal more of their own money than do public colleges to devote to merit aid. Even so, public schools are designating a greater portion of their institutional aid budgets to merit aid.

PELL GRANTS

Pell Grants are made by the federal government to eligible undergraduate students who can demonstrate a wide gap between their ability to pay and the cost of attending college. (See the following eligibility requirements.)

Just as with other types of financial aid, Pell Grants are based on need as determined by the personal financial information submitted on the grant application. This information is used to determine the amount of your family contribution.

The maximum Pell Grant for 1995–96 is $2,340. You would qualify for the maximum if your family contribution were determined to be zero. For a family of four, this would mean income of less than $25,000 *and* assets of less than $40,000.

 Even if you don't think you'll qualify for a Pell Grant, you should still apply. This is because many schools require a Pell denial before offering other forms of aid.

Once the application for aid is processed, you'll receive a computer-generated *Student Aid Report* (SAR), which you must then forward to the college(s) you are considering. Armed with your SAR, the college's financial-aid office can come up with a package for you. Don't get your hopes up: It's generally less than expected.

Is Your Child Eligible?

Eligibility requirements for a Pell Grant include the following criteria:

▶ Your child is a U.S. citizen or an eligible noncitizen.

▶ Your child is enrolled in an eligible program at an eligible school.

▶ Your child demonstrates need.

▶ Your child is not in default on any federal student aid loans (for instance, Perkins Loans, Stafford Loans), nor has your child borrowed in excess of the allowable loan limits.

▶ Your child has registered with the Selective Service. This applies only to men born after January 1, 1960, who are between the ages of 18 and 26. Call (708) 688-6888 for information on registering (or to check registration status).

▶ Your child has filed a Statement of Educational Purpose and signed an Anti-Drug Abuse Act Certification statement.

▶ Your child has a high school diploma or its equivalent, or can demonstrate "ability to benefit" from the course of study.

▶ Your child is making satisfactory progress in a course of study.

▶ Your child is not a member of a religious community, society, or order that directs a course of study or provides subsistence support.

Federal Supplemental Educational Opportunity Grants (FSEOG)

Students must demonstrate exceptional need; no repayment is required. These grants provide up to $4,000 per year only to students who have Pell Grants. It is important to file as early as possible because there is a limit on the funds awarded.

Federal College Work-Study Programs (CWS)

These programs provide jobs for undergraduate and graduate students who need financial aid. Work-study income helps defray the student's expenses; it is not a credit toward direct costs such as tuition, room and board, and fees.

Loans

A significant portion of the financial aid available for college and graduate studies comes in the form of government-sponsored loans. The government sponsors these loan programs through guarantees, reduced interest rates, deferment of payments, or by interest payments on the loan while the student is in school.

Table 5-11 outlines the major loan programs. Here's what some of the acronyms stand for: HPSL, Health Professions Student Loan; Perkins, formerly NDSL or National Direct Student Loans; Stafford, formerly GSL or Guaranteed Student Loan; and PLUS, Parent Loans to Undergraduate Students.

Table 5-11: Types of education loans

Program	Maximum borrowing	Interest rate	Need– Interest-Based		Subsidy		Grace Period	
			Yes	No	Yes	No	Yes	No
HPSL	*	5%	X		X		X	
Nursing	$10,000	6%	X		X		X	
Perkins†	$15,000	5%	X		X		X	
Stafford‡	$23,000	floating	X	X	X	X	X	X
PLUS	Cost of education	floating		X		X		X

Source: College Loans from Uncle Sam: The Borrower's Guide that Explains It All. *Octameron Associates.*

* Tuition plus $2,500 per year.

† $15,000 as undergraduate. $30,000 as a graduate/professional student, including undergraduate amounts.

‡ $23,000 as undergraduate. $65,500 as a graduate/professional, including undergraduate amounts.

Maximum Borrowing

In the Perkins and Stafford programs, the loan limits *include* any money the student borrowed under the program while an undergraduate.

Interest Rate

Some loan programs have floating rates; in most instances, they are tied to Uncle Sam's T-bills and carry a cap of 8.25 percent (Staffords), and 9 percent (PLUS). The rest have fixed rates (5 or 6 percent).

Need-based

To qualify for a loan, students must demonstrate need. Need is defined as the difference between cost of attendance and the family's ability to contribute to college costs.

Interest Subsidy

Uncle Sam pays interest on the loan (1) while the student is enrolled, and (2) during a grace period. The table does not reflect the interest subsidies paid to lenders to ensure that the loans are "profitable."

Grace Period

Students don't have to begin repayment until after a six- or nine-month period after a course of instruction. Uncle Sam pays the interest during this period.

DIRECT PROGRAM LOANS

The Student Loan Reform Act of 1993 established the Federal Direct Student Loan Program. This program allows students to borrow directly from their schools rather than from a lending institution.

To find out whether the school you are interested in participates in the Federal Direct Student Loan Program, call (800) 4-FED-AID. Approvals are given within 72 hours.

STAFFORD LOANS OFFER THE LOWEST COST

These low-interest loans—available to both undergraduate and graduate students and guaranteed by the federal government—are available through banks, savings and loans, credit unions, and some insurance companies. They can be either subsidized or unsubsidized. The maximum loan amounts for 1995–96 are the following:

	Dependent student	*Independent student*
Freshman	$2,625 per year	$6,625
Sophomore	$3,500 per year	$7,500
Junior, senior, fifth-year undergrads	$5,500 per year	$10,500
Graduate students	N/A	$18,500

▶ **Subsidized.** The government pays interest until six months after the student graduates or leaves school.

▶ **Unsubsidized.** These are not need-based. The interest is not deferred but can be added to the principal amount.

Students pay no interest on subsidized loans while they're enrolled in school *and* for six months after completing their course of study. This gives them time to find a job.

To qualify for a subsidized Stafford Loan, a family must demonstrate "remaining need." Remaining need is the gap between the cost of attendance, minus your family contribution, plus any other aid such as scholarships.

Unsubsidized loans are available to everyone, regardless of need. Stafford Loans carry a variable interest rate that changes every July 1. The 1995–96 rate is 8.25 percent The cap is 8.25 percent. The loan must be repaid within 10 years of graduation and is the student's responsibility.

For example, suppose that the cost of attendance is $9,500, your family contribution (parents' contribution plus the student's contribution) is $4,000 and you have a scholarship of $1,000. The remaining need would be

$9,500	College cost
(4,000)	Expected family contribution
(1,000)	Scholarship
$4,500	Remaining need

For those students who are currently repaying Stafford Loans, the federal government is offering a new program that will allow refinancing of an existing loan. Called the Federal Direct Consolidation Loan program, it carries a variable rate tied to the June 1, 91-day Treasury bill plus 3.1 percent. Recently, this figure was 8.25 percent. The cap is 8.25 percent. You can call (800) 4-FED-AID for details.

Good news/bad news:

Extended repayment, graduated repayment, and income-contingent repayment now are available to students with direct student loans. While these arrangements provide flexibility, especially for those with entry-level salaries, the long-term cost can be high. You should switch back to a standard plan of repayment as soon as possible, because extending costs indefinitely can jeopardize the student's children's education.

Consider federal student-loan forgiveness programs available through the Peace Corps and Vista.

PLUS Loans Are Your Next-best Resource

If your child has entered his or her junior year, you qualify for a Stafford Loan that will cover all remaining expenses. In our example, $4,500 is more than the current Stafford maximum for freshmen and sophomores. So what should you do?

PLUS (Parent Loans to Undergraduate Students) are available to parents, without regard to need. Because these loans are not need-based, their provisions are somewhat different from those of Stafford Loans.

PLUS Loans Are Unlimited.

Under the PLUS Loan program, parents now are eligible to borrow *any amount* (not to exceed the cost of attendance, minus other aid received) to pay for a child's education. These loans are available through banks, savings and loans, credit unions, and insurance companies. Under the Direct Loan Program, the school will assist the federal government by distributing the loan application, processing the loan, and delivering the loan funds. Some lenders do a credit check to determine whether the parent is "creditworthy"; others don't. Parents are responsible for repayment of these loans.

Under the new Federal Direct Student Loan Program, PLUS Loans can be obtained at reduced rates. As of July 1995, this direct rate was 8.98 percent with a cap of 9 percent. There is no difference in interest rates between direct and non-direct PLUS Loans.

PLUS Loans have a 3 percent origination fee. This means that you must pay up-front 3 percent of the amount you are borrowing. For example, on a $5,000 loan, the origination fee would be $150. Insurance fees vary from lender to lender and can cost up to an additional 1 percent of the amount of the loan, so it pays to shop around.

CAUTION Unlike Stafford Loans (which are need-based), there is no grace period for PLUS Loans—the interest clock begins to tick immediately. Repayment of PLUS Loans begins within 60 days of the date the loan is granted, and they can be paid back over 5 or 10 years. Repayment on former SLS loans may be deferred—with interest accumulating—until the student completes school and then must be repaid over 5 or 10 years.

Consolidation Loans

Consolidation Loans allow you to combine different types of federal student loans to simplify repayment. You can consolidate most federal student loans or PLUS Loans and make only one payment a month. You can even consolidate a single loan into a Direct Consolidation Loan in order to get a lower interest rate. The federally sponsored consolidation loans will continue to offer the benefits of deferment and forbearance. To find out more information, call the Direct Loan Servicing Center toll-free number: (800) 848-0982.

Be wary of private lenders that want to consolidate your loans. You will be paying additional fees and a higher interest rate for their services. In addition, you lose the deferment or forbearance that are available only with federal student loans.

How You Can Improve Your Chances for Aid

As you can see, the rules and processes for obtaining aid are complicated. Your chances of receiving aid should improve if you do the following:

▶ **Start early.** You and your child should begin to discuss colleges choices and the costs of attending various colleges early on—the junior year of high school at the latest.

▶ **Take advantage of free resources.** Your high school's guidance counselors should be able to help out, and the government publishes a variety of information. Also, get to know the college's financial aid officer(s).

▶ **Be neat, accurate, and well-organized when completing forms and applications.** An omitted or incorrect item on an application could cause unnecessary delays and result in less aid.

▶ **Shift income.** If you have control over when you'll receive income (bonuses, capital gains, commissions, business income, etc.), realize that more or less income in any given tax year could affect potential aid significantly. Keep in mind that financial-aid eligibility for the *current* school year (1996–97) is based on tax information from the *preceding* year (1995).

▶ **Shift assets.** It may help to shift assets away from the student and toward the parents (since the student's contribution percentage is expected to be larger), but don't concentrate too much effort on this because income is more significant than assets in determining aid.

▶ **Special considerations.** Death in the family, divorce, loss of job earnings, medical expenses, etc., will affect eligibility for aid and the amount of aid offered.

▶ **Use current forms and applications.** Formula and forms are revised annually.

▶ **Apply for aid *every* year even if you have been denied aid previously.**

▶ **Use cash/assets to reduce nonhousing debt.** To increase your loan potential by decreasing the value of your assets, consider paying off these debts with a home-equity line of credit. You also give yourself a tax break when you deduct the interest on the loan.

▶ **Pay cash for major purchases.** If you use cash instead of borrowing for a major purchase like a car, you will reduce your available assets and increase your aid potential by 5.6 percent of what you spend. Of course, *you should do this only if you need a car.* Restructure savings strategies by maximizing contributions to retirement plans—these are not used in financial-aid calculations, although your before-tax yearly contribution will be added back to total income.

▶ **Most important.** Do not offer information that is *not mandated.*

OTHER SOURCES OF FINANCING

PREPAID-TUITION PROGRAMS

College costs keep rising, so wouldn't it be great if you could pay for a child's future college expenses in today's dollars? In some cases, you can do that. Sometimes, parents can pay a predetermined fee to a university that will vary based on the child's current age. By the time the student enrolls in college, the tuition will be prepaid, regardless of the actual costs at that time. A great idea? Yes, but there are some disadvantages.

For example, if your child isn't admitted to the school—or chooses not to attend it— most of these plans return only your initial deposit *without interest*. In all the plans, you avoid any penalty if the plan is transferred to a sibling or if the child dies, is disabled, or earns a scholarship. Also, program restrictions may cap the interest rate if your child attends a non-participating college or decides to attend a school out of state.

Prepaid tuition plans were developed for private universities, but the concept has spread to public schools. Michigan, for example, has already established a program, and in a 1994 decision, the Sixth Circuit in *Michigan v. United States* has held that the Michigan Education Trust, a quasi corporation created by the state to help parents finance their children's college education, is *exempt from federal income tax*. The trust also obtained a favorable ruling from the IRS stating that the purchasers of the advance-tuition contracts would *not* be considered in actual or constructive receipt of income. The IRS stated that taxes are deferred until the contract is redeemed and then the earnings are taxable at the student's tax rate. Other states with prepaid tuition plans include Alabama, Alaska, Florida, Louisiana, Massachusetts, Ohio, Pennsylvania, Texas, and Virginia.

FOR THE LATE STARTER

If you're in a situation in which it's too late to set up an investment plan for education costs, you'll need to find more immediate resources. At this point, you may be tempted to dip into your retirement funds, but remember that even though your child's education *is* important, you'll still need money for your retirement years. Don't jeopardize *your* future! Consider a less expensive school. Or make your kids borrow. You could co-sign the loan, but your kids will be asked to repay the loan first. And, if your child gets a great first job, he or she could certainly repay the loan. Or, if your finances improve, you could help pay back the loan. At least, you'll have flexibility as to who will repay it. Here are some other alternatives:

LOANS

Mortgaging Your Home

Since current tax law has eliminated the deduction of interest on all personal loans, including student loans, borrowing up to $100,000 against the equity in your home may be a good option. If the loan is secured by your home, the interest on a home-equity line of credit will be tax-deductible *under current tax law,* and the money could be used to pay for college expenses. A number of financial institutions offer these loans, and you should shop around for the lowest fees and rates. But remember, if you take this approach, *you'll put your home on the line.* You'll want to be disciplined in paying off this loan.

 Check out IRS *Form 6251* on the alternative minimum tax (AMT), because interest on a home-equity loan that is not used to purchase or improve the home is not deductible for the AMT.

If you don't have enough equity for a home-equity line of credit, here are some other alternatives. Keep in mind, however, that the following loans are classified by the IRS as "personal" and are not tax-deductible.

School-Sponsored Loans

Many universities will lend parents as much as the full cost of a four-year education. Some of these institutions will even allow you to lock in the costs at current prices by establishing a line of credit to cover up to four years' expenses.

State-Sponsored Loans

About 20 states offer low-cost educational loans. For more information, talk to your child's high school counselor, as well as the financial aid staff at the college(s) you've selected.

Bank Loans

Many banks offer educational loans (for example, EXCEL℠ and SHARE) through sponsors such as the New England Education Loan Marketing Corporation (Nellie Mae) and the Education Resources Institute. Up-front fees typically are 5 percent of the loan amount.

The rates generally are pegged to the prime rate or a short-term Treasury-bill rate, plus 2 to 4.5 percent. The maximum that parents can borrow usually is $20,000 annually per child, and repayment periods range between 15 and 20 years. For more details, call Nellie Mae at (800) 634-9308.

Margin Loans

You can borrow against your securities by establishing a margin account with your broker. The interest is nondeductible. There is risk involved if you are highly leveraged and your investments drop drastically in value; in this instance, you may be forced to sell to meet the margin requirements.

Annuities

If you own annuities that were purchased before August 14, 1982, you'll be able to withdraw your initial investment first, which will be tax-exempt. In contrast, withdrawals from an annuity purchased after August 13, 1982, are taxable.

Life Insurance Loans

These are available from permanent-type life insurance policies. Typically, the interest compounds and is subtracted from your policy's cash value. If you don't pay the money back or die while the loan is outstanding, the amount of the loan will reduce the death benefit. Remember that the interest is not deductible if used for personal purposes, and that the interest cost might be more than the nominal interest rate cited by the insurer. If either the dividends or increases in cash value are reduced, you should consider that part of the cost of borrowing.

An Employer's Savings/Thrift Plan

If you're a participant in an employer's savings/thrift plan, often called a 401(k) plan, consider taking a loan from your account. The interest rates for these loans often are favorable, although *the interest isn't tax-deductible.* You generally will have to repay the loan within five years *or when you terminate service,* so be careful—if you leave your job (or it leaves you), you could have to pay back the loan immediately. Failure to do so could cause a taxable distribution and penalty. Under IRS rules, the amount you can borrow cannot exceed $50,000 or the greater of half of the account value.

OTHER SOURCES OF EDUCATION FUNDS

ASSISTANCE FROM GRANDPARENTS

Grandparents and others can take advantage of Code Section 2503(e), which exempts from gift tax *unlimited* amounts of tuition paid on behalf of another. This applies to nursing, elementary, secondary, and graduate school tuition, but does not apply to payments for living expenses, books, supplies, and so on. If the grandparents pay the tuition directly, this can prove to be a good estate-planning move as well.

OTHER ALTERNATIVES

Some employers offer help with tuition. Also check with foundations, religious organizations, fraternities or sororities, town or city clubs, community organizations, and civic groups—some may offer tuition assistance.

INDIVIDUAL RETIREMENT ACCOUNTS (IRAs)

You should borrow from your IRA only as a last resort effort because of the taxes and penalties you'll have to pay. If you receive a distribution or payout from an IRA, it will be taxed as ordinary income. And, except for a few cases, if you withdraw money before you've reached age $59^1/_2$, it also will be subject to a 10 percent penalty tax.

LETTING THE CHOICE OF SCHOOL HELP MANAGE THE EXPENSE

 Cutting costs:

1. Your child should apply to schools where he or she will be a top student—financial aid will be easier to get!

2. Get course credits where possible through tests and advanced-placement courses in high school.

Be sure to shop! Many schools offer discounts in one form or another—for example, to students over 25 or children of alumni. Your child clearly should be involved in this process. Many guidance counselors recommend that students, as high school juniors, visit local colleges to develop a sense of what they're like and how they differ. Will they opt just to go where their friends go? Or will they see their choice (subject to your approval) as an important step on the road to adulthood?

Lastly, consider seeking employment at the local university. Typically, after you work there for five years, your child's tuition is free. If your child prefers to go to another school, many times the university will pay half the tuition to the school of choice.

There are several other ways to save on college.

Community Colleges

Although starting a college education by attending a community college for a few years is an inexpensive route to a four-year degree, be careful if you're shooting ultimately for a prestigious school. Your child's academic performance must be stellar. Stanford University, for example, admitted just 188 students out of 1,197 transfer applicants in 1995.

Also check out courses to make sure all the credits will transfer. If one college has course offerings on a quarterly basis, and another on semesters, your child may have an excess of credits—or too few—when the time comes to transfer to the second institution.

The Military

Look into Reserve Officer Training Corps (ROTC) scholarships sponsored by the Army, Navy, and Air Force. The Army offers up to $12,000 toward tuition, plus fees and books. The Navy and Air Force offer scholarships that may cover full tuition, plus fees and books. In addition there also may be a monthly stipend. In return, the student must serve a minimum of four years after graduation in active duty, the Reserves, or both. Competition for these scholarships has become fierce in recent years, but considering the generous aid, it's worth investigating which colleges offer ROTC. The application deadline is usually in December.

Each of the U.S. service academies offers full rides—that is, tuition, room and board, all fees, books, and so forth—in exchange for a period of mandatory service.

The Army National Guard will "forgive" up to $10,000 in federal loans in exchange for six years of weekend and summer training. For more information, contact the professor of military science at the university's ROTC office or a representative at your local Army recruiting center.

PART-TIME JOBS

Have your child visit the campus student employment office. A work-study program can tailor an on- or off-campus job to fit your child's class and study schedule. Some schools help arrange co-op programs so that students can work in career-related jobs and receive either a salary or college credit.

THE NATIONAL SERVICE TRUST

This program provides $4,725 a year for up to two years of community service in one of four priority areas: education, human services, the environment, and public safety. You must complete 1,700 hours of service work a year. You can work before or after you go to college, graduate school, or trade school, and you can use the funds either to pay current educational expenses or to repay federal student loans. You'll receive a living allowance of at least $7,500 a year and, if necessary, health-care and child-care allowances. For more information, call Americorps at (800) 94-ACORPS.

STUDENT EDUCATIONAL EMPLOYMENT PROGRAM

The federal government often looks at educational institutions to find skilled individuals who could later work for the goverment. This program provides an opportunity to combine academic study with on-the-job experience. Most federal agencies use this program, setting up internships or fellowships to meet their specific personnel needs.

The Student Educational Employment Program has two components—temporary employment and career experience. It is available to all levels of students: high school, vocational and technical, associate degree, baccalaureate degree, graduate degree, and professional degree.

Check your school guidance office, or contact a U.S. Office of Personnel Management Federal Employment Information Center.

STUDENT/PARENT BUSINESS

Start an enterprise aimed at the student market. Deduct business expenses and the expense of college courses related to the business.

YOUR ACTION PLAN

▶ Ask your child (age 16 or over) to read this chapter.

▶ Use Table 5-1, the "monthly education calculator," to estimate how much you'll need to set aside each month.

▶ Review your spending patterns and see whether you can have a specific amount of money automatically withdrawn each month from your paycheck or bank account.

▶ Start a savings vehicle. It's important that you have this account even before you decide where to invest the money.

▶ Save any "found money" from bonuses, tax refunds, inheritances, etc.

▶ For children under age 14, invest primarily in growth mutual funds.

▶ Call (800) 4-FEDAID to receive *The Student Guide* free.

ADDITIONAL RESOURCES

AOL's Reference Service Press Funding Focus Forum

On-line listings of grants and scholarships. Keyword: RSP.

College Board Publications   (212) 713-8000

For the *College Costs and Financial Aid Handbook 1996*, write The College Board Guidance Publishing, 45 Columbus Avenue, New York, NY 10023.

College Costs Explorer FUND FINDER

A scholarship database put together by the College Board. Check with your high school guidance department, local library, or a college financial-aid office for access to this database. This database is now available on the WorldWide Web (http://www.collegeboard.org), or write to the College Board for more information.

Collegiate Choice   (201) 871-0098

To buy a $15 videotape to preview your college choice.

Consern (800) 767-5626

To find out about college loans.

Educate America Resource Network (EARN) (800) 733-GRAD

For free college cost analysis. Membership provides a number of benefits, including financial-aid assistance, scholarship information, money-saving consumer services, and tuition planning. Write 1055 Broadway St., Kansas City, MO 64105-9855.

Federal Student Finance Aid Information Center (800) 4-FED-AID
(800) 433-3243

For a free booklet, *The Student Guide: Five Federal Financial Aid Programs.*

National Association of College Admission Counselors (703) 836-2222

Octameron Associates (703) 836-5480

For guidance on receiving financial aid for children's college education; books, videos, software, and counseling services are available. "How to Pay for College" is a 40-minute videotape from NewsTeam Video and Octameron Associates that delves into the details of financing college. A companion book is based on Octameron's guide, *Don't Miss Out!*, and includes worksheets to help you calculate your family's expected contribution, as well as what you need to set aside monthly to meet future college costs. The video costs $30 plus postage and handling. The book costs $7.50 plus postage. Financial-aid counseling is available at hourly rates each Tuesday.

Stafford Loan (800) 433-3243

For the phone number and address of state agencies that might grant a Stafford Loan.

College Funding Strategies (203) 658-0444

90 HopMeadow St., Simsbury, CT 06070. This organization charges a one-time fee to help parents and grandparents set up savings and investment plans to prefund college expenses.

▼

BUYING A HOME

For anyone planning to buy a home, either first-time or repeat buyers, because the real estate market has changed dramatically and tax laws have also changed

Whether you're buying your first or your thirty-first home, there's no question that buying a home is one of the biggest financial transactions that you're ever going to make. It's not just the amount of money involved that makes the decision so stressful. There are additional considerations as well:

▶ **Commitment.** Unless you're investing in real estate, generally, when you buy a home, you're making a long-term commitment. You're probably borrowing a substantial amount of money that you will need to repay over the next 10 to 30 years. In addition to the mortgage, you're responsible for the upkeep and mainte-nance of your home, whether you do the repairs yourself or pay someone else to do them. These obligations may require adjustments to your lifestyle, especially if up until now you've been sharing low-rent apartments.

▶ **Emotions.** Buying a house has long been the classic American dream, but wrapped up in the dream are many different feelings. You may be looking to duplicate the home you grew up in, or, on the other hand, you may want the space and backyard that you didn't have as a child. And, if you have children, you want to find a home that they will also enjoy.

▶ **Purchase Process.** If you're a first-time homebuyer, you've unoubtedly heard horror stories from friends about their experiences. Buying a home is simply a bewildering experience that takes on a life of its own. From finding that perfect house to the actual closing, almost anything can and will happen. Even if your financing comes through without a snag and both you and the seller are reasonable people, assume that some hassles will occur before you move in. Obviously, the more knowledgeable and prepared you are about the process, the more likely you are to be able to minimize the problems.

There's nothing like falling in love with the perfect home to make you confront economic realities. Can you afford to buy your dream house, or will you have to settle for less, with the hope that you can buy up in the future? There's no easy answer. You have to consider the unpredictable economy generally and the sharp decline in real estate prices over the past decade or so, as well as your own situation—whether your job is secure, how much savings you have, and whether you have other major expenses such as college or medical bills.

THE SIX STEPS TO BUYING A HOME

Figuring out how to make the American dream a reality can be mind-boggling. Here are six steps that will help simplify the home-buying process:

1. HOW MUCH HOME CAN YOU AFFORD?

This is a crucial first question for anyone buying a home. Only you can answer this question. And your response is not how much money you will be able to borrow. Don't let a banker or mortgage broker answer this question for you. Remember, you have to consider not just the purchase price but the additional expenses you'll have as a home owner. Until you own a home, you can't begin to imagine how much you'll be spending on furnishings and repairs. You can be sure that you'll quickly be on a first-name basis with the clerks at your local hardware store or warehouse club. It doesn't matter whether you buy a newly built home or an older house; once you move in and start making the house "your home," inevitably, you'll find that you need to buy more items than you expected.

Rule of thumb:

All your monthly debt, including housing expenses, car payments, and insurance, should not exceed 36 percent of your gross income. Banks may be willing to lend you more, but you shouldn't exceed these guidelines. If you saddle yourself with higher debt payments, you may find yourself in trouble, particularly if you also encounter unexpected bills—for example, for home repairs or a sudden illness.

The experts say that you can afford to have 28 percent of your annual income as housing expense. In other words, according to the banks, your monthly mortgage *principal* and *interest* payments—plus property *taxes* and homeowner's *insurance* (PITI)—should not exceed 28 percent of your gross monthly income. And your *monthly house payment plus other debt should* not be more than 36 percent of your annual income. If your job is very secure and your finances are generally in good shape, then you can go slightly higher than the 28 percent, but you should pay attention to these guidelines and make sure you stay within the recommended range. If you're tempted to exceed these guidelines, thinking of the tax advantages as well the probability that your home will greatly appreciate in value and you'll be able to make a substantial profit when you sell it, think again. The booming real estate market of the early 1980s is long gone, so you should not base your financial plans on your home appreciating in value. Buy a home that you like *and* can comfortably afford.

The following table gives some examples of annual gross income, monthly gross income, and the amount of this monthly income available for your house payment (figured at 28 percent) according to lenders' standards.

Table 6-1: How much can you afford?

Annual Gross Income	Monthly Gross Income	28% of Gross Income
$15,000	$1,250	$350
$20,000	$1,667	$467
$25,000	$2,083	$583
$30,000	$2,500	$700
$35,000	$2,917	$817
$40,000	$3,333	$933
$45,000	$3,750	$1,050
$50,000	$4,167	$1,167

Once you know how much you can *spend* on your monthly house payment, you are on your way to finding out how much you can *afford*. And the amount you can afford will depend directly upon the interest rate. For example, you'll be able to buy a more expensive home if you're paying 9 percent interest as opposed to 11 percent. (See Table 6-3 in the mortage section, below).

2. Review Your Credit before You Apply for a Mortgage.

By looking at your credit report ahead of time, you'll have no surprises when you fall in love with that one perfect house and want to get a mortgage immediately. To get a copy of your credit report, call one of the leading credit bureaus: Equifax (800) 685-1111 or TRW (800) 682-7654. There may be things you can do that will help you qualify for a mortgage. You should look for:

► **Inactive credit cards that are listed as open.** You should cancel these cards and notify the credit bureaus. Having too much available credit can hurt you when you're applying for a mortgage. Banks will take these lines of credit into account when your application is renewed.

► **Inaccurate records of past accounts or delinquent records.** If there are inaccuracies or other information that you can explain—perhaps your credit record reflects joint accounts you had with a former spouse or card use when your credit cards were stolen—you should write to the credit bureaus and explain the circumstances.

3. Try to prequalify for a mortgage.

Even before you start your search, go to one or two local banks and see whether you can be prequalified. Although the bank will not give you a written confirmation that you will get a specific mortgage until all your financials are verified, it will tell you that, based on the information you have provided, you are likely to qualify for a mortgage of a certain amount. This knowledge can help you as you begin your house hunt.

4. Decide what you're looking for in a home.

This can be the $64,000 question, and it's likely that you and your spouse will have different priorities. Obviously, the two of you will have to sort things out before you finally choose a house. Make a list of your priorities before you start shopping for a home. Following is a sample priorities checklist:

Table 6-2: Sample Priorities Checklist

Type of neighborhood	Snow removal
Nearby homes/businesses	Square footage
Traffic	Number of bedrooms
Noise level	Number of baths
Safety/Crime rate	Closet/storage space
Age mix of neighbors	Basement (full, partial, slab)
Number of children	Garbage service
Pet restrictions	Fireplace(s)
Parking	Lot size
Zoning regulations	Garage (# of cars)
Neighborhood restrictions/covenants	Age of home
School district	Type of utilities:
Fire protection	(1)gas (2)oil (3)electric
Police protection	Air conditioning

If you're using a broker, you can give your list to the broker so that he or she will be on the right track when looking through the multiple-listings services or real estate ads. Of course, you should use your list as you begin your search, whether or not you're using a broker. You can look in the Sunday newspapers or community publications that list homes for sale. Drive through neighborhoods that interest you and look for OPEN HOUSE or FOR SALE signs.

Remember, the only questions that are stupid are the ones you don't ask. Don't overlook what appears to be obvious. For example, if you're looking at homes in a rural area, don't forget to ask about trash pick-up or water sewage systems. If you're concerned about the cost of utilities, call the utility and ask about bills for a particular size home for the entire year. Some brokers will also have this information.

Using a broker can cut down on the amount of legwork you'll have to do on your own. Even so, you should give a broker your price range along with the features you're looking for. Remember, too, that brokers are paid a commission by the seller from the sale. This means that you should filter all the information the broker gives you, knowing that he or she is acting on behalf of the seller. An alternative is to use a buyer's broker. In this case, you pay the broker a fee to represent you and help you negotiate the best deal possible. To find a buyer's broker, check the Yellow Pages or get a referral from one of the following:

The National Association of Real Estate Buyer's Brokers, Belmont, CA (415) 591-5446

Jerilyn Coats of Carriage Trade Realty, Wayne, PA (215) 687-0202

The Single Agency Realty Association (SARA), Germantown, MD (301) 353-1191

Buyer's Resource, Denver, CO (800) 359-4092

Who's Who in Creative Real Estate, Ventura, CA (800) 729-5147

Before you look at homes, you should read a guide on selling your home. What you're looking for are the tips that sellers employ to make their home more presentable. For example, sellers turn the heat up to make the house warmer; they take down personal pictures and items so that you can envision the house as you want it; they touch up the front of the house to enhance the home's appeal. In short, sellers polish their apple to maximize its appeal. Don't be blinded by the polish. See the house for what it is.

Since it's difficult to remember every feature of the homes you visit, pick up any fact sheets that the seller or broker has prepared. You should also take along a checklist to fill out. That way, at the end of a long day of house hunting, you can compare the checklists. If possible, you should videotape homes that you're interested in. You'd be amazed at what you see when you go home and watch the video in your own living room.

You should also visit homes at different times of the day. If you visit a house at night, you may not realize that trucks drive by frequently, kicking up gravel or dust onto the porch. My wife and I were once so transfixed by a beautiful home on the backside of the golf course that we practically made an offer on the spot. Later we came back by ourselves, without the broker, and stood outside and listened. You could clearly hear the traffic on the nearby freeway through the dense trees. In the winter, without the cushioning effect of the leaves, the noise would have been deafening. Obviously, we didn't buy that house.

Here's a detailed checklist to use when you're visiting homes:

Worksheet 6A: Your house-hunting checklist

Take a copy of this list with you and mark it for each house you look at.

The home	Good	Average	Poor
Square footage			
Number of bedrooms			
Number of baths			
Floor plan			
Condition of interior walls			
Basement			
Fireplace			
Cable TV			
Basement: dampness or odors			
Exterior condition			
Lawn/yard space and condition			
Fence			
Patio or deck			
Garage			
Energy-efficiency ratings*			
Screens, storm windows			
Roof: age and condition			
Gutters and downspouts			

The neighborhood	Good	Average	Poor
Appearance/condition of nearby homes/businesses			
Traffic			
Noise level			
Safety/security			
Age mix of neighbors			
Number of children			
Pet restrictions			
Parking			
Zoning regulations			
Neighborhood restrictions/ covenants			
Fire protection			
Police			
Snow removal			
Garbage service			

(continued)

* A comparison of the house to a regional average may be available through utility bills.

Worksheet 6A: (continued)

The schools	Good	Average	Poor
Age/condition	_____	_____	_____
Reputation	_____	_____	_____
Achievement test scores	_____	_____	_____
Play areas	_____	_____	_____
Curriculum	_____	_____	_____
Class size	_____	_____	_____
Busing distance	_____	_____	_____
Dropout ratio	_____	_____	_____

Convenience	Good	Average	Poor
Supermarket	_____	_____	_____
Schools	_____	_____	_____
Work	_____	_____	_____
Shopping	_____	_____	_____
Child care	_____	_____	_____
Hospitals	_____	_____	_____
Doctor/dentist	_____	_____	_____
Recreation/parks	_____	_____	_____
Restaurants/entertainment	_____	_____	_____
Church/synagogue	_____	_____	_____
Airport	_____	_____	_____
Highways	_____	_____	_____
Public transportation	_____	_____	_____

Date of visit: _____

Address of home: _____

Name of broker: _____

Other notes: _____

_____

5. NEGOTIATE THE PRICE.

Finally, you've found your dream house. Now comes the tricky part. How much should you offer for it? Obviously, you know the asking price. Discuss the following points with the broker:

▶ **The asking price.** Is it in line with prices in the area for similar homes?

► the name and address of someone who can verify your employment

You should be familiar with some common types of mortgages *before* you shop for a loan. Each has advantages and disadvantages, depending on your income level, the length of time you plan to own the home, and other factors. Ask your lender to explain each option before you make a decision.

Fixed-Rate Mortgage

With fixed-rate or "conventional" mortgages, the interest rate stays the same for the term of the mortgage, generally 15 or 30 years.

Advantage: Your payment is a stable monthly budget expense.

Disadvantage: Interest rates tend to be higher on fixed-rate loans than they are on other loans—at least initially.

Adjustable-Rate Mortgage (ARM)

With this type of loan, your interest rate and monthly payments usually start out lower than with a fixed-rate mortgage. However, your rate and payment can change either up or down as often as once or twice a year. The adjustment is usually tied to a financial index such as the U.S. Treasury Securities Index. Typically, there is an *annual* adjustment cap of 2 percent and a *lifetime* adjustment cap of 6 percent.

Advantage: With an ARM, you may be able to afford a more expensive home because your initial interest rate and payment will be lower.

Disadvantage: The possibility of upwards adjustments can price the loan payments out of your range.

Government-Insured Mortgages

The federal government backs two types of mortgages: FHA (the Federal Housing Authority) and VA (the Department of Veterans Affairs). The government insures the lender against loss in case the home buyer defaults on the loan. The FHA program was set up to put homes within reach of lower-income people. The VA program was set up as a benefit to armed services personnel. With an FHA-insured mortgage, you can purchase your home with as little as 3 percent down. With a VA-insured mortgage, you can purchase your home with nothing down.

Assumable or Nonassumable

You may find a home with a mortgage loan you can assume (take over) from the previous owner. This means that the bank or other lender is willing to transfer its old loan on the home to you, sometimes at the same interest rate, sometimes at a different interest rate.

Advantage: This can be a wonderful bargain, depending on interest rates. Loan paperwork usually is not complicated, so the closing is often quicker.

Disadvantage: Because the seller is usually liable on the note if you should default, sellers are less willing to negotiate a lower purchase price.

In addition to deciding which mortgage is right for you, you also must decide whether to use a mortgage broker. A mortgage broker represents many different lenders and can get you the lowest available rate. Using a broker can be a convenient way to shop for the best rate. If, on the other hand, you have a less-than-stellar credit history, you should approach a local bank or credit union. Typically, these institutions have more flexibility and may be willing to give you a mortgage because of your previous relationship with the bank.

Here's a worksheet to help you figure out what mortgage you can afford:

Table 6-3: Mortgage factors			
	Annual Mortgage Term		
Interest rate	**15 years**	**20 years**	**30 years**
4%	135.2	165.0	209.5
5%	126.5	151.5	186.3
6%	118.5	139.6	166.8
7%	111.3	129.0	150.3
8%	104.6	120.0	136.3
9%	98.6	111.1	124.3
10%	93.1	103.6	114.0
11%	88.0	96.9	105.0
12%	83.3	90.8	97.2

The factors in Table 6-3 should be used in the following exercise:

How much of a mortgage should you qualify for?

	Example	You
Line 1. Monthly payment you can afford (Example: $700 from **Table 6-1**)	$700.00	_____
Line 2. Annual property tax and hazard (Example: $1,900 + $350 = $2,250)	$2,250.00	_____
Line 3. Divide Line 2 by 12 (Example: $2,250 ÷ 12 = $187.50).	$187.50	_____
Line 4. Subtract Line 3 from Line 1 (Example: $700 – $187.50 = $512.50).	$512.50	_____
Line 5. Factor from **Table 6-3** (Example: 7% mortgage for 30 years)	150.30	_____
Line 6. Multiply Line 4 by Line 5 to determine the approximate mortgage you should qualify for (Example: $512.50 ×150.3 = $77,028.75).	$77,029.00	_____

 Self-employed?

Even if your salary qualifies you for a mortgage, lenders will want to analyze your business to be certain it will survive as long as the loan.

You will be required to produce:

▶ signed federal business income tax returns for the last two years

▶ signed year-to-date profit-and-loss statement

▶ two years' worth of balance sheets for the business, "reviewed" by a CPA

HOW MUCH CASH YOU'LL NEED TO HAVE

Even though the money you get from the lender will probably cover the majority of the purchase price, you still will have to come up with cash for the earnest money, the down payment, and the closing costs, which include a variety of fees.

EARNEST MONEY

When you make an offer on a home, the seller will probably require a deposit as proof that your offer is serious. The seller wants a deposit because the house will be taken off the market once a purchase agreement is signed. This "earnest money" is held by the seller's broker in an escrow account. If your offer is accepted, your deposit will become part of the down payment or closing costs. If your offer is rejected, the broker will return your deposit.

THE DOWN PAYMENT

The lender will expect you to pay a percentage of the home's price as a down payment. The higher your down payment, the lower the amount of your mortgage loan and corresponding monthly payments. Typically, down payments range from 10 to 20 percent of the purchase price. Many lenders will charge a mortgage insurance premium of 0.5 to 1 percent of the loan when the down payment is less than 20 percent of the purchase price.

CLOSING COSTS

These can average 3 to 5 percent of the price of your home, and include mortgage fees and other expenses.

APPLICATION FEE

This charge covers the initial processing costs and the checking of your credit report. It's negotiable. There may be a separate charge of $15 or $20 for the actual credit report.

TITLE SEARCH AND TITLE INSURANCE

This charge covers the cost of the title search: examining the public record to confirm ownership of the real estate. It also covers the cost of a title policy, which insures the policyholder for a specific amount against any loss caused by discrepancies in the title to the property.

 Ask the company carrying the present policy on the house whether it can issue your policy at a reissue rate. You could save up to 70 percent of what it would cost for a new policy.

Table 6-4: Typical costs for a home buyer*

	Sample range	Your situation
Application fee	$75 – $300	_____
Appraisal fee	$150 – $400	_____
Survey costs	$125 – $300	_____
Homeowner's hazard insurance (one year prepaid)	$300 – $600	_____
Attorneys' fees	$100 – $400	_____
Title search and title insurance	$450 – $600	_____
Structural and pest inspection fees	$175 – $350	_____
Loan-origination fees	1% of loan or less	_____
Prepaid interest (daily loan rate x loan amount x number of days from closing to month's end)	1 – 30 days' interest payments	_____
Mortgage insurance premium (if down payment is less than 20%)	0.5 – 1% of loan	_____
Points	0 – 3% of loan	_____
Taxes: School (some states) Property	*prorata*	_____ _____
Recording fees	vary by state	_____

* Because costs may vary from area to area and from lender to lender, this chart is an estimate only.

In addition to the title policy, title companies offer a fee policy to cover the difference between the amount of the mortgage and the purchase price of the home.

Most title insurance policies cover liens that exist before you buy (or refinance) your home. Subsequent liens, from either your original purchase mortgage or a home-equity loan, are not covered. When you finish repaying your home loan(s), be sure to obtain—from your county clerk's office or the local agency housing real estate records—a document confirming your lender's removal of its lien against your home.

ATTORNEYS' FEES

The lender usually will charge you for fees paid to the lawyer or company that conducts the closing for the lender. Typically, the closing will occur at the lender's attorney's office. You should have your own attorney to represent you at all stages of the transaction.

LOAN-ORIGINATION FEES AND POINTS

The origination fee is charged for the lender's work in evaluating and preparing your mortgage loan. Not all lenders charge origination fees. If yours does, this may be a negotiable item. Points are prepaid finance charges imposed by the lender at closing to increase the lender's yield beyond the stated interest rate on the mortgage note. One "point" equals 1 percent of the loan amount. For example, one point of a $75,000 loan would be $750. Points and origination fees may be deductible on your income tax return if you itemize deductions. (See IRS *Publication 936, Home Mortgage Interest Deduction.*)

Generally, points and origination fees can be deducted in the first year on original mortgages but not on refinancings. For refinancings, the deduction must be spread over the life of the mortgage.

> **Example:** A 30-year, $100,000 refinancing loan with 1% origination fee and 1 point. Total points are the equivalent of 2% of $100,000 or $2,000; $2,000 ÷ 30 = $66.67, so you may deduct $66.67 each year as prepaid interest.

Points and origination fees sometimes can be financed by adding them to the loan amount. But if you refinance again, you can deduct rather than amortize the remainder of the points you paid on the previous refinancing. If you've refinanced twice but didn't deduct the points from the first refinancing, file an amended tax return to capture the deduction.

APPRAISAL FEE

The lender orders an appraisal to make sure that the fair-market value of the property equals or exceeds the amount of the loan.

MISCELLANEOUS

You might also have a fee for a VA loan or FHA loan, your own attorney's costs, and private mortgage insurance.

CAUTION Stay away from mortgage insurance (credit life insurance) from the lender to cover your outstanding mortgage balance. It's too expensive! You're generally much better off purchasing a term or universal life policy on your life equal to the amount of your outstanding loan balance. Remember, too, that most of the fees associated with getting a mortgage are negotiable. Be outspoken and ask the banker to waive or lower fees, including the application, appraisal, and attorney's fees.

THE CLOSING

Even if you've used a broker or attorney to help you with your contract, you still have to pay attention to the details of the process. You should mark a calendar so that you don't forget any important dates. Make sure you talk regularly to your attorney or broker, or the seller.

Make sure the contract is very specific so that you won't be disappointed or suprised when you do your final walk-through inspection prior to closing. Obviously, the contract will include the price agreed upon, but it should also specify which items the seller has agreed to leave in the house. Any items not listed cannot be presumed to be part of the sale. You'd be amazed at the items that buyers and sellers forget—for example, the garage door remote!

Of course, to avoid hassles at the eleventh hour, it helps to remain on good terms with the seller.

When you do your walk-through, make sure the house is in the condition you expected. In fact, you may want to videotape the house and compare it to your original videotape. That way, there can be no dispute over what items are in the house or its condition.

YOUR ACTION PLAN

Before you start looking

▶ Get a copy of your credit report so that you can make any necessary corrections.

▶ Detemine how much you can afford to spend on your home.

▶ Decide what type of home you want, what features it should have, and where you want to look for it.

When you begin looking

▶ Shop around and tour at least six to ten homes in your "range."

▶ Apply for a mortgage—again, comparison-shop for the best rate and terms. Remember that everything is negotiable.

▶ Keep good records and copies of all relevant paperwork during the process.

RESOURCES

You can order an eight-booklet set developed by the Department of Consumer Economics and Housing at Cornell University that covers home buying, mortgage options, closing costs, and other topics.

Request the H.O.M.E. Series in writing from the Media Services Distribution Center, 7–8 Business and Technology Park, Cornell University, Ithaca, NY 14850. $6.50.

SELLING A HOME/ MOVING

For anyone selling a home

Few events are more exciting or more nerve-wracking than moving. Whether you're relocating to take a new job or simply moving across town, there are many issues—financial and logistical—that you must handle.

Suppose that you're selling your home and moving to a new one. As is the case with buying a home, you can choose to sell on your own or use a broker. If your home is in a highly desirable neighborhood and you don't anticipate having trouble selling it, then you may want to try to sell it on your own. You can place ads in a local newspaper or hold open houses. While you may not have to make major renovations, you do want your home to look as presentable as possible. There are some relatively easy ways to spruce up your home:

► **Paint your front door and have your lawn mowed and manicured.** It may seem obvious, but you want to make the best first impression on potential buyers.

► **Remove clutter from your rooms.** If you're a packrat who can't stand to throw anything away, at least put items away in closets or store some of your possessions in boxes in your garage or basement. The less you have in your rooms, the larger they'll look to visitors.

▶ **Use simple wallpaper or neutral paint to cover up your unique bedroom or bathroom.** You may love purple and black stripes, but chances are that other people prefer less bold colors.

▶ **Keep your kitchen in pristine condition, and make sure all your appliances work.** Most prospective buyers spend more time snooping around the kitchen than other rooms, so it should be terrific shape.

If you decide to use a broker, assume that the broker's commission—generally 6 to 8 percent—of the selling price is negotiable. Brokers may say that they only take a commission of X, but if the broker knows you're ready to sell your home yourself, he or she will probably be willing to take a lower commission. After all, some commission is better than none.

Tax Impact of Selling a Home

You've found a buyer for your home, and the sale looks like it will go through without a hitch. That's terrific. Now you have to make sure you comply with all Uncle Sam's rules on selling a house. Most of you will never face a tax liability on the profit from the sale of a home. Under the deferral-of-gain rules, when you sell your home and buy a more expensive one, any capital gain from the sale of the old home usually is deferred. In fact, assuming that you purchase a more expensive residence within 24 months, you *must* defer the gain under the tax law. It's likely that you'll keep deferring the gain from one home sale to another until you die.

After you die, your heirs will receive a share of the residence at a "step-up" tax basis. That stepped-up basis is equal to the current fair-market value of the homeowner's share of the residence. For example, suppose someone has a house that he or she paid $75,000 for, but which now has a current fair-market value of $100,000. After the owner's death, the heirs would claim as their tax basis the current fair-market value—$100,000. If the heirs immediately sell for its $100,000 market value, they won't have to pay any capital gains tax. But if the heirs sell the house for more than $100,000 and don't buy a new house within 24 months or buy one that costs less than the sale price, they will have to pay capital gains tax.

The following worksheet enables you to calculate the gain on your home. For a list of some items that may be included in your home's tax basis, review the *"Cost Basis in Your Home"* item inventory following the worksheet. Of course, you shouldn't include items in the property's tax basis unless they are included in the sale. You should be able to document these additions and improvements.

Worksheet 7A: Sale of a home

Based on IRS *Form 2119*

	Example	Your situation
1. Selling price of home*	$200,000	_____
2. Expense of sale†	12,000	_____
3. Amount realized. Subtract Line 2 from Line 1	188,000	_____
4. Basis of home sold†	50,000	_____
5. Gain on sale. Subtract Line 4 from Line 3	138,000	_____
6. If you are electing to use the one-time exclusion, enter $125,000 ($62,500, if married filing separate return). If you are not electing the exclusion or are not eligible for it, enter 0	125,000	_____
7. Subtract Line 6 from Line 5	13,000	_____
8. Fixing-up expenses‡	0	_____
9. Adjusted sale price. Subtract Line 8 from Line 3	188,000	_____
10. Cost of new home	150,000	_____
11. Add Line 6 and Line 10	275,000	_____
12. Subtract Line 11 from Line 9 (if a negative number, enter 0)	0	_____
13. Taxable gain. Enter smaller of Line 7 or Line 12	0	_____
14. Postponed gain. Subtract Line 13 from Line 7	13,000	_____
15. Adjusted basis of new home. Subtract Line 14 from Line 10	137,000	_____

* Do not include personal property items that you sold with your home.

† Include sales commissions, advertising and legal expenses. Also, loan charges, such as points charged to the seller.
Do not include fixing-up expenses.

‡ Enter the amount paid for work performed on your old home in order to help sell it. This would include expenses for work performed within 90 days before the contract to sell the home was signed to 30 days after the sale.

If you filed *Form 2119* when you originally bought your old home, use the adjusted basis of the new home from the last line of that *Form 2119* as the starting point to figure the basis of your old home. Then by using the list provided, add any capital improvements. If you did not file *Form 2119* when you originally bought your old home, use the cost of the home as the starting point.

For more information on selling and buying a home, see IRS *Publication 523, Tax Information on Selling Your Home,* and IRS *Form 2119, Sale of your Home.*

COST BASIS IN YOUR HOME

Use the following list as a reminder of items that can be included in the tax basis of your home.

Exterior	
Additional acreage or lots	Plants, bulbs, and seeds
Roofing additions and replacements	Topsoil and fill
Flashing	Grading
Gutters, leaders, drain pipes, and dry wells	Grass seed
Waterproofing	Fertilizers and conditions
Termite-proofing	Telephone and electrical outlets
Storm windows and doors	Retaining walls
	Fences and gates
Building additions	Play yard
Workshed—outbuildings	Driveway—paving or gravel
Aluminum siding	Walks
Breezeway	Pathways
Garage	Barbecue pit
Porch	Surveying of property
	Mailbox
Garden and land	Terraces and patios
Lawn sprinkler system	Cement staircase
Water well and pump	Swimming pool
Shrubs, bushes, and vines	Lamp post
Trees	

Interior	
Carpeting and padding	Bookcases, built-in furniture
Linoleum	Radiator covers
Flooring—wood, tile, etc.	Ventilators
Stairs that have been replaced or added	Window seats
Ceilings (acoustical)	Fireplace mantel
Cabinets	Closets
Closet shelves	Cupboards

Conversion of attic or basement to recreation or bedroom

Windows

Replacement

Screens

Storm sash

Window shades

Weather stripping

Venetian blinds

Inside walls

Alterations or plastering

Wood paneling

Wall tiles

Plumbing and sanitation

Sinks

Tubs

Floor drains

Grease traps

Hot-water tank

Pumps

Septic system

Hot-water pipe

Copper tubing

Cold-water pipe

Water supply system

Traps

Sump pump

Vent pipe

Heating and air conditioning

Cooling equipment

Air conditioning

Attic fan

Circulating system

Furnace and appurtenances

Boiler

Hot-water heater

Fireplace heater

Radiators and valves

Warm-air grills and registers

Space heaters

Automatic thermostats

Electricity and lighting

Circuit breakers

Fuse boxes

Lightning rods

Wiring system

TV antenna and wiring

Hardware, fixtures, and locks

For cabinets and closets

For doors

For windows

Lighting fixtures

For curtains and draperies

Hamper

Linen chute

Supply cabinets

Kitchen

Counter tops

Dishwasher

Drain boards

Food freezer

Range

Range hood

Garbage disposal

(continued)

Interior (continued)

Bathrooms

Tub hanger

Tub sliding doors

Unit heater

Towel racks

Shower controls

Shower cabinet

Mirrors

Medicine cabinet

Communication equipment

Call bells or chimes

Intercommunication system

Telephone raceways

Fire or burglar alarm system

Other items (if permanently attached)

Fireplace equipment

Workshop equipment

Mirrors

Dumbwaiter

Insulation

Legal and Tax Issues of Moving

There's no way you can avoid the hassles of moving. Your best defense is to stay organized and prepare yourself as much as possible ahead of time. You'll find a checklist to help you keep track of all the details on pages 110–12, but you should also be aware of the bigger picture. Moving has a significant impact on your tax bill—depending on where you move to and why you're moving. In fact, before you finalize your move, you should look into the tax rates in states or regions you're considering. The local tax department, a broker, or the Chamber of Commerce should be able to give you information on taxes.

Local Income Taxes

Prepare yourself for differences in tax laws. Not every state has a personal income tax, but taxes may be significantly higher in the state you're moving to than in your current state. Also, local municipalities sometimes levy income or earnings taxes, so relocating on one side or the other of a county or city line may affect your net income. Investigate whether your new state or locality uses the federal adjusted gross income in determining your tax liability. Many states offer itemized deductions that go well beyond federal deductions, so don't overlook them. You must determine what the appropriate withholding rules are at your new location. You may be required to make estimated payments or have more withheld than your final liability. Make sure you don't end up paying a penalty.

Some significant changes to moving deductions were made in the 1993 tax bill. First, these deductions are "above-line deductions" that are not affected negatively by the phase-out of itemized deductions. In addition, for moving expenses incurred after December 31, 1993, the following will no longer be deductible:

▶ expenses of selling or buying a residence (These expenses can, however, reduce the selling price or be added to the basis of a house.)

▶ meal expenses incurred while traveling or while living in temporary quarters near a new job

▶ cost of pre-move house hunting trips

▶ cost of temporary living expenses in the new location for up to 30 days

On the positive side, any *deductible* moving expenses reimbursed by your employer will not be required to be included in income. When an employer reimburses you for expenses that are no longer deductible (such as those listed above), the reimbursement will be included as income. How you report reimbursements from your employer will depend on whether your employer has an "acceptable" or nonacceptable plan. Your employer will give you a list of payments made for you.

A distance requirement must be met in order for a move to qualify as an adjustment to income. Your new workplace must be at least 50 miles farther from your old home than your old workplace was from your old home. For example, if your old workplace was 5 miles from your old home, your new workplace must be at least 55 miles from your old home. If you did not have an old workplace, your new workplace must be at least 50 miles from your old home.

A time requirement also must be satisfied. You must work full-time for at least 39 weeks during the 12 months following your move. You may, however, deduct your moving expenses for the previous year, even if you have not met the "time requirement" before that year's tax return is due.

For example, if you move in December of 1996, by the time your 1996 tax return is due (April 1997), you will not have met the time requirement. Nevertheless, you may deduct (adjust for tax years 1996 and beyond) your moving expenses for 1996 as long as you expect to meet the 39-week test by the end of the 12-month period following your move.

You do not have to meet the time requirement if you've been transferred for your employer's benefit. For more information on the moving expense deduction/adjustment, see IRS *Publication 521, Instructions for Moving Expenses.* Also, see IRS *Form 3903, Moving Expenses,* and its accompanying instructions.

DOMICILE

The legal definition of your domicile is the state in which you intend to maintain a permanent home. Your state of domicile impacts many factors, including the interpretation of your will and related property transfers, income taxes, personal property taxes, and marital rights issues. While the definition of domicile seems to be short and sweet, establishing a domicile takes some effort. You may have several permanent residences where you spend a significant amount of time, but only one domicile.

A domicile is the state in which you are registered to vote, maintain a driver's license and motor-vehicle registration, and pay personal property tax. Other indicators are the location of personal property, advisers such as attorneys or trust officers, and principal bank or securities accounts. Where you participate in religious activities and social clubs and have a will executed can also be factors in determining your domicile.

Failure to establish a domicile can be an expensive mistake. For example, if you relocate to a state with lower death taxes, you must establish domicile there if intangible personal property, such as stocks and other securities, are to be taxed in that state at your death. Otherwise, *both* your old state *and* your new state might seek to tax your estate.

The state of domicile determines property rights upon divorce or death. A move to a new state may bring the laws of both states to bear on your property rights. For example, moving to or from a community-property state will impose different sets of rules on the property acquired during marriage. Property acquired during marriage in the community-property state is subject to its laws even if the client later moves to a common-law state, and vice versa. Here's another peculiarity to the law. In the absence of a valid prenuptial agreement, you generally cannot disinherit your spouse. However, the extent of your spouse's inheritance rights or yours differs from state to state. In one state—Louisiana—you can't disinherit your *children,* let alone your spouse. If you have specific questions about your property, get legal advice in your domicile.

PROPERTY AND OTHER LOCAL TAXES

Most jurisdictions impose taxes on the value of real estate. Generally this tax is levied at the county or town level. In addition, virtually every state assesses real-property transfer or deed-recording taxes—usually at 1 or 2 percent of transaction value. It can be quite a shock to move from an area in which your property taxes were $600 a year, to a new location where your property taxes are $5,000 a year.

Many localities tax tangible or intangible property. The tangible property taxes are imposed on items such as automobiles that are physically located in the jurisdiction. Intangible taxes apply to stocks and other securities owned by a person whose domicile is that state. If you have a large investment portfolio, your choice of domicile can be very important.

Appealing Your Property Taxes

When you have a contract to buy a new house, you can mail a copy of the accepted contract to the local tax assessor's office if you want to appeal your property taxes. Appealing before you close on your new house is key because if the assessment is lower, you'll save on closing taxes and you'll also be able to put aside less money in escrow.

Your property tax bill results from multiplying the assessed value of your home by the local tax rate. You cannot change the rate. Therefore, your only hope for a lower property tax bill rests on "beating down" the assessment.

In some places, your assessment equals the full market value of the property. In other places, a percentage of that value is used. If you aren't certain how things work, call your local assessor's office and ask. The factor that is used to convert your market value to your assessed value may be called the tax multiplier or assessment ratio.

> **Example:** If the assessment ratio is 80 percent and you have a home worth $100,000, the assessed value should be $80,000. If the assessed value is $90,000, the property is being overassessed by $10,000.

An inflated assessment usually results either from an incorrect property description or an incorrect market value. The description of property includes the property's age, size, location, number of bathrooms, quality of construction, and so on. You can find the government's view of your home on the property record card in your local assessor's office. Overassessments often result from inaccurate record cards.

If there are errors, you can save money by correcting them, which will reduce the assessed value and your tax bill without a formal appeal. The assessor first will verify the new information.

Most communities limit formal appeals to a defined grievance period—anywhere from 10 days to two months after assessment notices are mailed. However, you may be able to get factual errors corrected at any time. Review any calculations that appear on your property record card, and ask the assessor's clerk to explain any you don't understand. Make sure your home is classified as residential (rental and business properties may be subject to higher taxes) and that you are getting credit for any exemptions you deserve, such as those for senior citizens and veterans.

Market Value

If the description of your property is accurate, you may still be able to show that the assigned value is too high. Your best evidence is the price you paid for it. However, arguing that home prices have fallen and that you got a good deal when you bought the home will not automatically translate into assessment relief.

Some localities do a general reevaluation annually. Others reevaluate less frequently. In Connecticut, for example, properties are reevaluated once every 10 years. You may appeal in subsequent years, but you must base your challenges on sales during the reevaluation period. In other states, such as California, current sales figures can be used to argue for a lower assessment. Always check the rules in your locality before you file an appeal.

The next-best evidence of the value of your home is the sale prices of similar properties. The information you need for comparison can be found on other property record cards—which are pubic documents—at the assessor's office. The assessor's office may have a file on recent sales, which will make your search a little easier. You can also get sales data from deeds at the county clerk's office or from local real estate agents.

Try to find properties near your house that are within roughly 20 percent of your home's square footage, with similar amenities and construction. You won't get far with an appeal on your one-story ranch by comparing it to the price of a French provincial on the other side of town.

Uniformity of Assessments

In some states, an assessment that accurately reflects your property's market value still can be challenged if it is high compared with assessments on similar homes. In other states, however, appeals based on fairness are a waste of time.

If you just bought your home and the assessment was set at or near the selling price, you may be able to get a reduction if comparable homes that have not been on the market recently enjoy lower valuations. The New Jersey Supreme Court, for example, has struck down "welcome stranger" spot assessments, and they may be outlawed in your area, too.

Hiring a Pro

Most homeowners who challenge assessments handle their own cases. There are professionals, however, who work on a contingency-fee basis and who will evaluate your chances on an appeal and actually file the appeal. The fee in these cases will usually be between 20 and 50 percent of your first year's tax savings.

If you are interested in hiring a consultant, look in the Yellow Pages under "Tax Consultants" or ask your real estate agent for references. A company called Inpho Inc., (800) 793-0852, will give you five minutes to search its database for the sale price of a property, all the properties on a particular street, or a dozen properties in a given price rage in your town. The service costs from $5 to $7.

Do

▶ Read all instructions about deadlines, forms, and procedures and follow them exactly. You don't want to lose on a technicality.

▶ Give the assessor advance notice of the evidence you intend to present.

▶ Verify that no unusual circumstances were involved in the sales of the properties you plan to cite as comparable to your own.

▶ Bring photos, both of your property and of the comparable homes.

▶ Have a supporting appraisal, if possible, perhaps from a recent mortgage refinancing or home equity loan application.

▶ Sit in on hearings before you take your case to an appeals board. That will give you a feel for procedures and an idea of how the hearing officers react to different arguments.

▶ Review evidence submitted by other taxpayers. These are public records, although you may have to pay a nominal fee to obtain a copy.

Don't

▶ Argue that your home should be valued at $195,000 rather than $200,000. Assessment is an art, not a science, and complaints about small differences will be ignored.

▶ Worry about bringing too much documentation. The more you have to support your case, the better. Have copies of your deed, original sales contract, closing documents, title report, survey, an appraisal, and so forth.

▶ Argue with the hearing officer. Just present the facts of your case clearly and succinctly, remembering that the board can consider only the assessment, not whether you can afford your taxes.

▶ Stake your case on emotion but on fact.

GIFT TAX RULES

Presently, six states—Connecticut, Delaware, Louisiana, New York, North Carolina, and Tennessee—have gift tax systems. If you are domiciled in any of these states, you should have any gift plans reviewed by an estate-tax attorney.

Every state has some form of death or succession tax, as well as probate procedures. The tax-base definitions (what your personal representative must include as part of your estate for tax purposes) vary, and your choice of beneficiary will trigger different rates and exemptions in each state. For example, some states allow the transfer of assets between spouses without any tax liability, while other states do not have an unlimited exemption for transfers to the surviving spouse.

You should also understand the difference between an *estate tax* and an *inheritance tax*. The estate tax is levied against and paid for by the estate; the inheritance tax is borne by the heirs. Some states impose whichever tax is higher, while others impose only one of the two. There is no federal inheritance tax, only an estate tax.

MOVING

All these details may seem daunting, especially if you're feeling overwhelmed by the mechanics of the move itself. Unfortunately, when you move, you're moving your financial life as well. Here's a summary of the important money issues involved in a move:

▶ Are you buying a home?

▶ Are you selling a home? Find out the tax implications. Can you postpone gains on the sale by moving to a more expensive house within 24 months? What is the tax cost of your house?

▶ Are you moving from a state with no income tax to a state with a high income tax? You may have to review your tax plans to fill out the proper withholding amount and redo your budget so that you can set aside more funds if you will have to pay more than you expected.

▶ Review your estate plans to make sure estate plan documents are legally valid in the state you're moving to. There may be different witnessing requirements, as well as laws governing who can inherit your property. State laws and taxation rules vary from state to state.

▶ Don't overlook the federal moving expense deduction if it applies to you.

RELOCATION

Sometimes, the decision to move is an easy one. There may be a great job opportunity somewhere else, or you may want to move closer to family and friends. Or maybe you're weary of the cold weather and want to move to a sunny, warm spot. However, whether you're offered a new position in another city or your present employer offers you a transfer, you should carefully consider all the factors before making a move.

The nonfinancial considerations are probably more apparent to you. For example:

▶ How does your family feel about moving? Are your kids involved in school activities that would be hard to duplicate elsewhere?

▶ Are there personal reasons that keep you in your current location?

▶ Are you ready for lifestyle changes? Sometimes, a small town sounds appealing, but will you miss the cultural and entertainment options available in a city?

Obviously, monetary issues are also an important part of a moving decision:

▶ Is the salary increase substantial?

▶ What is the cost of living in the new city?

▶ What is the tax bite in the new city compared to where you now live?

▶ Are the new company's benefits comparable or better than your current employer's?

▶ Will the company help pay your moving expenses?

YOUR ACTION PLAN

Two Months Before the Move

▶ **Establish a new bank account in your new location.** Order new checks as soon as you have a new address. If you will move within the month, have the checks held at the bank for you to pick up. Mail an initial deposit check to your new bank, and then have your old bank wire the bulk of your funds a day or two before the move. Many banks charge a $10 or $20 wiring fee.

▶ **Inventory your belongings.** If you need to file an insurance claim later, you'll be glad you did this. Record serial numbers of electronic equipment and walk through the house with a video or still camera and document your belongings. Keep the inventory with other important papers and take them with you to your new home. Obtain copies of medical and dental records so that you won't have to have tests repeated at your new location.

▶ **Obtain new business or professional licenses.** Contact state and local officials in advance to arrange for professional tests or reciprocity.

▶ **Review your taxes.** See a tax professional to project your tax bill, taking into account your new domicile as well as your moving deductions.

▶ **Keep records of your moving expenses.**

▶ **Contact your new bank.** Fill out forms authorizing it to send for disbursements of CDs and other time accounts that mature after you move.

▶ **Find out what documents your children will need to enroll in the local school.** Get copies of your children's school records, vaccination cards, birth certificates, citizenship papers, etc.

▶ **Get references of local professionals.** Get these from doctors, lawyers, contractors, etc. Ask your new employer or neighbors for their recommendations.

Two Weeks Before the Move

▶ **Travelers' checks.** Buy enough travelers' checks to cover expenses through your first two weeks in the new location. You won't be able to cash personal checks until you have an in-state driver's license.

▶ **Social Security benefits.** If you're receiving Social Security benefits, file an address change with the Social Security Administration. You can contact this office at (800) 772-1213.

▶ **Automatic investment programs.** Call your mutual fund's service number to switch direct monthly fund purchases from your current bank account to your checking account at your new bank.

▶ **Collect negotiable securities and other valuables from your safe-deposit box.** Make copies of all negotiable securities, and mail them to your new address. Carry the originals yourself.

▶ **Send your new address to your investment brokers.** Send change-of-address notices to mutual funds and other financial institutions you deal with directly.

▶ **Property and casualty insurance.** Call your insurance agent and confirm that you'll be covered for possessions you plan to move personally. Items that you take in your car probably will be the most expensive and most fragile. Coverage on these items should be through your homeowner's or renter's policy, *not* your automobile policy.

▶ **Renew prescriptions for drugs you take regularly.**

One Week Before the Move

▶ **Close out bank accounts.** Have your bank wire the funds from your savings account to your new bank, or ask for a cashier's check. Be careful with your checking accounts. Don't close them out if there are checks outstanding. Your bank can tell you what checks have cleared the account. Leave an amount that will cover outstanding checks, plus a cushion of about $100. You don't want checks to bounce because your math was off or because you had to pay a fee for not maintaining a minimum balance. Find out whether your bank credits interest on your money-market account daily, weekly, or monthly. Close the account after the last crediting.

After the Move

▶ **Notify the Internal Revenue Service.** Report your new address on IRS _Form 8822_, which you can obtain by calling (800) 829-3676.

▶ **Notify your old state's tax department.** You'll probably have to file two state tax returns in the year of the move.

▶ **Go to the Department of Motor Vehicles.** Get your new driver's license, registration, and tags. Don't put this off, or you may end up paying extra fees for late registration.

▶ **Review your estate plan.** Have a lawyer in your new state review your will, powers of attorney, living will, and other legal papers. A will written in another state is still valid, but the lawyer may recommend revisions based on local tax law and probate procedures.

▶ **Reexamine your previous investment decisions in light of your new state's taxes.** If you moved from a state with income tax to a state with none, you won't get as much of an advantage from your tax-free municipal bonds.

▶ **Re-shop your automobile and homeowner's policies.**

▶ **Get a safe-deposit box.**

CHANGING YOUR JOB

For anyone voluntarily leaving a job and for those who unexpectedly lose a position

Changing your job can be stressful, and much of the stress is due to suddenly shaky finances. Whether you're about to leave a job—or your job is about to leave you—you can take a number of steps to help smooth the transition and help you ride out a period of unemployment before you get a new position. These steps fall into two categories: financial and professional.

Obviously, if you have some notice that you're going to lose your job—if you know your company is planning layoffs or closing—you should bolster your finances as much as possible beforehand. You've got to prepare yourself for the loss of your regular income—your paycheck.

ADD TO YOUR CASH RESOURCES

▶ **Decrease your 401(k) plan contributions to the miniumim required to get the company match.** Put the after-tax difference in an emergency fund, if you don't already have one.

▶ **Establish a home-equity line of credit.** Do this while you're still working, because the bank will want to verify employment.

▶ **Eliminate all unnecessary payroll deductions,** such as savings bonds or United Way. Use this cash to bolster your savings.

▶ **Borrow against your 401(k) plan only as a last resort,** since you'll usually have to repay the loan when your job is terminated. Unpaid loans are subject to income taxes and tax penalties.

▶ **Replace group term life insurance.** Use personal term or universal life insurance or plan to take your group policy with you if it has terms that allow you to do so.

PRIORITIES WHEN YOU'RE OUT OF WORK

▶ **Lump-sum contributions.** If you will receive a lump-sum pension or savings plan distribution, depending on your age, you may want to leave your money in the company plan and withdraw it even though you will have to pay a 20 percent penalty, or you can transfer that money *directly* into a separate IRA. Invest in a money-market fund if you feel that you will need to make a withdrawal. IRAs are exempt from mandatory 20 percent federal withholding. In addition, the funds still will be eligible for rollover to a new employer's savings plan. Withdrawing money from an IRA should be considered *only as a last resort,* because it jeopardizes your retirement, and the amount you withdraw may be subject to penalty taxes, if you are younger than $59^1/_2$.

▶ **Apply for unemployment insurance.** Contact your state's unemployment office immediately upon termination, to begin the process of applying for and collecting unemployment benefits. Check to see whether your state allows you to collect both unemployment and Social Security benefits.

► **Review your insurance coverage.**

► **Medical coverage.** You may be able to cover yourself and your family through your spouse's employer's plan. If this is not possible, you may be able to continue your current medical coverage under the COBRA law. This is less expensive than trying to replace your group coverage with private coverage. Look into switching to a health maintenance organization (HMO); they usually have low per-visit charges.

► **Life insurance.** If you lose coverage under your employer's plan, the most economical way to maintain coverage is to get personal term or universal life insurance. If you're in good health, you may want to "re-enter" your policy for a lower rate or purchase new insurance at that lower rate. Be sure to get a clean bill of health from your doctor before submitting to the insurer's medical test, and make sure the new policy is effective before canceling the old one.

► **Auto and homeowner's insurance.** To lower your premiums, increase deductibles on auto and homeowner's insurance.

Spending Priorities for "Fixed Expenses"

If you're laid off or if your job search is dragging on longer than you expected, do the following:

► Pay monthly rent/mortgage and home-equity-loan bills first.

► Pay utility bills second.

► Make minimum payments on credit cards, department store cards, and gas cards.

► Restructure your debt. If your mortgage is really a strain, see whether you can renegotiate the terms with your lender. Your bank may let you refinance without paying additional closing costs. Borrow against your home-equity loan to pay off a high-rate auto loan only if you can make the payments comfortably.

Discretionary Spending

▶ Eliminate all unnecessary expenses such as extra phone and cable TV services.

▶ Become the consummate tightwad—use discount coupons, carpool, and shop at warehouse clubs.

▶ Drop unnecessary insurance such as life coverage for your kids.

When You're Laid Off

These days, with so many two-income families, it's not uncommon for one spouse to be out of work for periods of time. Whereas you may be able to meet your day-to-day expenses, you'll take a big hit in your long-term savings for retirement. Remember, when you're not working, you're not accruing a pension benefit. And, over the long run, one person's pension may not be enough to support both of you. That's why you have to reassess your savings and investment choices. You have to set priorities between maintaining your current style of living versus being able to afford a similar style in the future. You shouldn't assume that you'll quickly find another job at the same or a higher salary. Depending on your field, income, and where you live, you could be out of work for an extended period of time. That's why it's so important for you to make financial choices carefully during this time.

Whether you expected to lose your job or suddenly find yourself unemployed, it's important that you take some time to assess your situation before you make any dramatic decisions. While you were working, you may have been too busy to review your finances. Now, out of necessity, you must understand exactly where you are—in terms of savings, investments, and assets. In fact, now is the time when you'll probably fully accept the importance of financial planning. However, since this is an uncertain time and you're anxious about finding a job and paying all your bills, you should get help, whether from a friend or a planner.

Losing one's job can be a large blow to the ego because people often define themselves by what they do for a living. You may want to join a support group in which you can share your feelings about losing your job. People are often angrier and more discouraged than they realize at the loss of a job. Talking with others who have gone through the same loss can help rebuild your self-esteem as you realize what you've accomplished during your career and what skills and abilities you can offer a future employer.

For better or for worse, your life is intertwined with your finances. You may not be working, but your life—and your family's—continues. You'll have to make some changes, but you shouldn't immediately assume that all your plans have to be canceled or put on hold. For example:

▶ **Vacation.** It's nearly summer and you've just been laid off. You always go away during the summer, but now you don't see how you can. Remember, once you start a new job, it will be tough to take a vacation for several months. But you're entitled to take a vacation now. You may not be able to stay at the five-star resort, but you can still take your family camping or drive to the beach. If you've been re-engineered out of the workforce, re-engineer your vacation.

▶ **College.** If your child is in or about to start college, don't panic. There are ways to work out payment plans. First, notify the school's financial-aid office. Your change in status is a reason to review your financial-aid package. Tell your child that he or she may have to get a part-time job or work over the summer instead of travel.

PROFESSIONAL STRATEGIES

Use the following checklist to help you through the transition.

IF YOU'VE BEEN FIRED

▶ **Negotiate your departure, if this is an option.** Don't immediately sign anything with your employer. Negotiate what kind of severance package is available. Is there outplacement assistance? For how long? Can you choose the outplacement firm? Will your employer pay for job-search calls and trips? Are there benefits for re-education or tuition assistance or training?

▶ **Obtain a list of employment lawyers if you feel you lost your job through discrimination or breach of contract.** You may be able to negotiate a larger severance package.

As You Look for a New Position

▶ **List your dreams and desires.** Why have you been doing the kind of work you've been doing? Would you rather do something else? What do you really want? *Clarify your goals and values.*

▶ **Consider alternatives.** Is now the time to start a new business, go into private consulting, or find a job related to a hobby of yours? Don't put yourself in a "box"; consider taking a new career direction. Will this require additional training or education? Will your employer pay for this in lieu of outplacement?

▶ **Prepare a résumé of accomplishments and skills.** Don't merely list your positions. Spell out your professional experience and be sure to list your full range of talents and abilities. *Don't* make the mistake of selling yourself short!

▶ **Obtain copies of performance appraisals** and bring them to interviews.

▶ **Compensation:** Be realistic; don't "price yourself out of the market."

▶ **Looking for work is a contact sport.** The majority of jobs are still found by networking, so make a list of contacts and maintain them. But don't expect others to find a job for you. Ask your supervisor to send a letter of recommendation/ reference to his or her contacts. Remember that classified ads contain only between 5 and 15 percent of job openings. Remain active and visible in professional organizations.

▶ **Outplacement services can provide emotional support and help you fine-tune your résumé and brush up on interviewing skills.** They will also provide self-assessment programs to show you how to apply your job skills in different industries. Outplacement will not find you a new job. It will, however, help you clarify your goals, collect data on employers, and market yourself. Some services offer classes, whereas others have individual counselors.

▶ **Maintain a list of "headhunters" who may be able to place you with a new employer.**

Remember, everyone changes jobs at some point in their lives. Once you find another position, you should focus on repaying your bills, building up your emergency fund, and then getting your savings and investment goals back on track.

YOUR ACTION PLAN

Before Losing Your Job

▶ Bolster your savings by decreasing your 401(k) contributions.

▶ Get a home-equity line of credit.

▶ Eliminate unnecessary payroll deductions.

▶ Reduce discretionary spending.

When You're Out of Work

▶ Pay your mortgage or rent bills first.

▶ Pay utility bills second.

▶ Make minimum payments on credit cards, department store charge cards, and gas cards, respectively.

▶ Eliminate all unnecessary expenses such as cable TV, extra phone services, and magazine subscriptions.

▼

Planning for Your Retirement

*For anyone concerned with retirement planning,
both before and during the event*

*For people who are many years away from retirement and
for those who wish they had started to plan ten years ago*

Poverty or Prosperity

It's doubtful that you would consciously overlook the basic retirement goals of security and financial freedom. Nevertheless, this happens when you fail to prepare adequately. If so, you are making at least one of the same basic financial mistakes:

▶ You fail to plan.

▶ You don't learn how savings and protection vehicles work.

► You depend on someone else—bankers, brokers, insurance agents, accountants—to be responsible for your financial future.

► You procrastinate.

► You don't understand the difference between savings and investing.

► You assume that there is a system and your employer will work it out and take care of you.

DID YOU KNOW THAT . . .

► Only 5 percent of all Americans are financially independent at age 65?

► Seventy-five percent of all retirees have to depend on family, friends, and Social Security for their only source of income?

► Seventy-four percent percent of all Americans age 65 and older have incomes of less than $15,000 a year; 57 percent have incomes of less than $10,000 a year?

Women face additional retirement worries for several reasons:

► Women live longer than men.

► Women still earn less then men.

► Women often drop out of the workforce when they have children, thereby losing pension benefits for extended periods of time. This can account for a loss of as much of one-third to one-half of the value of a woman's 401(k) plan, making the woman more reliant on a spouse's retirement plan.

► Women often give up their rights to their spouse's pension benefits in divorce proceedings, or the spouse elects the single life option pension benefit.

► An increasing number of women are single parents who must pay attention to housing, child care, tuition, and other expenses for their children, and as a result, they don't plan for their own retirement.

> ## THESE ARE THE STARTLING STATISTICS FOR WOMEN:
>
> ► The average income for women over the age of 65 in this country is $7,300.
>
> ► Eighty percent of retirement-age women currently are not covered under a pension program.
>
> ► Forty percent of out-of-pocket costs for retirement-age women are health-related.

Poverty or prosperity: The choice is yours. Have you set aside enough for retirement? Have you thought about retirement at all? Although it may seem far away, many of you will spend one-third of your lives in retirement. Saving enough money to cover living and health-care expenses for that amount of time is an enormous challenge. But you can make it easier if you use time to your advantage by starting to save today!

ELEVEN MYTHS OF RETIREMENT PLANNING

Following are some common assumptions that virtually everyone makes about retirement. But if you believe in only one of these assumptions, wake up, you're in trouble. Relying on these assumptions to make your retirement plans is just plain stupid. Creating a plan based on false assumptions is worse than not making any plan at all. Here's a list of the 11 most dangerous myths to watch out for when developing your plans.

Myth 1

Social Security should provide enough income to replace my salary during retirement.

Social Security was never designed to replace all your earned income. In fact, the higher your preretirement income, the lower the percentage of your pay that will be replaced by Social Security benefits. As a general guideline, Table 9-1 shows what you can expect from Social Security.

Table 9-1: Projected Social Security benefits

Average Earnings	Estimated % of Pay Replaced by Social Security Benefits
$30,000	55%
$50,000	37%
$61,200	24%*

* of that portion of your pay subject to Social Security tax

Various changes to Social Security including reductions in benefits or postponment of the beginning of benefits are under discussion. Uncertainty about your benefits is all the more reason to save, save, save!

Myth 2

My company-sponsored pension plan is all I'll need for retirement and to meet my future cost of living needs.

Don't count on it. At best, the plan will replace some percentage of your pay, provided that you remain with the company for a considerable length of time, such as 20 or 25 years. If you leave prematurely, the payments will be reduced drastically. Lifelong long employment is a thing of the past. These days, it's more likely that you will switch jobs several times during your career, and these moves will have a significant impact on your pension plan buildup. In the past, people often worked for the same employer for 30 to 40 years. Today, however, people are more likely to work for half a dozen or more companies over the same time period.

Also, the trend among corporations today is to offer "defined contribution" plans rather than "defined benefit" plans. This puts the responsibility for future payments and current investment risk squarely on your shoulders. All your employer promises to do is put money in an account. You have to make contributions as well as choose how to invest the money. Your employer has shifted the responsibility to you.

Even if you are entitled to collect a substantial pension benefit, chances are that it will not be increased annually for inflation. What may *start out* as a pension that's sufficient to meet your expenses may quickly become inadequate, even with a modest inflation rate of 3–4 percent.

Myth 3

My living expenses won't be nearly as high after I retire, so I won't need to replace that much of my current income to maintain the same standard of living.

For most retirees, this is simply not true. Although you may eliminate some work-related expenses such as commuting costs, and dry cleaning, you will probably find that you replace them with other costs. You will spend more on leisure activities, groceries, and casual wear, according to a study from Georgia Tech. Assume that you will need 70 to 80 percent of your preretirement income.

Even more significant are the effects of inflation. Perhaps you've arranged to have your mortgage paid off by the time you retire. Great! But what about your real estate taxes, homeowner's insurance, utilities, and maintenance expenses? They comprise a larger portion of home ownership expenses than you may realize. You're still going to be responsible for these costs, and they are heading in only one direction: up!

What about medical expenses? As an active employee (or as a self-employed person), you probably are covered under your company health plan or a group health plan. Even if you are required to contribute to the cost, your company probably subsidizes the majority of it. Companies that now offer postretirement insurance may amend their plans in the future. They may require retirees to pay the full cost of coverage, or they may terminate their plans altogether. Furthermore, you should assume that the cost of medical insurance will rise a measure that exceeds the rate of inflation.

Myth 4

I expect to live only 10 to 15 years after I retire, so the funds I have accumulated should be more than enough to live comfortably.

While it may be true that some of you will live only 10 to 15 years beyond retirement, many of you will live a lot longer. The average life expectancy for men currently is 84; for women, 88. This may translate into 30 years of retirement—and a 30-year war against increasing living expenses. To be safe, you should assume that you'll live to age 85 or even 90.

Myth 5

I plan to live off my interest and/or dividends only, without ever touching my retirement savings principal.

Unfortunately, it usually doesn't work out this way. Look at the following example:

Table 9-2: How Inflation Erodes Your Principal Annual Expenses

Year	Principal Balance	Annual Earnings (7%)	(4% Inflation)
1	$100,000	$7,000	$7,000
2	100,000	7,000	7,280
3	99,720	6,980	7,571
4	99,129	6,939	7,874
5	98,194	6,874	8,189
6	96,879	6,782	8,517
7	95,144	6,660	8,857
8	92,947	6,506	9,212
9	90,241	6,317	9,580
10	86,978	6,088	9,963
11	83,103	5,817	10,362
12	78,558	5,499	10,776
13	72,845	5,099	11,207
14	66,737	4,672	11,655
15	59,794	4,183	12,121
16	51,856	3,630	12,606
17	42,880	3,002	13,110
18	32,772	2,294	13,634
19	21,432	1,500	14,179
20	8,753	613	14,746

As you can see, with a 7 percent earnings rate and a 4 percent inflation rate, you will need to start drawing on your principal in the second year of retirement. And by year 20, you will have exhausted all the principal and interest. So your plan to live just on income is impossible to maintain unless you accumulate a *very* large nest egg.

Myth 6

If worse comes to worst, I can always sell my house to increase my retirement savings.

Yes, but this should be one of your last options, unless you decide that you want to live in a smaller house to simplify your life. Even if you are thinking about renting someplace smaller, the cost of renting versus owning may not make a sale worthwhile because of the tax advantages associated with owning. And once you sell your home, especially if you haven't reached age 75, you've lost a valuable reserve in your retirement arsenal. The bottom line: Don't automatically assume that you will be better off by selling your home. Examine all your options. For example, where will you move? Remember that when you move, you will have the expenses of moving, paying rent, or taking on a new mortgage.

Myth 7

I won't need to "save" any more after I retire.

This is absolutely untrue! You should always save some percentage of your annual income, even during retirement. Most people should spend less than their full income until age 75. This is especially critical if you aren't receiving a pension benefit or if your pension benefits won't be indexed for inflation.

To calculate the amount of your annual income that you can afford to spend, complete the worksheets in Appendix 1.

You can save money by cutting expenses. But you can also keep working. You may continue to earn money through part-time work or self-employment. The additional income, though less than your preretirement pay, will go a long way toward fighting inflation and building a cash cushion. The longer you can afford to leave your retirement funds intact—and growing—the better off you'll be.

Myth 8

I'll be in a better position down the road to save for retirement. I'll make up for what I should be saving now.

If this were true, you would be on easy street. However, it's almost impossible to make up for lost time because of the effect of compounding: The longer you save, the more your money grows. Look at the following example: Person 1 saves $2,000 a year from age 20 to 30. The money earns 10 percent over those 10 years. This person doesn't add to the $20,000, and at age 60, the value of this account is $556,197. Person 2 saves $2,000 a year from ages 30 to 60, with the money also earning 10 percent a year. The value of Person 2's retirement account at age 60 is $328,988. Person 2 saved three times as much as Person 1, but ended up with much less money!

The problem with delaying is that it puts off the day you begin serious saving. There is always something new, whether it's a vacation, car, or something for your home, that you can spend your money on. What happens if your cash flow never really improves? What if you become disabled or get a divorce or lose money in a bad investment? And, if you're in your 40s and 50s, you may be earning more money, but you also may have children to put through college. Also, don't overlook the higher insurance premiums you'll pay as you get older. Or corporate downsizing may force you to retire early. Don't just assume that you will be able to play catch-up down the road; the odds are against you.

Myth 9

During retirement I should invest only for safety because I can't afford to make up for any losses.

Remember, you may be retired for a period of 20 to 30 years—certainly long enough to recover from any investment setbacks. Although your investment strategy should be more conservative during retirement, a portfolio invested solely in liquid interest-bearing instruments (for example, CDs, short-term bonds) is every bit as dangerous to the retiree as one entirely invested in growth stocks. The risk, although of a different type, can be just as devastating. The reason? Inflation.

Inflation does not affect all investments equally, as you'll see. If you compare the annual performance (total return) of various investment options from 1950 through 1995 with the inflation rate, the disadvantages of investing strictly for safety become more apparent.

Table 9-3: Stocks, Bonds, and Treasury-Bills vs. Inflation

Total annual returns, 1950–1995

Common stocks (S&P 500)	11.9%
Long-term corporate bonds	6.1%
Long-term government bonds	5.7%
Three-month Treasury-bills	5.1%
Inflation rate (CPI)	4.0%

If you had invested all your retirement savings during that period in three-month Treasury-bills—the "safest" investment there is—you would have barely kept pace with inflation and likely fallen behind after the impact of paying income taxes.

The bottom line: Don't be recklessly conservative. Don't invest all your savings for growth *or* safety securities.

Myth 10

Medicare will cover most of my medical expenses during retirement.

Unfortunately, this is not the case! First of all, Medicare coverage doesn't even *begin* until the first day of the month you reach age 65, *and* you must be entitled to receive a Social Security benefit. If not, you pay a monthly premium—currently $42.50 per month for Part B only—to receive coverage.

Second, Medicare does not cover all expenses. Medicare basically consists of two types of coverage. Part A helps pay expenses when you are hospitalized or in a skilled-care nursing home, depending upon the length of your stay; but you must pay a deductible. In limited circumstances, it also covers the cost of home health care. Part B is designed to cover doctors' visits, prescription drugs, medical supplies, and certain types of therapy. It covers about 80 percent of these costs (after the deductible), and you pay the remaining 20 percent. Unlike Medicare Part A, there is also a monthly premium. With health care costs rising faster than most other expenses each year and with the gaps that exist in Medicare coverage, your medical expenses may represent a significant percentage of your postretirement expenses. Plan accordingly!

Myth 11

Things work out in the end.

Sadly, they often don't. Many employees assume there's some master plan that guarantees that pensions plus Social Security plus outside income will be enough when they retire. But there is no such master plan unless you construct it. Planning for a secure retirement is your responsibility.

If you're an employee, your company merely provides some benefits. It's up to you to take advantage of those plans, combined with your outside investments, to have enough for retirement. Remember, company plans are subject to change. Pension plans may be discontinued, you may get laid off, the cost of medical coverage may continue to shift. You can't assume that what's available to your coworkers today will be available to you when you retire.

BUILDING YOUR NEST EGG— PRERETIREMENT DO'S AND DON'TS

Do invest a minimum of 10 percent of your gross income, but aim for closer to 20 percent each year, toward retirement. Depending upon your age when you start saving, you may have to save more than 10 percent. Start with what you can afford, even if it's only 3 percent. Then make a promise to yourself to increase your savings by an extra percent per year.

If your employer offers a 401(k) savings or thrift plan, **do** take full advantage of it. Currently, 57 percent of all companies offer these tax-deferred plans. You should make the maximum before-tax contribution allowed, currently $9,500. This number is indexed for inflation and will occasionally change. You should also check with your plan administrator to find out whether any other plan limits apply to your contributions. But, at a minimum, contribute enough to take full advantage of any company match. Of all companies offering 401(k) plans, approximately 71 percent provide a company match based on some percentage of the amount contributed by the employee.

If you are self-employed, **do** consider setting up a Keogh or Simplified Employee Pension plan (SEP). Even employees who moonlight, such as a teacher who tutors in the evening, may fund a Keogh.

There are several types of Keoghs you may choose from:

▶ **Profit Sharing.** This is the most flexible form of a Keogh plan and a good choice if you cannot be certain of your annual self-employment income. You may contribute and deduct up to 13.04 percent of your net self-employment income, to a maximum annual contribution of $30,000. The advantage of a profit-sharing Keogh is that you're not committed to that amount. If you have no income, you don't have to make a contribution.

▶ **Money Purchase.** This plan is best if you expect a steady stream of income each year. You may contribute and deduct up to 20 percent of your income to a maximum of $30,000. However, you are required to choose your contribution percentage in advance and continue with it.

▶ **Combination (Money Purchase/Profit Sharing).** This type of plan gives you the best of both worlds: flexibility and the right to make the largest contribution. You choose a fixed percentage that you will contribute each year under the money-purchase provisions. Then, if your cash flow allows it, you can contribute additional money to your profit-sharing plan.

▶ **Defined benefit.** You choose the annual income you believe you'll need at retirement, and an actuary will tell you how much you'll need to contribute each year to reach that goal. The advantage of this plan is that you are not restricted by any dollar or percentage contribution limits. The disadvantages are that you must retain an actuary, which increases your administrative costs considerably, and you must meet IRS-mandated minimum plan-funding requirements.

You may set up a Keogh with a bank, credit union, insurance company, brokerage firm, or mutual fund company, depending on the investment vehicles you prefer. Although you may contribute to several Keogh accounts (subject to the annual limits discussed above), fees and commissions might make it preferable to have only one account.

Do make annual contributions to an Individual Retirement Account (IRA). If your employer offers a savings or thrift plan, it makes more sense to contribute *first* to that plan and then to an IRA if your cash flow will allow it. That's because your company plan may match a percentage of your contributions. Since this is *free money*, you should take advantage of it. Second, you can defer taxes on your company 401(k) savings plan contributions, but, depending on your adjusted gross income, your contributions to an IRA may or may not be deductible.

Currently, you may contribute up to $2,000 to an IRA per year; up to $2,250, if you have a nonworking spouse, but not more than $2,000 to one IRA. Follow these guidelines to determine whether your contributions are deductible:

▶ If neither you nor your spouse is an active participant in a company retirement plan, regardless of your income, your contributions are entirely deductible.

▶ If you and/or your spouse are covered under an employer's plan, but your adjusted gross income is less than $40,000 ($25,000 if you're single), your IRA contributions are completely deductible.

▶ If you and/or your spouse are active participants in company retirement plans and your adjusted gross income is between $40,000 and $50,000 (between $25,000 and $35,000 adjusted gross for single filers), you may deduct a portion of your IRA contributions. For each $50 of income over $40,000 ($25,000 for singles), your deduction is reduced by $10, until the deduction is completely phased out at $50,000 of adjusted gross income ($35,000 for singles).

If you're not sure whether you're an active participant in a company plan, one way to check is to look at your Form W-2 from the prior year. If a box labeled "pension plan" is marked, you are an active participant.

Even if you find that you're *not* entitled to a deduction for your IRA contributions—and assuming that you're making the maximum before-tax contribution to your 401(k) savings/thrift plan (or Keogh)—consider making *nondeductible* IRA contributions because your IRA earnings compound tax-free until you take the money out (without penalty as early as age $59^1/_2$ or as late as age $70^1/_2$).

Do invest a portion of your retirement savings in common stocks or stock mutual funds. Professional pension managers have known for years that the key to financial success lies in diversification of assets. In other words, invest in a mix of stocks, bonds, and cash-equivalent investments.

Unfortunately, the majority of all savings plan participants invest their money in GICs (guaranteed investment contracts) or BICs (bank-insured contracts). These investments usually pay a fixed rate of interest, and the principal is guaranteed by the life insurance company or bank that issued the contract. Remember that any guarantee is only as sound as the institution that backs it. But although these investments generally are safe, most will not provide you with the return over inflation that you need for the long haul.

So how much do you invest in stocks, and how much do you invest in bonds? To get a rough estimate of how to split your investments, we suggest that you follow our Age Rule of Thumb. Invest a percentage equal to your age in fixed-income investments: fixed-income funds in your company savings plan, certificates of deposit, bonds, or bond mutual funds. Then invest the remaining percentage in equities: stocks or stock mutual funds. As you age, the idea is to increase the fixed-income side of your portfolio while decreasing your exposure to stocks. For example, if you're 40 years old, then you should allocate *no more than 40 percent* of your retirement savings to fixed-income investments.

Don't invest too much of your retirement savings in any one stock or industry. You've heard the saying over and over: *Don't put all your eggs in one basket.* As a general rule, you should diversify within asset categories by investing in several types of stocks and bonds. For instance, when investing in stocks, select a large-capitalization, a small-capitalization, and a foreign stock fund. When it comes to choosing a bond investment, select short-term holdings that mature within 5 years. Steer clear of long-term securities that mature in 12 or more years, or medium-term instruments that mature in 5 to 12 years, because the added risk you will undertake outweighs the potential added gain.

You also should diversify *over time*. If you need to make adjustments to your current allocation or if you will be investing a large sum of money all at once, such as a lump sum from your retirement plan, you should consider spreading it out over time.

Do consult with an adviser *before* you retire, to make sure that you'll have enough money to retire. If the outlook is not promising, take action immediately. There are a number of variables you can control to make your retirement situation work out:

▶ Retire later.

▶ Develop an income during retirement.

▶ Reduce your retirement living expenses.

▶ Save more, and increase your retirement investments to more than 10 percent of your annual income.

▶ Take more risk, and change your investment mix to include more stock funds, to improve long-term returns.

APPROACHING RETIREMENT

There are certain steps you can take now to ease the transition from having a paycheck provide a regular stream of income to relying on your assets for income:

ESTIMATE YOUR RETIREMENT LIVING EXPENSES

This is critical. You wouldn't think of taking a cross-country trip without taking a road map with you. But that's what you'd doing if you didn't have a realistic estimate of how much money you'll need to live. If you don't know this basic information, you won't be able to make the other decisions that go hand-in-hand with retirement, such as which payment options to elect from retirement plans, or how to invest your retirement savings. Regardless of your circumstances—whether you've saved for your retirement or not—this estimate is necessary.

REQUEST AN ESTIMATE OF YOUR BENEFITS FROM SOCIAL SECURITY

You do this once every three years while you are working, but it is especially important to do so the closer you are to retirement. Either go to your local Social Security Administration office or call (800) 772-1213 to request a *Form SSA-7004*.

Social Security benefits will probably represent between 24 and 55 percent of your annual retirement income. The higher the percentage, the more important it is for you to understand how the Social Security system works. You should know, at the very least, *how much you can earn* while collecting a Social Security benefit, *how early retirement* affects your benefit, and *how to apply* to Social Security.

EVALUATE YOUR RETIREMENT-PLAN OPTIONS

You may be entitled to a company pension benefit. If so, this is a good time to find out what your payment options are. Can you get a lump-sum settlement? If so, what is the "discount rate" used to calculate it? Generally, the lower the discount rate, the higher the value of the lump sum. You may want to take the lump sum and roll it into an IRA.

FIND OUT ABOUT AVAILABLE JOINT-AND-SURVIVOR OPTIONS

What is their *cost* to you? In other words, by how much do they reduce your benefit? Does your company provide cost-of-living adjustments to the monthly pension?

Does the pension pop back up to full amount if the beneficiary dies first? Some companies have pop-up provisions because they're only paying for one person, but many don't have these provisions.

What are your options for savings or thrift plan distributions? Can you *defer* your distribution—leave it in the company plan after retirement? If you're happy with the investment alternatives, and you can still transfer funds from one to another, this is a great way to avoid IRA fees and commissions.

EVALUATE YOUR HOLDINGS IN COMPANY STOCK

If your company offers an employee stock ownership plan (ESOP), you may reduce your holding by up to 25 percent of the account value at age 55. At age 60, you may liquidate another 25 percent of your account. This is a great way to keep from being underdiversified.

REVIEW YOUR INSURANCE POLICIES

Find out what your life and medical insurance coverage will be when you retire. If you're fortunate and your employer offers medical and life insurance to retirees, find out the eligibility requirements and the cost. Compare the cost of company coverage with policies from other sources, such as a spouse's plan or personal coverage outside of your company plan.

PROTECTING YOUR NEST EGG AFTER RETIREMENT

As we've said before, a pension (if you're lucky enough to have one), along with Social Security, usually won't provide enough to maintain your standard of living once you retire. You'll need a third source of income to ensure a comfortable retirement: personal savings.

Hopefully, you've been accumulating your nest egg faithfully. But have you thought about how your funds should be invested *after* retirement? After all, this money may have to last for 20 to 30 years. Here are essential strategies to follow:

FOCUS ON YOUR REAL RATE OF RETURN

You may have been doing this all along, but it is especially critical for retirees. Inflation can undermine your return. If you're earning 5 percent on your investments, you're actually *losing money* once you account for inflation and income taxes. Since 1926, common stocks comprise the only asset class that has outpaced inflation and produced a positive net after-tax return.

How do you calculate your real rate of return? Look at this example: If a particular investment is yielding 8 percent and your combined federal/state tax rate is 30 percent, your *after-tax return* is 5.6 percent. If inflation is running at 4 percent, you are left with a *real rate of return* of just 1.6 percent.

Table 9-4: Calculating Real Rate of Return

Nominal yield on investment	8.00%
Multiply by 1 *minus* your combined federal/state tax, e.g., 30% tax rate: 1-.30 ×.70	
After-tax return	5.60%
Subtract inflation rate–	4.00%
Real rate of return	1.60%

So the number you need to focus on is 1.6 percent, *not* the 8 percent figure you probably were quoted by your financial institution.

DIVERSIFY, DIVERSIFY, DIVERSIFY

As a retiree (or soon-to-be retiree), you can't afford to take the same risks as those who are years away from retiring. You may not have sufficient time to recover from investment setbacks, or you may not have the earning power to replace lost funds. But you also need higher returns to guard against inflation. There is no single investment that will meet all your needs! Your best bet is a combination of fixed-income securities (to provide stability of principal and income) and equities (to provide the opportunity for growth and serve as a hedge against inflation). Just as you did before retirement, you'll still need *to diversify among asset categories, within asset classes,* and *over time.*

RETIREMENT RECAP

If you do nothing else, take this advice! The following four points summarize the essentials of retirement planning. If you have started to do even one of these steps, you're on the right track. And if you have addressed these four issues, then, you're in control of your retirement finances. Not only is the planning process *your* responsibility, but you need to start now no matter how old you are.

The key to a financially comfortable retirement largely depends on how well you:

▶ **Save and invest on your own to supplement company benefit plans and Social Security.** Save at least 10 percent of your gross income for retirement. Make this a priority. If you can't start off saving that much, start saving whatever you can afford, and work toward the goal of 10 percent or more!

▶ **Plan for inflation.** Inflation is the retiree's worst enemy. Once you know the impact that inflation will have on your post-retirement income, you can plan ahead and invest some of your retirement nest egg in assets that can outpace inflation.

▶ **Start to save early.** Don't underestimate the value of time; use it to your advantage. Even if you could save 10 percent of your income when you're age 50, you would't be able to build an adequate nest egg, so start saving *today*.

▶ **Diversify your investments.** This is critical to building your retirement nest egg. You need a *balance* of stocks, bonds, and cash-equivalent securities. You should not only diversify your holdings during your accumulating years but also during your retirement years, while you're drawing down your funds.

Will you retire in poverty or prosperity? The choice is yours.

YOUR ACTION PLAN

Ten Years or More Away from Retirement

▶ Start saving for your retirement today. Ideally, you should save each year a minimum of 10 percent of your gross income.

▶ Take full advantage of any matching program offered in your company savings plan.

▶ If self-employed, set up and fund a Keogh or SEP.

▶ Diversify your retirement investments among and within investment classes.

▶ Follow the Age Rule of Thumb:

> Invest a percentage no greater than your age in fixed-income investments.

> Invest the remaining percentage in equities.

▶ Make deductible or nondeductible contributions to an IRA.

Within Ten Years of Retirement

▶ Project your retirement living expenses.

▶ Call Social Security at (800) 772-1213 and request an Earnings and Benefit Estimate *(Form SSA-7004)*.

▶ Check with Social Security to find out when you'll be eligible for a full Social Security benefit.

▶ Make an accurate statement of all available retirement assets, including income and other assets (See Appendix 1, Retirement Worksheet).

About to Retire

▶ Start the Social Security application process two or three months before you want to begin receiving your benefit.

▶ Compare IRA options before selecting an investment for your rollover contributions.

▶ Elect an IRA direct rollover (rather than a 60-day rollover) for any lump-sum distributions.

▶ Evaluate your post-retirement insurance coverage to determine whether they're adequate.

▶ Consider obtaining a Medigap policy to supplement your Medicare coverage.

Upon Retirement and Within the Next Twelve Months

▶ At age 65, sign up for Medicare. Part A is free and Part B carries a monthly premium.

▶ Review your medical coverage.

▶ At age $70^1/_2$ (or April 1 following the year you reach age $70^1/_2$), calculate and withdraw your minimum distributions from your IRA.

▶ Closely examine your retirement plan distribution options. Make sure you understand the tax consequences of each option.

▶ Elect IRA rollover if you haven't done so yet.

▶ Start Social Security payments if you can and want to.

ADDITIONAL RESOURCES

American Association of Retired Persons (AARP)   (202) 434-2277

For membership information or an index of publications, call the number shown, or write AARP Fulfillment, 601 E Street NW, Washington, DC 20049. Request *AARP Publications and A/V Programs: The Complete Collection,* #48.

Bureau of Public Debt   (202) 874-4000

For information on how to purchase Treasury securities directly from the Federal Reserve, write Department F, Washington, DC 20036-3998.

National Center for Women and Retirement Research   (800) 426-7386

To receive information, audio, video, and printed materials that help women address financial and other planning needs.

Pension Benefit Guaranty Corporation   (202) 326-4000

2020 K St. NW, Washington, DC 20006-1806

Social Security Administration   (800) 772-1213

Call to receive *Form SSA-7004, Request for Earnings and Benefit Estimate Statement.* Send the completed form to Wilkes-Barre Data Operations Center, P.O. Box 20, Wilkes-Barre, PA 18711.

PERIODICALS

To obtain two free publications on Social Security, *Your Social Security (Pub. 05-1003)* and *Understanding Your Social Security (Pub. 05-10024),* write the Dept. of Health & Human Services, Baltimore, MD 21235.

To obtain free booklets on Medicare, *A Brief Explanation of Medicare, Your Medicare Handbook, Medicare/Medicaid—Which Is Which,* and *How to Fill Out a Medicare Claim Form,* contact the Health Care Financing Administration, Baltimore, MD 21207; (410) 786-3000.

The Internal Revenue Service publishes a number of free publications about retirement. Call the IRS at 800/TAX-FORM, and ask for *Tax Information for Older Americans (Pub. 554), Pension and Annuity Income (Pub. 575), Individual Retirement Arrangements (Pub. 590),* and *Social Security Benefits (Pub. 915)*.

The Continuing Retirement Community: A Guidebook for Consumers tells how to choose a retirement community and offers some suggestions about the questions you should ask before signing a contract. $4; available from American Association of Homes for the Aging, Attn.: Publications, 901 E St. NW, Suite 500, Washington, DC 20004. (Also ask for a free list of accredited facilities.)

Mercer Guide to Social Security and Medicare provides a thorough, understandable overview of the Social Security and Medicare programs. $10; William M. Mercer, Inc., Social Security Division, 1500 Meidinger Tower, Louisville, KY 40202.

▼

GETTING A DIVORCE

*For anyone considering a divorce or who is separated
or already divorced*

Divorce is simply a reality in today's world, in which one of every two marriages breaks up. This is a particularly challenging life event because it's such an emotional time. Divorce signifies the end of a relationship. You're losing a part of your life—your marriage. It's a time of uncertainty: You don't know what the future will bring, especially with regard to your finances. You will have to take your joint financial identity and break it down into separate parts. This difficult task becomes more difficult because of all your feelings. It would be much simpler if you could wait until you're calmer or less angry or hostile to make decisions about your finances. Usually, though, you won't have the luxury of waiting. That's why—even if you barely paid attention to such things before—you must find out what insurance coverage you have, as well as what amounts and types of savings and investments you both have. You'll also have to learn about the tax laws that relate to property, child support, and alimony.

Once you're certain that you want a divorce, you'll have to decide whether you need to consult an attorney or can use mediation. In most divorces, each spouse will need his or her own attorney, especially if there are children or a lot of assets. The attorneys are essentially adversaries who will negotiate on behalf of their clients. On the other hand, if you've been married for only a short period of time, and have no children and relatively little property, you should consider using mediation. This is often an effective, low-cost way to negotiate a fair property settlement. To find a local mediator, contact the American Arbitration Association, 140 West 51st St., New York, NY 10020, telephone (212) 484-4000.

You'll have to address three key issues: budgeting, division of property, and child support or alimony.

BUDGETING

Budgeting will probably be your top priority because divorce proceedings put such a strain on finances. If a separation or divorce seems imminent, you'll need access to money to tide yourself over until you and your spouse reach a settlement.

▶ **Start putting some of your paychecks into a separate account.** If you are the nonworking spouse, it may be a good idea to move half of the money from a joint account into a separate account. But, don't take all of it, because a court may look at this as bad faith on your part.

▶ **Next, each spouse should destroy any powers of attorney that they gave each other.** In addition, you should notify your financial institutions in writing that you revoke any powers of attorney that your spouse may have had. Send a certified letter to your spouse stating that these powers of attorney are no longer in effect. You should also terminate or freeze your home-equity line of credit; this typically can be done unilaterally. Go to the bank in person and get a letter from the lending institution verifying the termination.

▶ **Inform credit card companies that you wish to stop the credit lines on all joint cards, and apply for individual credit.** You're trying to prevent your spouse from running up additional debts on these cards. Remember, at the time of divorce, you may receive not only half the assets but half the liabilities—including mortgage and credit card debt—that were incurred during the marriage.

CAUTION Your divorce decree should address the subject of joint debts, such as mortgages, directly so that personal liabilities are clearly established. Failure to do this may impair the credit of one or both spouses.

PROPERTY

Generally, marital assets are shared equally. Inherited assets, however, are often kept by the person who inherited them. That's why it's usually a good idea to keep marital assets and inherited assets separate.

Before any agreements are made or any property is divided, you'll need to take a detailed inventory of your income, assets, and liabilities. You'll have to make full disclosure to your attorney. If a divorce or separation seems likely, you'll want to secure evidence in the form of documentation early. Each of you will have to provide:

► **Payroll stubs.** In addition to salary, they will indicate whether money is being deducted for savings and retirement accounts.

► **Five years' worth of state and federal income tax returns.** If you cannot find your copies, get them from the IRS (use IRS *Form 4506* to request copies) or the state tax office.

► **Financial statements that you and your spouse keep.** Typically, these are filed with a bank when you apply for mortgages and other loans.

► **Copies of appraisals done for insurance purposes** on real estate and valuable personal property, such as jewelry, paintings, and antiques.

► **Deeds, bank statements, check registers, loan documents, credit card statements, mutual fund reports, statements from stockbrokers, statements of employee benefits, and insurance policies.**

► **A copy of your credit report.** This is important because you may not know about all debts or credit cards that your spouse has.

When you're considering what assets you want to keep, pay attention to the tax issues and look beyond the current value of these assets. For example, suppose that Jim and Anne own a house and 1,000 shares of XYZ stock. They agree one will take the home and the other the shares. Since both assets are worth $100,000, the exchange appears to be fair. But it's not. The house has a basis (tax cost) of $20,000, and the stock has a basis (tax cost) of $80,000. When Jim and Anne sell their respective properties, they each will receive $100,000, but one is going to pay taxes on an $80,000 profit and the other is going to pay taxes on a $20,000 profit. After paying taxes, one person keeps a lot less money than the other. You should be concerned with the net value of an asset—the value after you pay taxes.

PENSIONS

Although you may focus on the division of the more tangible assets such as your home and furnishings, pensions and retirement benefits are likely to be very significant assets. Especially if one spouse earned a significantly higher salary or only one spouse worked, these assets be a sizable portion of the family assets—as much as 70 percent of the assets, all in one person'a name. Obviously, the division of property varies according to circumstances and individual financial needs. *But, if you are a woman, you should be aware that the leading cause of financial difficulty for single women in retirement is not having a pension benefit.* They either lost it in a divorce settlement or their spouse took the single life option payment, and there's no money left now.

The spouse who doesn't have the pension benefits is generally entitled to 50 percent of these assets. You have to decide, however, whether you want these benefits and if so, how you want them paid. You might be able to take a lump sum in cash now or elect to receive a percentage of the pension when it is paid out in the future. You may be inclined to let your spouse buy out your pension rights with cash now: If you're worried about whether the pension will be around in the future, this may be a good option.

However, since the pension is often the only other significant asset beside the house, you should get advice from an attorney or financial planner. Generally, if you're the nonemployed spouse, you should not take a cash settlement. Instead, you should negotiate to receive a percentage of the total pension benefit, including any future increases for inflation and any special incentive payments that your spouse's employer may offer.

Here's an example showing the importance of pension benefits. Anne chose to be a stay-at-home spouse. She has, in effect, given up those years of work experience that cannot be replaced. Anne, a college graduate, is age 52, and while she may find work to support herself modestly, she is not likely to get a high-paying job with a pension. Accumulating enough money for her retirement will be virtually impossible. But all is not lost. Under a federal law known as the Retirement Equity Act of 1984, Anne has protection. That act permits all qualified, tax-deferred, employee pension and retirement benefits to be shared in defined portions between divorcing spouses. Generally, the employee-spouse who has earned the benefits suffers neither a penalty nor a loss of the plan's tax advantages.

As a result, Anne's former spouse, Jim, is allowed to assign and share a part or all of his qualified retirement plans with Anne, without being assessed taxes normally imposed on distributions from these plans. In addition, Jim won't face a penalty tax for premature withdrawal of money in the retirement plan before age $59^{1}/_{2}$.

Anne may receive these funds (or have them allocated to her under the existing plans) and will not pay taxes as long as she keeps them in the existing plans or puts them in another tax-deferred retirement plan, such as an IRA.

To take advantage of these favorable tax rules, the spouses will have to receive a qualified domestic relations order (QDRO). Such an order generally may not violate any of the employer's plans' limitations regarding the form and amount of benefits and the persons to whom benefits are paid. A QDRO can't require the plan to provide any form of benefit or option that is not otherwise provided under the plan. For example, if a pension plan provides for benefit distribution only in the form of a joint-and-survivor annuity, a QDRO can't require payment in the form of a lump-sum distribution. If Jim wants to work until he is 65 but the pension plan allows benefit payouts to begin at age 55, Anne can start to take out her money when Jim is age 55. She does not have to follow what Jim does. However, Anne could not start her benefit any earlier than the plan would allow Jim to start his.

CUSTODY

If you have children under the age of majority, either 18 or 21, depending where you live, you must decide who will have custody of the children. Courts today are more inclined to grant generous visitation rights to the noncustodial parent. In some states, grandparents have been awarded visitation rights as well. Still, by naming one person custodial parent, the court is saying that that parent will have primary responsibility for the child. This parent will be legally responsible for the child's physical well-being and will make decisions related to the day-to-day education, activities, and other aspects of the child's upbringing. Deciding which parent is the "best" is not simply an issue of who loves the child and can provide the best guidance, but who is the best provider financially. In fact, today courts are more inclined to grant motions of joint custody.

Suppose that each parent shares custody of their children. But even in these situations, one parent is often designated as the primary custodian. The parent who has custody for the greater part of the year generally gets the dependent exemption on his or her income tax return. However, the noncustodial parent gets the dependency exemption for the child if:

▶ the custodial parent signs a written declaration that he or she will not claim the exemption for the child, and this declaration is attached to the noncustodial parent's return (use IRS *Form 8332, Release of claim to exemption for child of divorced or separated parents*), or

▶ the divorce decree or separation agreement went into effect after 1984 and unconditionally states that the noncustodial parent can claim the child as a dependent, or

▶ the decree or agreement executed before 1985 provides that the noncustodial parent is entitled to the exemption, and he or she provides at least $600 for the child's support during the year.

CHILD SUPPORT

Although your marriage may be over, your financial obligations to your children continue until they are adults. Support varies according to state and parental income. All states are required to have guidelines specifying the percentage of a parent's income that must go toward child support. Both parents' incomes are counted in these guidelines.

If you're negotiating child support, don't forget to seek a cost-of-living adjustment (COLA) for long-term child-support payments. This will ensure that your child's standard of living will not fall because of inflation. COLAs can be tied to an index such as the Consumer Price Index (CPI).

If you're the parent paying child support, you may find it most convenient to arrange *automatic* withdrawals from your bank account to your ex-spouse's bank account. In this way, a major source of friction can be avoided.

 Make sure that child-support payments are secured with adequate life insurance. Temporary maintenance payments and alimony also should be secured by term life and disability insurance. If your ex-spouse has this kind of insurance, you or your lawyer should ask to see proof of it, including the payment book for the premium, as well as a copy of the policy showing your ex-spouse as owner of the policy.

The federal law that sets guidelines also provides for national enforcement of child-support agreements. Some states will automatically withhold child-support payments (but not alimony) from a parent's paycheck.

Unfortunately, some parents may try to skip out on their responsibilities. If you face this situation, there is help available. You should review the federal publication, the *Handbook on Child Support Enforcement*, prepared by the Federal Office of Child Support Enforcement. It's available for free by writing to: Handbook Dept. 638M, Consumer Information Center Pueblo, CO 81009.

A private support group that helps parents collect their child-support awards is the Association for Enforcement of Child Support, 723 Phillips Ave., Suite 216, Toledo, OH 43612, or call (800) 537-7072.

CAUTION Don't confuse custody payments with college expenses. You should have a separate agreement with your ex-spouse about paying for your kids' education.

Paying for college is not considered a parental obligation in most states. Colleges and universities may base scholarships and aid on *both* parents' income (including the income of stepparents).

ALIMONY

Years ago, when there were fewer two-income families, alimony was a bigger issue. Alimony was awarded to the nonworking spouse for a long period of time. Today, however, alimony awards are more likely to be for very limited durations of time. Alimony is seldom granted for more than five years. Instead, rehabilitative support (sometimes called *separate maintenance*) is often ordered. This is support to the spouse so that he or she can receive training, education, or experience that will enable him or her to earn a living.

Restorative alimony—if it's awarded—is to ensure that the separating spouse will be able to maintain the style of living he or she is accustomed to. This would be awarded to someone who is unlikely to be educated or enter the workforce.

If traditional alimony is appropriate (typically, in marriages of long duration in which one spouse stayed home), the spouse seeking alimony should also include a demand for an *income escalator*. That would entitle the alimony recipient to a share of the payor's future increases in total compensation, as well as cost-of-living increases. The theory is that, without the support of the stay-at-home spouse, the working spouse could not have attained his or her position and the accompanying salary.

The tax laws governing alimony are complicated, and you should talk to an attorney or accountant to make sure you comply with the regulations. Not all payments to a spouse are considered alimony. Some are considered child support and are not tax-deductible. Other payments are alimony and *are* deductible to the person paying the alimony; they are taxable income to the person receiving the payments. Also, you can't use the laws to give you a higher deduction. For example, you can't pay two years' worth of alimony ahead of time.

 The value of a CPA:

A CPA well-versed in matrimonial issues can be just as helpful as an attorney, particularly in the valuation of stock options, personal business interests, and pending inheritances. Call the American Institute of Certified Public Accountants (AICPA) at (800) 862-4272, extension 5, and ask for the names of specialists in your area. If you need help valuing an intangible asset, such as an ownership interest in a small business, you may wish to hire a valuation consultant. Call the Institute of Business Appraisers at (407) 732-3202.

OTHER BENEFITS

▶ **Health insurance.** Some advisers recommend that separation agreements require one partner to provide health insurance to the former spouse and children if that partner was doing so before the divorce. Under federal law, health- and life-insurance coverage provided by a spouse's employer may be continued at group rates for up to 36 months after the divorce, regardless of who pays for it. This doesn't apply if you are covered by another group plan.

▶ **Social Security.** Divorce doesn't affect Social Security benefits accrued during marriage, as long as the marriage lasted for at least 10 years. This is true even if your ex-spouse remarries and his or her new spouse is collecting a Social Security benefit from the same account. Contact Social Security at (800) 772-1213 for more information.

▶ **Prenuptial agreements.** If you waived your rights to a portion of your spouse's pension in a prenuptial agreement, there still may be hope. A recent federal court decision ruled that such a waiver—while valid *after* the wedding—is invalid if signed before the marriage.

YOUR ACTION PLAN

During Separation/Before the Divorce

▶ Put aside some savings in your own name. Establish your own credit by getting a credit card of your own.

▶ Cancel powers of attorney for your spouse, and notify creditors, banks, and brokerages that you and your spouse are separated.

▶ Consult an attorney or look into mediation if you have no children and few assets.

▶ When splitting property, consider your tax liability on property such as houses or stocks.

▶ Make sure you don't give up the right to your spouse's pension.

▶ Use COBRA to extend health insurance for yourself and your children, or look into getting policies on your own.

After the Divorce

▶ Prepare a new will.

▶ Change your beneficiaries on all life insurance policies, retirement accounts, pension plans, IRAs, and so forth.

▶ Take your spouse's name off your savings account, brokerage account, and mutual funds.

▶ If you have children and are planning to remarry, consider a prenuptial agreement to protect the assets you want your children to have.

▼

HELPING AGING PARENTS

For aging parents and those helping them out

Dealing with the financial issues of aging parents may present some of the most difficult and challenging financial situations you'll ever experience. This is not helped by the fact that you may live far away and you're probably busy with your own family, perhaps struggling to pay college bills. Most significantly, though, acknowledging that your parents need help means realizing that they will now depend on you. And most of us simply don't want to face the fact that Mom and Pop won't always be around. Unfortunately, there's no way around this certainty. It's scary and unpleasant, but you have to face it.

Since there's no easy way to initiate a conversation with your parents about their finances and health issues, you may try to postpone this discussion until there's a crisis. However, waiting until there is an emergency is the worst thing you can do. Trying to sort out your parents' finances when one or both of your parents are ill or incapacitated would be an ordeal. You need to talk with your parents when they're healthy and alert, not later on when they may be unable to spell out their wishes or when family conflicts over property can make a tense situation even more difficult. Approach your parents with a positive perspective. Remember, you're trying to make their life easier and help them preserve more of the assets that they have worked so hard for.

Especially if you don't live near your family, chances are that you and your parents haven't talked about finances in a long time, and you may not have discussed money matters when you were growing up either. Suddenly, you have to ask them about their savings, insurance, and other legal matters. You may feel awkward asking your parents pointed questions, but wouldn't you rather they share this personal information with you and other family members rather with than strangers?

An Agenda for Discussion

Whether you and your siblings sit down with your parents or you talk with their lawyer or financial planner, it's important that you get details on the following:

► **Important documents.** Find out where your parents keep their wills, trust documents, and other important personal papers such as insurance policies and marriage certificates. The papers may be in several locations, including safe-deposit boxes or with an attorney, but you, a close family friend, or an attorney should have access to them if the papers are needed.

► **Secret hiding places.** Don't assume that all your parents' money or valuables are in a bank, brokerage, or safe-deposit box. It's not uncommon for people who lived through the Great Depression to stash cash in hiding places or keep older coupon bonds without ever clipping the coupons to get interest.

► **Your parents' net worth.** This is a basic financial worksheet with an account of income and assets.

► **All pension and savings plans.** Ask your parents to review or get a copy of their most recent statement from all their pension or retirement plans. Also, read the plan description so that you understand all the payout options. Find out whether your parents are presently receiving payments under a single-life annuity or joint-and-survivor annuity. Ask whether they received a lump-sum payment. If they haven't started to receive payments, which type of payout schedule would they prefer? Also, when can they receive full benefits?

▶ **Social Security.** If your parents haven't begun to receive benefits, send in a Request for Earnings and Benefit Estimate Statement, *Form SSA-7004*, to get a projection of what those benefits will be.

▶ **Investment Income.** Review statements and account records to find out what income and dividends your parents receive now and what they should expect to get in the future.

▶ **Expenses.** Break out their expenses into their fixed and variable components. Also note the frequency—monthly, semiannual, or annual—of expenses using the following categories:

housing	clothing
food	gifts
medical/dental	recreation/hobbies
transportation	other
insurance	

EVALUATING INSURANCE COVERAGE

Given the rising cost of medical care and the increasing premium cost, you must address the way in which your parents will pay for medical expenses. No matter how well-prepared your parents may think they are, they should know that even a short stay in a nursing home can deplete savings. You should understand and review:

▶ **Health insurance.** The federal Medicare program is available to everyone at age 65, whether they are retired or working. Medicare consists of two parts: Part A is hospital insurance; Part B is supplementary medical insurance. Generally, Part A covers hospitalization, some related inpatient-care costs, and home health services. Part B covers doctors' fees, most outpatient hospital services, and some related services. Presently, there is no monthly charge for Part A, but there was a monthly premium of $42.50 for Part B in 1996.

▶ **Long-term care.** This is a concern for many elderly people but especially for
women, who are more likely than men to live longer and require long-term care.
Depending on where you live and the type of care you need, long-term care costs
range from $5,000 to $8,000 a month. The average stay in a nursing home is three
years. Medicare will cover very little of these costs. Therefore, you should consider long-term care insurance. These policies have become more popular recently
but are still expensive. If you can, you should buy these policies well in advance
of the time you will need the coverage. People buying these policies when they're
in their 50s pay from 20 percent to 60 percent less than someone age 65. Long-
term insurance covers nursing-home care, home care by visiting nurses, home
health aides, home-delivered meals, chore services, and adult day-care centers.

▶ **Medicaid.** This is a federally funded program that is administered by each state.
A patient with no spouse or dependents must turn over to the nursing facility all
his or her income and assets, including Social Security benefits, except for a
personal allowance of $30 to $50 per month.

Example: An elderly woman has $25,000 in CDs, and her annual income from
Social Security and interest totals $1,250 per month. Nursing-home costs in her
area are $5,000 per month, so her monthly income is insufficient to cover her
expenses. She will eventually need help from Medicaid. When she enters the
nursing home, however, her $25,000 in assets will exceed her state's asset limit
for a single person—$3,000. When she first enters the nursing home, she must
spend $1,200 of her monthly income on her care (she can keep $50 for personal
needs). To cover the rest of her nursing-home expenses, she will have to "spend
down" her savings. When she has spent $20,500 of her $25,000, she is eligible for
Medicaid. She can keep the remaining $4,500 (the $3,000 asset allowance, plus
$1,500 for burial). After she depletes her assets, she will continue to apply her
monthly income to nursing-home costs, but Medicaid will pay the balance.

Medicaid once meant complete poverty for the spouse who was not in the nursing
home. Today, however, that spouse can maintain a modest standard of living. Based on
federal guidelines, each state will determine how much of a couple's assets the spouse
may keep, from a minimum of $14,964 to a maximum of $74,820. When a couple's assets
are under the minimum, the spouse at home can keep the entire amount. The couple's
home, household goods, and personal effects are not counted toward the asset limit, and
the spouse at home can continue to live in the family house.

After both spouses are dead, however, the state can recoup from the sale of the family residence the amount of money its Medicaid program paid.

States also may dictate how much income the spouse at home can have. The federal limits are a minimum of $1,230 and a maximum of $1,870.50 per month. Both asset and income limits are adjusted each year for inflation.

Other types of insurance include:

▶ **Life insurance.** Parents shouldn't be paying for coverage they no longer need. They may still need life insurance if one spouse is much younger or if they have dependents such as a disabled child.

▶ **Property and casualty insurance.** Homeowner's insurance should include the replacement cost of the dwelling and depreciating contents, a personal-articles floater for appreciating contents, and valuables that *definitely would be replaced* if lost or stolen. Don't pay to insure things that probably wouldn't be replaced. Liability coverage of at least $300,000 is recommended.

Raising deductibles can be a good way to lower premiums for both auto and homeowner's insurance. With auto coverage, be sure to consider $100,000/$300,000 in bodily injury liability, $50,000 in property damage, uninsured motorist and medical expense payments coverage, plus *high deductibles* for comprehensive and collision coverage. For instance, a $250 deductible should be raised to $500 or $1,000, as long as this money would be available in case of an accident.

"Umbrella" or excess liability coverage of $1,000,000 should be maintained, *especially for elderly parents who drive*. This provides protection against lawsuits.

WAYS TO INCREASE INCOME

Pensions are smaller than they used to be, and Social Security payments may also shrink, so your parents' income is unlikely to cover their expenses. Here are some ideas for increasing income:

▶ **Switch investments.** If most of your parents' money is in T-bills, savings bonds, CDs, or passbook savings accounts, consider switching these funds to money market funds, which generally have higher returns. Tell your parents to look at their situation. They're probably in a lower tax bracket, and they may have less need to invest for long-term growth.

WARNING Be careful! EE Savings Bonds issued before March 1, 1993, are guaranteed a minimum 6 percent interest rate. However, if you switch them to HH Bonds (the kind that pays interest semiannually), you'll receive the new 4 percent guarantee.

For more information on redemption dates and guaranteed minimum interest rates, write to the Superintendent of Documents, U.S. Government Printing Office, Washington, DC 20402. Ask for the schedule of interest dates for Series E and Series EE bonds.

▶ **Tap their home value.** This is an option if your parents are "house-rich but cash-poor." Suggest that they replace their existing home with a smaller one if they have too much room. After all, if your parents no longer need a large house, whey should they pay to heat and insure it as well as pay property taxes? The more home you own, the more you pay. This is a good time to encourage your parents to simplify and lessen their responsibilities. Plus, they could use the profit from the sale to bolster income.

▶ **Investigate a "reverse mortgage."** This is a way to tap the equity in a home without selling it or making regular loan payments. The lender lends a fixed amount each month, based on the owner's age and the home's appraised value. The lender maintains a loan account for the accumulating debt that is settled by the sale of the house at death or at the end of the loan term.

CAUTION There may be high up-front and monthly service charges, so be careful!

▶ **Borrow against insurance.** If your parents have cash-value life insurance, they probably can borrow against it to supplement income. Any amounts that haven't been repaid are deducted from the policy proceeds when the insured dies.

▶ **Cash gift to parents.** Under the gift-tax exclusion, you can make a gift of $10,000 per year per parent ($20,000 for a couple) without tax consequences to you as donor.

INCAPACITY

Although you may dread asking your parents to spell out their wishes for treatment if they become incapacitated, you should do so. To make certain that you parents' desires are considered, have them prepare the following documents when they are still healthy and of sound mind.

DURABLE POWER OF ATTORNEY

This document must be drawn up when someone is considered mentally competent. It can be crucial if a parent becomes unable to conduct his or her own affairs. It enables the powerholder to make financial decisions, sign tax returns, and transfer assets for the incapacitated person. If your parents have many different brokerage or bank accounts, you should check with the institutions ahead of time to find out whether they will honor a durable power of attorney. Some may require you to use their forms.

LIVING WILL

With this document, people can state clearly what they want—and don't want—done to keep them alive if they are seriously ill or injured. While not legally binding, a living will can help families avoid having to make decisions in the middle of a health crisis.

HEALTH-CARE PROXY

Also known as the health-care power of attorney, this document delegates the responsibility to make medical decisions for the signer if he or she cannot make such decisions. These decisions include what treatments to administer and what treatments to withhold.

WILLS AND TRUSTS

Although your parents may already have a will or trusts, you should remind them to update these documents. This is especially important if your parents have retired and moved—say, from New York to Florida. They should redraw their will or at least have an attorney in the state they live in review it, and the attorney should also review the trusts. Make sure your parents know about any potential estate or income taxes on their assets.

▶ **Wills.** A will puts three important personal decisions in writing: how one wants property distributed; who is to act as the *executor*, the person responsible for carrying out the will's instructions; and who will become the guardian of minor children.

▶ **Trusts.** There are two types of trusts your parents may want to consider: a *living trust*, which is established during a person's life and can be used along with a durable power of attorney to ensure that important financial affairs continue to be managed in the event of disability; and a *testamentary* trust, which can be part of a will and which takes effect at death.

▶ **Letter of instruction.** This document is intended for beneficiaries and trustees. It is not legally binding, but is designed to help family members handle funeral arrangements and other last wishes.

WHEN YOU LIVE FAR AWAY

Hopefully, you're able to stay in touch and visit your parents even if you live far away. However, if you're unable to see your parents as much as you'd like or as much as they need, you can still help them. A new type of professional—a geriatric care manager—can assist with financial, medical, and legal issues. To find a care manager, ask attorneys or doctors for referrals. Or send a self-addressed, stamped envelope to: The National Association of Professional Geriatric Care Managers; 1604 N. Country Club Rd., Tucson, AZ 85716.

Care managers are generally paid by the hour, with fees ranging from approximately $65 to $150. Before hiring a care manager, ask whether he or she is licensed locally and check references.

You should also see whether your employer offers any elder-care benefits. A handful of corporations have started to offer services ranging from counseling to caregiver referrals, because an increasing number of workers are helping to care for elderly parents.

YOUR ACTION PLAN

▶ Talk with your parents about their finances and health concerns while they are healthy.

▶ Find out where your parents keep their valuable documents.

▶ Review your parents' insurance and beneficiary designations.

▶ Make sure they have updated their wills, named a durable power of attorney and health-care proxy, and have a living will.

▶ Look at ways to increase your parents' income, including dropping unnecessary insurance coverage, switching investments, and selling their home.

DEALING WITH THE DEATH OF A LOVED ONE

For anyone who must take charge of his or her family's finances

For widows, widowers, and others involved in helping to organize and settle the estate of a spouse, parent, friend, or other relative

For executors of wills

Experts agree that coping with the death of a loved is the most stressful event you'll ever go through. The emotional impact is, of course, obvious, but there are also many financial consequences. After all, you're never really prepared for your spouse's death. Over a lifetime, you will buy car after car or several houses but, hopefully, you will deal with the death of a loved one only once. You're the person left behind who has to pick up the pieces and move on. While you're in an emotionally fragile state, you face many difficult questions and you're expected to make many important financial decisions.

Death is a public event. Friends and relatives come to the funeral. Others read obituary notices. Fortunately, this means that you'll have the support of many people. But it also means that you'll be a target. Some people in the financial services business will see this as an opportunity. They know that you may be getting death benefits from pensions or life insurance policies and will attempt to become your "trusted adviser" in the hopes of generating business. You won't believe how many uninvited offers of help you'll receive. Whom do you trust and whom do you turn to?

 CAUTION If you do get calls from solicitors who say they know you or knew the deceased, say that you already have an adviser and that you'll call back when you're ready to discuss financial matters. Beware of anyone who insists you need to make new professional arrangements immediately.

These days, more and more companies offer counseling for widows or widowers of employees. The employer pays for this counseling, during which you meet with an objective confidential advisor who is not selling any products. If you're not sure whether the deceased's employer offers this type of benefit, ask about it. Even if it's not generally offered, the employer may be willing to arrange it.

There are a lot of decisions that you're not going to be prepared for. Typically, one person in a family handles the financial affairs. It may not be clear-cut, but usually one spouse has primary responsibility for the kids while the other spouse handles money matters. If the latter dies, the survivor suddenly has to assume two roles with double the responsibility. It's difficult. You will have to confront many issues, such as:

▶ Will I have to sell the house?

▶ What about the kids and their college bills?

▶ What about debts and medical expenses?

There will be many questions that you won't be able to answer. That's okay. *You must resolve not to make any major financial decisions immediately.* You will need to maintain health insurance and other coverage and, of course, pay certain bills. But you shouldn't make other significant decisions about your money right away.

You should focus on grieving and helping your family adjust to the new situation. And you should take inventory of your assets, income, and liabilities and gather as much information about your finances as possible so that you'll be better prepared to make decisions in the future.

ARRANGING THE FUNERAL

Check for funeral instructions, but keep in mind that they may be in a separate letter elsewhere. Or, if the deceased had been ill, he or she may have prearranged the funeral. Check with a local funeral director to see whether any plans were made.

 CAUTION Have someone watch your house during the funeral; burglars read obituaries to find out when a house will be empty. Change the message on your answering machine so that it doesn't have a phone number. Your message should be generic, without first names, so that solicitors won't call you by name, as if they know you.

There are ways to save money on your funeral, according to the Continental Association of Funeral and Memorial Societies, which has been advising consumers for 30 years. Here are some tips on arranging an inexpensive funeral:

▶ **Coordinate the funeral yourself.** Forty-three states (as of 1993) permitted families, religious groups, or friends to bypass the funeral home and make all the funeral arrangements.

▶ **Consider cremation.** Cremations, which cost an average of $2,000, now account for 20 percent of all funerals. Memorial services can be held at a church or home.

For more information, you can write to:

Continental Association of Funeral and Memorial Societies
6900 Lost Lake Road
Egg Harbor, WI 54209
(414) 868-3136

National Self-Help Clearinghouse
Graduate School and University Center
City College of New York
Room 620 N,
25 West 43nd Street
New York, NY 10036
(212) 642-2944

The Association for Death, Education and Counseling
638 Prospect Avenue
Hartford, CT 06105
(203) 586-7503

The Foundation of Thanatology
630 West 168th Street
New York, NY 10032
(212) 928-2066

How Much Will the Funeral Cost?

The National Funeral Directors Association reported that costs for the average funeral in 1995 were as follows:

Item	Cost
Casket (18-gauge steel, sealer, velvet interior)	$ 2,143
Staff cost and overhead	953
Embalming	322
Use of chapel for wake or memorial service	258
Use of chapel for funeral service	308
Hearse	145
Limousine	74
Transfer of remains to funeral home	118
Makeup, hair styling	117
Acknowledgment cards	21
Total	**$ 4,459**

Use this list to see what's reasonable. If someone quotes you $10,000, walk away or ask why it's so costly.

What to Expect Financially

For most widows and widowers, the period after the death of a spouse is one of financial as well as emotional adjustment. In addition to the loss of long-term income from a spouse's earnings or retirement benefits, the survivor faces funeral expenses and, often, sizable medical bills. Many surviving spouses receive lump-sum payments from several sources: life insurance, Social Security, veterans' benefits, employee benefit plans, and so on—with life insurance often accounting for about 75 percent of the total. These payments may provide a financial cushion for a time, but survivors must be careful to use assets wisely in order to keep as much income as possible over the long term.

In the difficult weeks after the funeral, you will have to pay bills, fill out a variety of forms, contact government agencies, acknowledge gifts, and take care of other details—even though you'd rather not do any of these things. The following checklist will help you sort out what you must do.

First Things First

Get Death Certificates

You should get 10 certified copies of the death certificate. Usually, the funeral director can get them for you. You will need to send one each to Social Security, the IRS, and any bank or brokerage in which the deceased had an account.

Keep Track of All Documents

Don't throw away canceled checks or receipts, and make sure to keep old insurance policies. Some may have cash value even if they appear to have expired. Check to see whether there was life insurance linked to loans, mortgages, and credit cards. You'd be astonished by how much money in death benefits goes unpaid because dependents aren't aware these policies exist. Go through the membership cards of the deceased, and if the membership is current, check with the professional, trade, or fraternal organizations to see whether there are life insurance, death benefits, or annuities. Many social organizations, associations, and unions have group life insurance plans that provide special benefits for surviving spouses. Some of these groups will assign a member to visit a family if assistance is needed. You'll need to notify these organizations of a member's death (a sample letter is provided at the end of this section) or cancel and see whether you can get a prorated refund of the dues or subscription if the membership was just renewed. Don't throw away any mail until you're sure you've got all the paperwork under control. If you're moving or handling matters for someone who lived elsewhere, give your forwarding address so that you'll continue to get important correspondence.

Locate the Estate Documents

You need the original will plus any *codicils* (amendments) and trust agreements. Look around the deceased's home, or check with his or her attorney. If you think that a document is in a safe-deposit box, check with the bank. Some hometown bank directors are compassionate, and if the banker knows you, he or she may let you open the box, but, legally, safe-deposit boxes must be sealed when someone dies.

Find the Original or Certified Copies of Certificates

This includes marriage certificates, birth certificates, divorce decrees, military service papers, Social Security cards, and income-tax records. Organize these papers into folders under general headings so that you can find them quickly. You'll need these papers in order to apply for Social Security benefits—including the $255.00 death benefit—or to ensure that benefits for any eligible survivors will be continued. If you don't have originals or certified copies, you can get certified copies at the office or department of vital records or statistics. All states have such offices; check your phone book.

 Let Uncle Sam help if you need proof of age, residency, or family ties to qualify for government benefits or collect an inheritance. The Bureau of Census Personal Search Unit will search its records. Write to the Bureau, Preparation of Data Division, P.O. Box 1545, Jeffersonville, IN 47131.

Hospitalization/Medical Insurance

You will need to decide whether to continue or convert any hospitalization and medical insurance your spouse had. Delaying this decision could have very costly consequences. Among your options are the following:

1. **Most group hospitalization and medical plans continue for a fixed number of months after the person covered by the insurance dies.** A federal law known as COBRA lets you, as surviving spouse, continue to buy medical insurance through your spouse's employer's plan for up to 36 months. This is called *continuation*, which is different from *conversion*.

2. **Most group plans also allow the surviving dependents to *convert* individual policies without a medical exam.** They may also cover preexisting conditions. But converting a policy can be expensive. It may be cheaper to buy your own individual policy elsewhere. You should compare costs and policy features before making a choice.

3. **Make sure you file claims for any bills incurred by your spouse.** Ask your spouse's employer whether your spouse had a medical care reimbursement account. If so, find out how much money is in the account and make sure you use it to reimburse yourself for out-of-pocket expenses related to the deceased's care.

 You should file claims for accrued vacation pay, unpaid salary, and accumulated sick pay.

Benefits

You should contact your spouse's benefits or human-resources coordinator and obtain benefit claim forms for pensions, savings plans, employee stock ownership plans, stock options, and deferred-compensation plans. Most companies are very responsive and want to help you. As a survivor, you may be eligible for various benefits. To claim them, however, you must be ready to prove your relationship to the deceased. Have a copy of your marriage certificate handy. Having the necessary documents will save you time processing claims. You'll want to research benefits available through Social Security and the various organizations in which your spouse was active, particularly veterans' programs and groups connected with former employers. If the deceased worked for a long time for another employer, there may be additional survivors' benefits due to you. A sample letter requesting information on these benefits is provided at the end of this section.

 Keep copies and stubs for any checks you receive from your loved one's employer. But, be careful: If you're a surviving spouse, you're permitted to roll over certain employee benefit plans into IRAs. However, you must complete the rollover within 60 days of receiving the funds. You should ask for a *direct rollover* to avoid the mandatory 20 percent federal income tax withholding on the distributions.

LIFE INSURANCE PROCEEDS

If your spouse was covered by personally owned life insurance, contact the insurance company whose name and address are on the policy or the agent who sold the policy.

If you are the beneficiary, you'll need to fill out a statement of claim and provide the following to the insurance company:

▶ the name and address of your spouse

▶ a copy of the death certificate

▶ the policy number

▶ the policy amount (sometimes called the death benefit or face value)

▶ your spouse's occupation and the date of his or her last day of work (if it is a group life plan)

▶ your spouse's birth certificate (or other birth documentation) and possibly yours, depending on how you want the proceeds to be paid

The insurance company may ask for additional information about the cause of death, such as an attending physician's statement or a police report. Since the insurer is required to file information on taxable payments with the federal government, the company will also need your age, address, and Social Security number. However, you as spouse-beneficiary will not have to pay income tax on the insurance proceeds. But the money then goes into your estate, and if your estate is worth more than $600,000, your children or other heirs will have to pay taxes on the money. Regardless of who the beneficiary is, the death benefit will be free of income taxes as long as the policy was not sold during the insured's life.

Selecting a Payment Plan

Insurance proceeds generally are paid in a lump sum, but there may be reasons for you to choose another method of payment. If no method of payment was specified by the insured, you may select among several "settlement options" (also called "modes of settlement"). If you are the beneficiary, discuss these options with your insurance representative. Following are the most common options:

▶ lump sum

▶ payment of interest only. The principal is left with the insurance company until a final decision is made.

▶ payment of equal installments until the proceeds are depleted

▶ payment of periodic income for a specific number of years

▶ payment of income for life

▶ withdrawal by check

Under this last option, the insurance company simply mails the beneficiary a checkbook with a balance equal to the death benefit. The beneficiary then writes checks from this account. The beneficiary may write a check for the entire balance at any time. These accounts generally earn money market rates of return.

If you're uncertain of what your finances will be in the future, you should probably take a lump-sum payment, which you can then deposit in a bank account. Then, when you have a better handle of your savings and debts, you may be able to go back to the insurer and choose to take another form of payment. Before making a decision, ask the insurer what the cost will be and whether you have to meet other conditions if you want to choose an alternate method of payment in the future.

 Missing Policy Queries:

If you think that your spouse may have had life insurance policies that you can't find, you can write to the American Council of Life Insurance, Policy Search, 1001 Pennsylvania Ave., NW, Washington, DC 20014.

Include a self-addressed, stamped envelope and request that its member companies search their files. The search is free and will take about six weeks.

PROBATING THE ESTATE

Probating your spouse's or relative's estate is the next step. This process can be crucial to your financial well-being because a speedy probate will free up cash and other assets.

Each state has its own probate laws, which govern the transfer of property and assets of a deceased person. The probate courts in each state (in some states, these are called the Surrogate's Court) clear the transfer, and the process can take several months or years. An attorney or the clerk of the court can advise you whether probate is necessary. You may be able to start probate yourself or do it yourself. Don't immediately hire an attorney.

If you're the executor or executrix, you are the person legally responsible for managing the estate. (Executors are frequently beneficiaries as well.) While you can get people to help you and advise, your personal involvement is important.

The steps to file are as follows:

▶ **File the will.** If there is a will, it should be filed with the probate court. The court then formally appoints the executor named in the will. Without a will, the deceased is "intestate" and the probate court will appoint an *administrator* to act as executor. The executor's duties include making a list of the deceased's assets, collecting debts, paying the debts of the deceased, managing and distributing property, and submitting a final accounting to the court. Don't underestimate these duties—they can be a lot of work.

▶ **Giving information to the court.** Initially, the court will need the will, names and addresses of children, and a list of assets. It also may require copies of your marriage certificate and documents on any previous marriage(s). You'll also have to fill out various forms.

▶ **Assets may be frozen.** During the legal sorting-out period, bank accounts and other assets may be "frozen," safe-deposit boxes sealed, and other steps taken to protect the interest of heirs and conserve assets subject to taxes. Banks often will allow you, as surviving spouse, to withdraw funds to meet daily expenses until the estate is settled. If the bank does not allow assets to be withdrawn, the court can order the release of estate assets to you.

▶ **Finding an attorney.** If the estate is small and not complex, you can handle probate procedures without legal assistance. However, obtaining legal assistance usually is advisable. If you don't have a family attorney, you can call the local bar association for recommendations. Or you can ask a bank trust officer whether he or she knows an attorney who is an expert in probate and estate law. It's usually a good idea to talk with two or more attorneys—and investigate fees—before choosing one. Find out whether the attorney charges an hourly fee and how many hours he or she expects to spend on your estate section. Be very wary of any

lawyer who wants a percentage of the value of the estate; you should pay for the
work the lawyer does rather than simply giving them a large amount of the estate
for filing papers on your behalf. A well-organized estate plan can reduce the
number of hours the attorney will spend on probate. In certain circumstances,
probate help may be available from legal aid societies.

▶ **Assets not subject to probate.** The clerk of the probate court can provide general
information on which assets should be included in probate. Although laws vary
from state to state, many states exclude certain joint property from passing
directly to a widow or widower. For example, your jointly owned home or your
joint bank account, life insurance proceeds payable to a named beneficiary, U.S.
savings bonds, and assets in certain types of trusts are generally excluded. In fact,
much of one's estate can pass probate-free.

▶ **Even if no assets will pass through probate, filing for it has another advantage.** Many states have laws that prevent creditors of the deceased from collecting
debts after a specified period of time. The time period, however, is usually contingent on filing for probate.

▶ **If there is no will.** Each state's laws of descent determine the division of an estate
if there is no will. They usually provide for you, as surviving spouse, and your
children to receive shares of the estate. In some states, a widow with one child
receives half of the estate and the child the other half. If there is more than one
child, the widow receives one-third and the children equally share two-thirds.
Probate court will assign an administrator, which may be you, but may assign
someone else. You may want to hire an attorney if you don't like the person who
is named.

Fees associated with probate are strictly regulated by statute. They are based on the
amount of an estate in the deceased person's name alone and the amount that may
have been owned with others, such as survivorship property. For the latter, there is
often a reduction in probate fees.

▶ **Estate taxes.** Each state taxes estates according to its own law. Many states
simply assess a "death tax" based on the federal tax, but some states have their
own inheritance or estate taxes. The federal government does not tax estates
valued at less than $600,000. There is no estate tax on any amount left from one
spouse to the other because of the unlimited *marital deduction.* (*Note:* This

applies only to surviving spouses who are U.S. citizens.) However, there can be taxes at the second or surviving spouse's death.

Appraisals of securities, other than publicly traded securities, businesses, and other assets will be necessary. For income tax purposes, the value of your capital assets steps up to the fair market value of the assets on the date you die. If you think an estate will be subject to federal taxation, you should contact a tax attorney or a CPA, because federal-estate tax laws and regulations are complicated. The estate includes employee benefits such as deferred compensation, a savings plan, or stock options and other securities.

Other Benefits to Which You May Be Entitled

Workers' Compensation

Families of workers who die as a result of a work-related accident or illness may be eligible for benefits under the workers' compensation program administered by each state. Generally, such benefits are based on a percentage of the worker's wages. Contact your state labor department or compensation commission if you need assistance.

Social Security

Social Security is not just a program for retired people. Benefits are paid to widows, widowers, children, and other surviving family members. Funeral directors usually send death notices to the Social Security Administration, but this does not constitute a claim. *The surviving spouse should apply for benefits as soon as possible* by contacting the nearest Social Security office. The phone number will be listed in the telephone directory under "U.S. Government, Department of Health and Human Services." Benefits also can be applied for by mail. A sample letter is provided at the end of this section.

There is often a two- or three-month period between completion of paperwork and payment of the first check. *It's important to apply quickly because back payments are limited to a 12-month period.*

Initially, the Social Security office will need the deceased spouse's Social Security number, *W-2* forms for the previous year, birth and marriage certificates, and children's birth certificates. *Don't delay filing if some of the documents are missing.* The Social Security office can help in securing replacements for missing documents.

▶ **Death benefit.** The Social Security Administration pays a one-time death benefit of $255 if the deceased was covered by Social Security. This is payable to either you as the surviving spouse or your dependent children.

▶ **Monthly benefit.** Monthly Social Security benefits are payable to widows and widowers age 60 and older. Widows and widowers of any age who are caring for children under age 16 (or any age, if disabled before age 22) are entitled to benefits. A child is eligible for benefits if a deceased mother or father worked in a job covered by Social Security for the required length of time (which varies based on year of birth). Children under 18 (or 19 if still in high school or any age if disabled before age 22) also are eligible for benefits.

If your family's size will produce a total benefit that exceeds the family maximum, the rate of payment to each family member is reduced to fit the limit.

▶ **Earnings restrictions.** Anyone under age 70 who is receiving Social Security payments is restricted as to how much he or she can earn in annual pay without reducing benefits. Income from other sources—dividends, interest, retirement plans, and rents—does not affect benefit payments. Each year, the earnings restriction is changed based on inflation, so it's a good idea to check with Social Security for the most current restrictions.

Veterans' Benefits

Benefits available to survivors of veterans include reimbursement of some burial expenses, pension payments, and education assistance. Payments depend on whether the veteran died from causes connected with military service, whether the veteran served in war or peacetime, and whether the discharge was honorable.

To check on these benefits, call or visit your local U.S. Department of Veterans' Affairs (VA) office or contact local veterans' organizations or the American Red Cross for assistance. Many states have toll-free numbers for the VA, listed either under "U.S. Government" or available from directory assistance.

The VA will need either a veteran's claim number ("C" number) or a copy of a discharge certificate (*DD Form 214*) from military service plus military service number or branch of service, and dates served. A death certificate, marriage certificate(s), and birth certificates for children also may be required. A sample letter is provided at the end of this section.

▶ **GI life insurance.** If your spouse was covered by GI life insurance, write to one of the two VA centers that handle claims. A sample letter is provided at the end of this section.

In the East:	In the West:
U.S. Department of Veterans' Affairs	U.S. Department of Veterans' Affairs
P.O. Box 8079	Federal Building, Fort Snelling
Philadelphia, PA 19101	St. Paul, MN 55111

▶ **Funeral and burial benefits.** Families of veterans who served in wartime and families of certain peacetime veterans are eligible for a $150 burial-expense payment. These veterans also are entitled to an internment flag.

▶ **Wartime veterans.** People who served in the Spanish-American War, the Mexican Border Period, World Wars I and II, the Korean conflict, Vietnam era, certain time periods surrounding the Grenada and Panama invasions, and the Gulf War are eligible for burial in any national cemetery except Arlington. Check with the VA on dates of eligibility. Peacetime veterans who qualify for the same benefits include those who were disabled in the line of duty or who were receiving payments for service-connected disabilities at the time of their death or discharge.

▶ **Headstones or grave markers.** Both wartime and peacetime veterans are eligible for free grave markers or headstones. Apply at a local VA office.

▶ **Pensions.** Spouses and unmarried children of veterans are eligible for monthly payments from the VA if a veteran's death was connected with military service. These payments depend on the veteran's rank; there are additional payments for children.

Depending on financial circumstances, spouses and children of veterans whose deaths are not connected with military service may be eligible for pensions. The VA frequently adjusts the amounts. A sample application letter is provided at the end of this section.

▶ **Education benefits.** Spouses of veterans whose deaths or disabilities were connected with military service can apply for education benefits for themselves and their children. The VA provides education counseling for children and, on request, for widows and widowers. Monthly payments vary for students enrolled in apprenticeship training, in cooperative programs, or in VA-approved schools or colleges. There also are provisions for cooperative work-study programs. Payments can continue for up to 45 months of schooling or the proportional equivalent for part-time students.

- ▶ **GI home loans.** Unmarried widows and widowers of veterans of World War II, Korea, and Vietnam who died of service-connected disabilities are eligible for GI loans to acquire a home.

- ▶ **Aid and assistance.** Surviving spouses also may be eligible for an "aid-and-assistance" benefit if they are patients in a nursing home, helpless, blind, or require regular aid in the home.

INCOME TAX RULES

There are special income tax provisions for widows and widowers. For example, you may file a joint return in the year of your spouse's death rather than file as a single person, which generally produces a lower tax rate.

- ▶ For two years after a spouse's death, if you have at least one dependent child and have not remarried, you may use a special tax bracket as surviving spouse.

- ▶ At the end of the two years, you may file as head of household, if you still claim your child as your dependent.

- ▶ If you are widowed before your spouse receives pension benefits, you may be entitled to a $5,000 exclusion against annuity or pension income. The method of computing this benefit is rather complicated, but the IRS or a tax expert can help. Various IRS publications may also be useful. (See *Publication 575—Pension and annuity income*.) Call (800) TAX FORM to get this form.

- ▶ Anyone over age 55—widowed or not—is entitled to a special one-time exclusion of $125,000 gain when selling a personal residence (see Chapter 7).

ADJUSTING TO A NEW FINANCIAL SITUATION

You have to learn how to maintain financial stability for yourself and your family. You may be working for the first time or have to adjust to living on only your income, as well as savings. This can be intimidating, especially if you are doing this on your own for the first time. Use the following tactics to get started:

▶ **Take a clear look at how much money is coming in and how much is going out for everyday expenses.** Check on big bills that need to be paid, and, if money is tight, cancel credit cards and subscriptions and get refunds. Transfer title and insurance on automobiles, and obtain a list of items in your spouse's safe-deposit box.

▶ **Figure out what funds, if any, are available for emergencies or special goals, such as retirement or a child's education.** Even before probate is completed, an attorney can project what cash and other assets you are likely to receive from the estate. Federal agencies can estimate the size of monthly benefit payments such as Social Security before the checks are issued.

▶ **Mortgages, loans, and some credit card debt may have been insured against the death of the borrower.** If so, then you will have fewer worries about whether you can cover these payments. However, if these debts were not covered by insurance, don't assume that you're headed for the poorhouse. Some lenders will extend repayment periods or reduce the amount of your monthly payments until you're better able to make payments easily. But it's up to you to contact the lender and explain your circumstance. Be sure to tell them whether payments will be late and the reason why.

▶ **If you can meet your current expenses, you'll want to start a regular savings program.**

GETTING FINANCIAL ADVICE

If you're managing or helping someone else manage a large sum of money, you should consider talking to a professional. A life insurance agent or attorney may be able to recommend a financial adviser if the estate is unusually complex. Advisers are available from several sources:

▶ Most banks have money-managing services.

▶ Most brokerage firms have investment-management or consulting services.

▶ Many insurance companies have financial-planning services and offer various forms of annuities.

▶ There are also independent counseling firms that will develop overall investment plans for a fee.

▶ Financial counseling may be available through an employer as part of a survivor support benefit.

 CAUTION Don't invest in anything you don't understand. Ask yourself: "Will this investment pay more than a savings account?" and if not, "What other advantages does it offer?"

LOOKING AHEAD

It's important—especially for the sake of your children and other loved ones—to make the financial adjustment to your spouse's death as easy as possible. Now that you're on your own, single rather than part of a couple, you have to readdress all your financial decisions.

Protecting your children will be your priority:

▶ If you have no will, see an attorney and make one so that your property will pass to those you wish.

▶ If you have minor children, name a guardian and trustee of assets.

▶ If you want to protect your minor children and other dependents from financial worry over income in the future, you may need additional life insurance.

▶ Make certain you and your children have enough health insurance.

▶ Decide whether you want to move to a smaller home or relocate on your own (see Chapter 7).

▶ Review your auto insurance. If you sell one car, drop your coverage.

▶ Drop membership in clubs that you don't need.

▶ Reestablish your own credit, especially if you were the nonworking spouse.

▶ Review your investment strategies. Investments that were appropriate for you and your spouse may no longer be appropriate for your tax bracket.

▶ Tell someone in your family or a trusted friend where you keep your important papers. Make sure you tell someone you expect to outlive you.

You should get a release from the IRS saying that the deceased has fully paid all of his or her tax obligations. When you file a tax return for the deceased, you must check a box stating that this is a final return for the last three years. You will have to file an estate tax return, and when the probate court releases all assets and the estate is closed, the IRS will send you this release.

SAMPLE LETTERS

When requesting survivor benefits by mail, you may find it difficult to phrase questions so that you get the information you need. The following section contains sample letters that can make this job easier.

SOCIAL SECURITY

Social Security Administration

(Address)

(City) (State) (Zip)

Gentlemen:

I understand that (funeral director) has informed you that my (deceased/relationship), (full name and Social Security number), died on (month, day, year). I would like to schedule an appointment with your representative.

I have secured copies of the death certificate, our marriage certificate, our birth certificates and those of our dependent children, our Social Security numbers, and evidence showing my (deceased/relationship's) recent earnings.* If you require any additional documents or information, please inform me when you set a date for the appointment.

Sincerely,

(Signature)

(Typed name)

(Address)

(City) (State) (Zip)

---

* You should proceed with this letter even if you don't have all these items in hand. It's important to get the process started as soon as possible.

VETERANS' PENSION BENEFITS

Veterans' Benefits Office

U.S. Department of Veterans' Affairs

Munitions Building

Washington, DC 20025

Gentlemen:

Please send me instructions and forms necessary to apply for the Veterans' Pension Benefits due me and my children because of the death of my (deceased/relationship).

(Name in full)   (Branch of service)   (Dates of service)

_____ died _____

(Service number)   (Date of death)*

Very truly yours,

(Signature)

(Typed name)

(Address)

(City)   (State) (Zip)

---

* Expedite mailing this letter and subsequent applications for benefits since, under certain circumstances, benefits start from the date the application is received by the appropriate government agency and **not** from the date of death. Use certified mail, return receipt requested, to ensure receipt.

Government Life Insurance

Eastern United States

U.S. Department of Veterans' Affairs

District Office

P.O. Box 8079

Philadelphia, PA 19101

or

Western United States

U.S. Department of Veterans' Affairs

District Office

Fort Snelling

St. Paul, MN 55111

Gentlemen:

Please send me instructions and forms necessary to apply for life insurance benefits to which I am entitled because of the death of my (deceased/relationship).

(Name in full)   (Branch of service)   (Dates of service) was insured under policy no.

_____ and died _____

(Service number)   (Date of death)

Very truly yours,

(Signature)

(Typed name)

(Address)

(City) (State) (Zip)

COMMERCIAL INSURANCE

(Insurance company)*

(Street address)

(City)   (State) (Zip)

Gentlemen:

Please send me instructions and forms necessary to complete and file a claim for life insurance benefits to which I am entitled as beneficiary, due to the death of my (deceased/relationship).

(Name) was insured under policy no.

_____ and died _____

(Service number)   (Date of death)

Very truly yours,

(Signature)

(Typed name)

(Address

(City)   (State) (Zip)

_____

* If life insurance policies are held with different companies, use same format as above for each company.

CIVIL SERVICE BENEFITS

Civil Service Commission

1900 East Street, NW

Washington, DC 20415

Gentlemen:

Please send me instructions and forms necessary to apply for Civil Service benefits due me and my children because of the death of my (deceased/relationship), who died.

_____   _____
(Name in full)   (Date of death)

Very truly yours,

(Signature)

(Typed name)

(Address)

(City)   (State) (Zip)

EMPLOYER

(Personnel officer)

(Company or organization)

(Street address)

(City)   (State) (Zip)

Dear Sir or Madam:

This is to advise you that my (husband/wife), (full name), died on (month, day, year). I understand that he or she may have been covered by a life insurance plan through your organization. Please send me a list of the documents you will require and whatever information you will need from me as beneficiary.

                                        Very truly yours,

                                        (Signature)

                                        (Typed name)

                                        (Address)

                                        (City)   (State) (Zip)

ORGANIZATION

(Secretary)

(Organization name)

(Street address)

(City)   (State) (Zip)

Dear Sir or Madam:

This is to advise you that my (husband/wife), (full name), died on (month, day, year). I understand that (he/she) may have been covered by a life insurance plan through your organization. Please send me a list of the documents you will require and whatever information you will need from me as beneficiary.

> Very truly yours,
>
>
> (Signature)
>
> (Typed name)
>
> (Address)
>
> (City)   (State) (Zip)

Your Action Plan

▶ Find any letters of instruction about funeral arrangements, and locate the will.

▶ Contact the deceased's employers, and ask about any benefits you are eligible for.

▶ Make arrangements to continue health coverage for yourself and your family.

▶ Contact your spouse's former employers, credit card issuers, unions, and other organizations and ask whether you're entitled to any survivor benefits from insurance coverage.

▶ Make sure you write or revise your will to spell out distribution of your assets. Name a guardian or trustee if you have minor children.

▶ Tell a family member or friend where you keep your will and other valuable papers.

▶ Take a long hard look at your finances. Decide what changes you must make to adjust to the loss of income.

▶ Start a savings and investment plan that matches your new needs.

DECLARING BANKRUPTCY

*For anyone who feels overwhelmed by credit problems
and is considering bankruptcy*

WHAT DOES BANKRUPTCY MEAN?

Bankruptcy is both a life event and a financial process. It occurs when your debt payments and necessary living expenses exceed your income and assets. In addition, you haven't been able to work out a solution to your debt crisis on your own, and you need protection from creditors. You're in credit hell and feel overwhelmed, especially if you're relatively young or simply inexperienced at handling your money.

Bankruptcy is a very serious option, and if you're thinking about it, you should have already tried everything to solve your problems. You should turn to bankruptcy only as a last resort. You should never assume that bankruptcy is an easy way to get out of credit trouble. Not only does it impact your current financial life, but after you file for bankruptcy, you may find it difficult to get credit and even rent an apartment. Bankruptcy is a serious black mark on your credit record. You should carefully consider these consequences before you decide to file for bankruptcy.

What Leads to Bankruptcy?

Various situations lead you to bankruptcy. The most common situations include:

▶ **A failed business.** You started a business and racked up a large amount of debt, thinking that the profits would just start rolling in. Unfortunately, that never happened, and now you're left with the bills and no profits.

▶ **Poor debt management.** You've succumbed to the powerful temptation to use and abuse your credit cards. Now you've got large unpaid balances on several cards and no way to pay off your bills.

▶ **Lack of income.** You lost your job and have spent your severance and your emergency fund, and you don't know when you'll find another position.

▶ **Family health problems.** You or one of your dependents has been critically ill, and you've accumulated hundreds of thousands of dollars in medical bills not covered by insurance.

▶ **Divorce.** You and your spouse have split up. Suddenly, you've got to support two households and foot legal fees and child support—all on your salary, which hasn't gone up along with your expenses.

▶ **Lawsuits and legal proceedings.** Even if you have a strong balance sheet, a lawsuit can sink you. If you've been personally sued and don't have sufficient insurance coverage, legal fees and judgments can quickly consume all your savings and more.

Some of these situations are beyond your control. Obviously, you hadn't counted on getting sick or being sued by your neighbor. Or, your business may have been thriving until there was a devastating flood or the town's leading employer—and your biggest client—moved away. On the other hand, if you have contributed to your problems—either indirectly by not getting enough insurance or directly by overspending—you have two issues to deal with:

1. Will declaring bankruptcy solve your present problems?

2. How will you work on avoiding these problems in the future?

BEFORE YOU FILE FOR BANKRUPTCY

Even if you're certain that you've exhausted all other possibilities, make sure that you do the following before you file a bankruptcy petition:

▶ **Get professional advice from a planner, lawyer, or accountant.** Don't immediately go to an attorney who specializes in bankruptcy. In fact, if you've already consulted a bankruptcy attorney, you should get a second opinion from a lawyer who has nothing to gain from you going through bankruptcy.

▶ **Take another hard look at your income, debts, and other assets.** See whether there's not some alternative, including selling your car, moving, or getting a second job, that would be a better option than bankruptcy.

▶ **Contact your creditors and offer to work out a repayment plan.** Often, creditors are willing to make some arrangment with you when they know that your next step is bankruptcy. After all, if you declare bankruptcy, your creditors will have to wait for the court proceedings and will probably be able to collect only a small portion of the outstanding debt.

▶ **Consult a credit counselor.** Make an appointment with a local nonprofit consumer counseling service that charges no or very low fees. Even if you haven't been able to negotiate with your creditors, legitimate consumer credit services often can.

TWO TYPES OF BANKRUPTCY

There are two types of personal bankruptcy: Chapter 7 and Chapter 13.

Chapter 7

This type of bankruptcy is sometimes called "straight bankruptcy" and can be used by both individuals and businesses. Under this type of bankruptcy plan, a portion of your assets are liquidated and converted to cash and distributed to your creditors by a court-appointed trustee, usually an attorney or accountant. You cannot file more than once in six years under Chapter 7.

A key advantage of Chapter 7 filings is that you're allowed to keep some of your property—it is exempt from the assets that are liquidated by the court. It's important that you check with an attorney familiar with bankruptcy law in the state where you live.

There are different sets of state and federal exemptions. In some states, you can choose whether to file under state or federal, but in most states, you can file only according to state exemptions. Federal exemptions include:

▶ $15,000 in home equity (If you live in a $100,000 mansion, you will have had to borrow against $85,000 of your home's value before you can declare bankruptcy.)

▶ $2,400 in auto equity (You can't drive around in a Mercedes if you're declaring bankruptcy.)

▶ $400 per item in household goods, up to $8,000

▶ $8,000 in accrued loan value on any life insurance policy

▶ $1,000 in jewelry (The bankruptcy judge won't be happy about seeing you in court wearing a Rolex.)

▶ Your right to government benefits, including, veterans, Social Security, and public assistance

▶ The value of your qualified pension, savings, and profit-sharing plans

The dollar amounts of these exemptions are doubled if you're filing for bankruptcy with your spouse.

CAUTION California has an interesting set of rules. Because of the state's high property values, there are two different standards for homeowners and renters. For example, if you don't own a home, you're allowed to keep additional personal items to make up for what you would otherwise have in home equity.

Chapter 13

This form of bankruptcy proceedings is sometimes called the "wage-earner plan" because it can be filed only if you have some steady source of income. Chapter 13 can be filed by individuals, including sole owners of businesses. Under this type of filing, you agree to repay your debts from your current assets and your income, usually over a three-to five-year period. Chapter 13 can be filed at any time, provided that you don't have more than $750,000 secured debt or more than $250,000 in unsecured debt.

THE BANKRUPTCY PROCESS

To file for bankruptcy, you have to file a petition and other forms with the county clerk, spelling out your assets, liabilities, and living expenses. If you're filing a Chapter 13 petition, you must also file a debt-repayment plan. (Filing this plan immediately prevents creditors from trying to garnish your wages or seize other assets.)

Under Chapter 7, your creditors will meet with the court-appointed trustee. After this meeting, the trustee collects your assets, excluding any of the exempt items, which are then sold by the trustee—quickly and expediently. The cash raised by this sale is distributed among your creditors according to the schedule set by the trustee. After the cash is distributed, your bankruptcy is discharged. This process usually takes from three to six months. Generally, creditors can't try to collect unless you illegally defrauded a creditor. However, even under Chapter 7, you are still liable for the following:

▶ Court-ordered child support and alimony

▶ Debts owed to the federal government for taxes or student loans

▶ Debts from fradulent activities, such as ripping off investors in your business

▶ Court-ordered restitition

▶ Cash advances or luxury items purchased against your credit cards in the three months before you filed for bankruptcy. (The court would see this as an effort to hide assets.)

▶ Any debt arising from you driving under the influence

▶ Marital debts arising out of divorce, such as money you owe to an ex-spouse as part of a property settlement

With a Chapter 13 filing, you formulate a plan to repay most or all of your debt, according to your income and amount of credit. For unsecured debt, you must repay at least as much as your creditor would have gotten if you filed under Chapter 7. For secured debt, you must repay the amount of the claim that the creditor agrees to accept. You present this to the court for approval. When the court approves your plan, it notifies your creditors of your intent to pay, thereby putting creditors on notice that they will get paid under these terms and that they should accept these terms. If your plan is approved, you must begin to make payment to the trustee within 30 days of filing the plan.

Filing Chapter 13 serves to forestall aggressive legal proceedings that creditors may use to collect their money. It also protects you from harassment by collection agencies.

WHICH TYPE OF BANKRUPTCY IS PREFERABLE?

If you're uncertain which type of filing to make, ask yourself the following:

1. **How serious is your debt situation?** If you have no source of income, liquidation under Chapter 7 provides complete protection from your creditors. However, if you're working or have another regular source of income, such as a pension, you can probably work out a repayment schedule and renegotiate the terms of your loans and get more time to repay them.

2. **Are there cosigners on your loans?** Consider the consequences of your filing. If you file Chapter 7, your cosigners have no protection from creditors.

3. **What will happen to your credit report?** Chapter 13 shows your willingness to work yourself out of debt. It's a court-approved plan that you have committed to follow. Chapter 7, on the other hand, is a more desperate step that isn't viewed as favorably by creditors.

WHAT HAPPENS AFTER BANKRUPTCY

Although filing for bankruptcy today doesn't carry a stigma as powerful as a scarlet letter, it's crucial that you accept responsibility for your actions. You must recognize that you were forced to seek protection through bankruptcy because your financial plan failed. You should now set your personal financial performance as your highest priority. You should monitor your cash flow so that you can reestablish good credit.

 And you must aim at all costs to avoid filing for bankruptcy again. Repeated bankruptcy filings can be very damaging in the long run.

ANSWERS TO THE MOST COMMON QUESTIONS ABOUT BANKRUPTCY

What about collateral on a loan?

If property has been pledged as collateral for a loan, it may have to be surrendered to the creditor. Or arrangements may be made to pay for it during or after the bankruptcy period.

What debts are not guaranteed protection under bankruptcy?

Child support, alimony, most taxes, student aid, and student loans are not protected under either bankruptcy filing.

Do cosigners on loans receive protection?

Cosigners under Chapter 13 receive the same protection as the person who filed the bankruptcy petition, but under Chapter 7, cosigners are not granted any protection.

Can someone back out of a bankruptcy filing?

After you file either type of petition, you can ask the court to dismiss the case. Also, you can switch a Chapter 13 plan to a Chapter 7, provided that you have not filed a Chapter 7 petition within the previous six years. In addition, if your finances suddenly improve— you win the lottery or get a new job—you can go back to court and amend your petition.

How long does a bankruptcy filing remain on a credit report?

Bankruptcy remains on credit reports for about 7 to 10 years. However, lending institutions are often willing to extend credit after two to three years, if you have demonstrated financial responsibility in paying your obligations. If your circumstances have changed since you filed for bankruptcy—marriage, a new job, or a spouse who is also working— the lenders may view you as less of a credit risk than you were in the past.

Does an attorney have to be involved in the bankruptcy process?

You can file the petition yourself and fill out the other necessary paperwork, but you should have legal guidance to make certain that you comply with all the state and court regulations.

Your Action Plan

Before Filing for Bankruptcy

▶ Make an accurate list of your assets, liabilities, income, expenses, cash flow, and net worth.

▶ See an attorney.

▶ File your petition if you have decided you have no alternative.

After the Bankruptcy

▶ Pay close attention to debt management.

▶ Avoid the habits or behavior that led you to declare bankruptcy in the first place. (Obviously, you have little control over some problems, such as ill health.)

▶ Make sure you have adequate health, life, disability, and liability insurance.

▶ Begin to rebuild and maintain your emergency fund.

▶ Don't borrow beyond your means.

▶ Get a secured credit card. Using money in a bank savings account as security, apply for a secured card and then charge and repay some bills using the card. Then you'll be able to get a gas card on which you can charge only small amounts. You're aiming to rebuild your credit record to show a report of current payments. Within several months or so, you'll be able to get unsecured credit cards and cancel the secured accounts. You want your credit report to be full of "C's," which are better than "A's" in school. With your record of payments all "Current," then you'll be able to get an important loan in the future, when you need it.

▼

FINANCIAL PLANNING WHEN YOU'RE TERMINALLY ILL

For the terminally ill person, as well as his or her spouse, loved ones, and friends

You are very ill, and your doctors have told you that you have from three to six months to live. Of course, you're hoping that you outlive their predictions, and your first priority is treating your illness. Although finances may seem unimportant at this time, unfortunately, you must face your situation and get your affairs in order—for yourself and for your family members. You will have to deal with medical expenses, insurance, and estate planning. And you shouldn't hesitate asking friends, relatives, and social service agencies for help. If you're employed, talk to your employer's human resources department. In addition to providing explanations of your medical benefits and life insurance coverage, the department may offer other counseling services.

There are several key issues that you must act on when time is of the essence.

PROVIDING FOR MANAGEMENT OF YOUR AFFAIRS

If your illness is progressing much more quickly than anticipated, you'll need to make sure that your financial and legal affairs will be handled if you become unable to make decisions. You should authorize someone to act as your attorney to make decisions on your behalf if you are unable to do so. This is know as giving someone "power of attorney." You give this person either limited power—for example, to pay your bills—or a range of authority to make all financial decisions.

 To make certain the document clearly specifies the decisions you want the power of attorney to have, you should consult an attorney. The document will have to be filed in court; a lawyer will also know whether your state has any other requirements for power of attorney documents.

The person you designate as your attorney "in fact" will likely make decisions in the following areas:

▶ **Employee benefits.** For example, if you become incapacitated at a time when a stock option should be exercised or else will expire worthlessly, the power holder can make this exercise on your behalf. Retirement decisions also may come into play. For example, if you're incapacitated, the power holder can elect to retire or collect disability on your behalf. Along with this decision come other elections, such as pension payment options, conversion privileges on life insurance lost at retirement, distributions from other qualified and nonqualified employer plans, and retiree medical elections. Give a copy of the power of attorney to your company's personnel office. This way, personnel officials are less likely to challenge decisions by your agent (the power holder).

▶ **Donation of assets.** Your agent's ability to donate your assets to family members or your favorite charity can reduce your taxable estate. Recent court cases have ruled that a power to donate must be expressly stated in a power of attorney. You can make gifts up to the maximum limit of the exclusion, until the date of your death. If you're in a coma, the power of attorney can make gifts and donations, including, but not limited to, gifts under exclusion. You may want to limit the donations to a class or category of individuals or a particular charity, and such a decision may require the approval of all adversely affected individuals. Donating assets via a power of attorney can help your family members avoid taxes on your property.

 CAUTION This ability to donate is generally not included on a standard power of attorney form.

▶ **Successor agents.** The power of attorney should set out procedures for when, why, and how successor agents will be determined.

▶ **Limits.** The power can be limited to a future time or event. This way, the agent cannot exercise it while you (the power giver) are still competent.

▶ **Durability.** The power should state that it remains in effect even after the principal is no longer competent to grant it. If it is not a *durable* power of attorney, it becomes invalid when the principal becomes incompetent, thereby defeating its purpose.

A power of attorney eliminates the need for a lengthy court process, during which you could be delared incompetent. If a court decided that you were legally incompetent—that is, unable to handle legal matters—it would appoint a representative, sometimes called a *guardian* or *conservator*.

While a power of attorney can authorize medical treatment or act as your personal representative in legal matters, you may want to set up a revocable (grantor) trust to handle all legal matters. There are some advantages to this type of trust, such as protecting your assets after your death, so check with your attorney.

Making Medical Decisions When You Can't Have a Voice in the Process

Hospital decisions generally fall into three critical areas:

Authorizing Procedure

This is known as a health-care proxy. A durable power of attorney deals with all health-care measures whether or not the patient is terminally ill. In this respect, a health-care proxy goes well beyond the power of a living will (see below). The distinction is that the proxy delegates *all* health-care decisions to the power holder, while a living will delegates authority for medical decisions *only in life-threatening situations*. End-state medical care in an acute situation is extrememly expensive and can be a financial and emotional drain for you as well as your family. By making your instructions about resuscitation, invasive procedures, and forced feeding very specific in your health-care proxy, you will make your intentions very clear.

Discontinuing Life-Sustaining Procedures

A living will document is an instruction or directive dealing with orders for the care of someone who can't communicate and is in a terminal condition. It's usually limited to refusal of extraordinary life-prolonging procedures. Many states now have standard forms for living wills. You may want to contact your attorney to have a living will drafted for yourself. Or contact the not-for-profit organization, Choice in Dying, at 200 Varick Street, New York, NY 10014; (800) 989-9455. Choice in Dying will, for a nominal fee, send you a form drafted to meet your state's living-will standards, and also offers terminal-care counseling and referrals to attorneys.

For more details on the subject of living wills and health-care proxies, write to the American Association of Retired Persons, AARP Fulfillment, 601 E Street, NW, Washington, DC 20049. Request two free publications, "Making Medical Decisions Q&A" (D155-25) and "Shape your Future with Health Care Advanced Directives" (D-15803). Their phone number is (202) 434-2277.

Anatomical Gifts

A person's body or specified organs may be donated to a qualified organization or recipient. Arrangements made with the recipient before the individual's death can ensure that the body or organs will be utilized as designated. Many states have organ-donor programs administered through the Department of Motor Vehicles.

EMPLOYEE BENEFITS

You should carefully review all your benefits policies so that you are aware of the full extent of the coverages as well as any limitations to the policies. This is true of pension plans as well as insurance policies.

▶ **Retirement benefits.** If you're eligible for retirement, compare the financial advantages of electing early retirement versus continued disability. You should also compare the advantages of electing to retire with a 100 percent survivor annuity versus a 50 percent joint-and-survivor or single life annuity.

 Be very careful when you select a survivor annuity if your priority is maximizing your survivor's income. Although disability income may exceed the 100 percent survivor annuity, over the long term the 100 percent survivor annuity could provide more dollars than the disability pay followed up by a reduced survivor annuity. Disability pay ends when you die. On the other hand, a 100 percent survivor annuity or a 50 percent joint-and-survivor annuity can maximize income for your survivor. Your life expectancy isn't the issue, so you should base your decision on your survivor's financial needs.

▶ **Life and disability policies.** Review these policies for flexible arrangements that can help you. You may be able to increase your coverage without meeting any medical guidelines. Some policies let you change beneficiary designations. Many newer policies carry provisions that allow terminally ill people to receive a cash payment from the policy while they're alive. If you're strapped for cash, perhaps for costly medical treatment, this may be a good option.

 Remember that you are reducing—if not eliminating—the death benefit, which your dependents might need.

At retirement, many companies reduce the amount of life insurance available to retirees. Typically, group term-life coverage lost at retirement is convertible without a physical exam to whole-life or other forms of permanent insurance. The new insurance will be more expensive, but this shouldn't be an issue when the insured is terminally ill.

REDUCING DEATH TAXES

There are a variety of ways you can reduce the federal and local taxes that could be owed on your estate when you die. Gifts are a time-honored method of transferring wealth and can be a very efficient tax-avoidance method. The property given may be exempt from taxation, and all income and appreciation accrued after the gift is made will escape transfer (gift and estate) taxes.

► **Gifts of $10,000 per donee.** A terminally ill person may use the annual gift-tax exclusion of $10,000 per donee, which can significantly reduce an estate's size. For example, a person with 3 married children and 10 grandchildren who is diagnosed as terminally ill on December 15 and who dies on January 15 could donate up to $320,000 to his heirs free of federal, state, and gift taxes (3 children, plus 3 children-in-law, plus 10 grandchildren equals 16 donees; times 2 years' worth of donations, equals 32 donations; times $10,000 for each donation equals a $320,000 reduction in the person's estate).

A married person may give up to $20,000 annually if gift-splitting is elected between the spouses. Also, you can pay the medical and tuition expenses of your children and grandchildren, and such payments will be exempt from the gift tax as long as they are made directly to the health-care or educational organization.

► **Using the $600,000 unified credit exemption equivalent.** Everyone has a unified credit of $192,800 against gift and estate taxes. The exemption equivalent of this credit is $600,000—which means, in effect, that the first $600,000 transferred by an individual, whether by gifts or through death, are effectively exempt from federal gift and estate taxes.

Although the credit is not scheduled to decrease, Congress may cut it in the future. Therefore, the credit may never be worth more than it is today. So you might consider making a gift of up to $600,000 of property today and using the unified credit to eliminate the gift-tax liability. This may be a particularly good idea for high-yielding assets. By transfering these assets, you will avoid the increasing estate taxes caused by the accumulation of income that is not expected to be spent before a person's death.

► **Basis considerations.** A terminally ill person should be very careful before transferring any asset with a basis well below its current value. When someone gives property to another person, that person (the *donee*) takes the donor's basis (a carryover basis). Therefore, if the donee sells for a gain, the donee ends up paying the taxes on the appreciation.

When property is transferred by reason of death, the recipient generally takes a basis in the property equal to its fair-market value as of the date of the decedent's death (a stepped-up basis). Therefore, if the recipient sells the property—even the very next day—he or she will have little, if any, taxable gain. When property is given during a lifetime, the expected estate-tax savings (*i.e.,* on any appreciation) must be balanced with the fact that the donee will take the same basis as the donor. In other words, to receive the benefit of reduced estate taxes, you, as donor, may be transferring to your donee a potential capital-gains tax.

Let's consider this illustration to help clarify the issues:

John, a widower, has a gross estate valued at $620,000. He hasn't used any of his $600,000 unified credit, so he'll be able to shield most of his estate from taxes. But he's concerned about the remaining $20,000 in value. Assume for simplicity's sake that the $20,000 comprises his 500 shares of XYZ Corporation common stock, with a current market value of $40 per share, and that its price remains stable. He paid, on average, $10 per share when he bought the stock, so his total *basis* is $5,000. John has held all his shares for at least one year.

If John dies without disposing of the shares (either through an outright sale or a *lifetime* gift), the $20,000 value of the stock will generate an estate tax liability of $7,400. (Under current federal estate tax rates, this "tier" of estate value is taxed at 37 percent.) The estate will have to sell 185 shares (at $40 each) to pay the taxes. John's son Jack, the sole heir, will receive 315 shares worth $12,600. Jack's *stepped-up basis* will be $12,600. If Jack immediately sells all his shares at $40 each, he won't have to pay capital gains tax. Why? His "per-share" *basis* is $40, so he has neither a gain nor a loss.

If John instead gives all his shares to Jack, via two separate, annual *tax-free* gifts of $10,000 each (or 250 shares per calendar year), he will remove the $20,000 in value from his estate. Jack, the donee, will get his father's $5,000 basis. If Jack sells all 500 shares after receiving the second gift, he'll have a $15,000 *long-term* capital gain (if an asset is sold at a gain, the don*ee*'s holding period effectively began when the don*or* acquired the shares), subject to taxes at a maximum of 28 percent. The capital-gains liability is at most $4,200. If Jack's total taxable income, including the gain, is in the lowest marginal bracket (15 percent), his capital-gains tax liability attributable to the sale would be only $2,250.

If John wants to maximize Jack's gain, he's better off making lifetime gifts of his stock now rather than letting it pass through his estate. The following illustration summarizes his findings:

John wants to maximize the transfer of wealth—here represented by 500 shares of stock in XYZ Corporation—to his son Jack. He can either make a lifetime gift of the share or pass them on to Jack through his estate. Which method is best?

Table 14-1: Transferring Wealth Between Generations

Distribution Gift	Through Estate	During Lifetime
John's beginning share value		
Number of shares	500	500
Times: market value per share	$40	$40
Equals: share value	$20,000	$20,000
Shares distributed or "gifted to" Jack		
Shares received by Jack	315	500
Times: Market value per share	$40	$40
Equals: Value of shares received	$12,600	$20,000
Result of Jack's sale of these shares		
Jack's sale proceeds	$12,600	$20,000
Less: Jack's basis	$12,600	$5,000
Gain on sale	$0	$15,000
Tax liability		
Estate (at 37%)	$7,400	N/A
Personal (at 28% long-term capital-gains rate)	$0	$4,200
Total tax liability	$7,400	$4,200
Net benefit (or wealth transferred) to Jack	$12,600 ($20,000 less $7,400 estate tax)	$20,000 (less $4,200 taxes capital-gains tax)

Note that the $3,200 in tax savings equals the amount of wealth transferred to Jack. John's estate pays 37 percent on the entire $20,000 in value, whereas Jack pays 28 percent only on the $15,000 in *appreciated* value. A reconciliation of the difference follows:

John's estate		
Value "Tier"	*Tax Rate Applied*	*Computed Tax*
First $5,000	37%	$1,850
Remaining $15,000	37%	$5,550
Total Tax Liability		**$7,400**

Jack		
Value "Tier"	*Tax Rate Applied*	*Computed Tax*
First $5,000	NONE	$0
Remaining $15,000	28%*	$4,200
Total Tax Liability		**$4,200**

* This is the maximum long-term capital-gains rate. If Jack's taxable income, including this gain, falls into the 15 percent bracket, this latter tax rate will apply and the computed tax will be $2,250.

To determine what's best for your situation, you should consider the following:

1. The donor's *basis* in the property

2. The property's current market value

3. The dollar difference between items 1 and 2—that is, the donor's net *unrealized* gain or loss

4. The total value of the donor's estate

5. How much, if any, of the unified credit the donor has used, and how much remains to "shield" the estate from taxes

6. The dollar difference between items 4 and 5—that is, the excess amount, if any, of the estate's value over the unused unified credit

7. The donor's marginal income tax bracket

8. The donee's expected marginal income tax bracket if he or she were to dispose of the property

If the value of John's estate, *including the XYZ stock,* is less than $600,000, he'd want to hold on to the shares and distribute them through his estate and *not* "gift" them or sell them. Why? Because otherwise he'd make permanent a tax liability that would vanish; if he gifts them now, Jack gets his father's $5,000 basis. An immediate sale would produce a $15,000 gain and associated tax liability of $4,200, per our illustration. If the shares remain in his estate, their basis will be *stepped up* to the $40 market value per share and, because the total estate value is under $600,000, no estate tax would be due. Remember, don't do anything without considering *basis*!

Consider selling assets with a high basis and low value for current income tax-loss purposes. (*Note:* Incurring losses in excess of gains will be deductible only up to $3,000 per year. A decedent's unused capital loss is not eligible for carryover.) This high basis will be reduced to the fair-market value if the asset is held until the individual's death. Assets with a low basis and a high value should be held until death, to give the heirs a stepped-up basis.

Marital-Deduction Gifts

There are several benefits to transferring property by gift to a spouse:

▶ **There is no federal gift-tax liability.** Since all transfers to a spouse qualify for the marital deduction, they are not considered taxable gifts.

▶ **Such gifts avoid probate expenses.** All property transferred to a spouse by gift will not be part of the terminally ill person's probate estate. If the property was located in another state, the need for ancillary probate will have been avoided.

▶ **With marital-deduction gifts, no federal estate tax return is needed.** If the gifts to a spouse result in the decedent's estate having a value of less than $600,000 at the time of his or her death (before the distribution of any taxable gifts), no federal estate tax return will be required.

▶ **State death taxes can be avoided.** Gifts to a spouse may reduce state death taxes. This will be the case only in states that don't have marital deductions in their death/inheritance-tax statutes.

Charitable Contributions

Gifts that meet charitable objectives may provide a method to reduce both income and estate taxes, but this is an extremely complex area that requires expert legal assistance. Whatever your objectives both for charitable gifts and retention of current income, you should discuss your methods and tactics with an estate-planning attorney.

SIMPLIFYING YOUR SITUATION

Some strategies may not benefit you but can help your survivors. Among these tactics are the following:

▶ **Domicile.** Because some states don't have death taxes, changing your domicile to such a state may be worthwhile from a tax perspective. Again, check with an experienced estate-planning attorney before deciding on such a move.

▶ **Liquidity.** You should make funds available for pre-death and post-death expenses.

▶ **Social Security.** Contact your local Social Security office to determine eligibility rules for disability and death benefits.

▶ **Safe-deposit boxes.** Don't overlook any items kept in safe-deposit boxes. Determine who you want—and who you don't want—to have access to the boxes.

▶ **Bank accounts and investment assets.** Decide who you want to have access to your bank accounts, money-market accounts, and other assets.

▶ **Claims and litigation.** It may be a good idea to preserve a dying individual's testimony relating to claims or litigation regarding his or her estate and affairs through a formal, legal deposition or other means.

YOUR ACTION PLAN

▶ Make arrangements for the continued management of your situation. Update your will, create trusts if necessary, and designate a power of attorney.

▶ Make your decisions about ongoing medical care very explicit by using legal documents such as a living will, health-care proxy, and a durable power of attorney. If you want to, specify that you want your organs donated.

▶ Consider benefit elections for your retirement plans and life insurance policies.

▶ Review your health insurance in view of your medical condition.

▶ Talk to a social service agency if you want to make arrangements for hospice care.

▶ If your estate is valued at more than the $600,000 federal uniform credit exemption, do planning to reduce your estate taxes. Consider making gifts to family members or transferring assets to family members in lower tax brackets.

CHAPTER 15

PREPARING FOR THE UNEXPECTED— HANDLING DISASTERS AND WINDFALLS

For anyone who has suffered a severe financial setback and for those who unexpectedly receive a large sum of money

Virtually all life events have some impact on finances. When the life event is drastic or disastrous—you lose your job, you're in an accident or become seriously ill, or you're sued—you may find yourself headed toward financial catastrophe. Fortunately, there are strategies that will enable you to overcome financial reverses and get back on your feet.

On the other hand, when you face a much happier problem, such as a sudden windfall of money, your finances are also thrown into a tailspin. Both situations are financial extremes, and when they occur, you'll probably need to get professional advice and counseling.

What is a Financial Disaster?

You may think that missing one or two payments on your credit card bill means that you're headed for money woes. If you've always paid your bills in full on time, this problem may, in fact, be distressing. But a true financial disaster is far worse. A financial disaster means that you've experienced a significant financial loss, in which your debt far exceeds your income. When this happens, you're really in trouble.

You're probably all too aware if you're headed for disaster. If you've been ill, you've watched your medical bills accumulate. If you've been out of work, you've used up all your savings. In these situations, you may feel as if you're treading water—moving but going nowhere. You feel overwhelmed because there seems no way out of a very bad situation. You have little or no income. The bill collectors are hounding you, and you're worried that you may lose your home. Everything appears hopeless because you don't see any way out of this terrifying money crunch.

Crucial Steps to Coping with Financial Disaster

Despair is your biggest enemy, and you must not succumb to it. Although you may think there's no way you can dig yourself out of this bottomless pit, you have to keep fighting and fighting . . . There *is* a solution to every financial problem. It may not be easy—you may have to file for bankruptcy—but you must believe that there is a way out.

Along with recognizing that there is an end to your woes, you have to accept responsibility for yourself and your problems. Since no one cares more about finding a solution than you, you can't give up and blame someone else or circumstances beyond your control. You have to pick yourself up and take positive steps toward your future well-being.

Taking responsibility for your situation doesn't meant that you have to confront your problems on your own. In fact, you probably won't be able to see the practical solutions; you'll only see what you can't overcome—difficulties that seem to grow larger than life every day. That's why you may have to get some help.

 You may need to talk to someone other than your spouse or a family member, someone who isn't directly involved in your life. This is not the time to let shame or embarrassment prevent you from reaching out.

Sometimes, it helps to make a list of everyone you know. Call ten people with whom you feel comfortable. You'll be surprised by how helpful people can be; your friends may know others who can assist you during this difficult time.

You should, of course, involve your family. You may feel that you'd rather not burden your children, especially if they're living on their own or have their own families. But remember, extreme situations call for drastic measures. If you've been supporting your kids in graduate school or helping to pay their rent, you may have to reduce or cut out this financial contribution. Sit down with your family and explain the circumstances, and see what adjustments everyone can make to the situation. Although your ego may take a bruising and you may not really want to tell your children that money is tight—you should spell out the cash flow situation for the next 6 to 12 months. See whether your kids can pitch in to help or take less money from you. If you're lucky, your kids may even offer to help out, if their circumstances permit.

Likewise, if you're feeling besieged by calls from creditors or doctor's offices, ask a friend or someone else to act as a go-between with your creditors and help mediate the problem. See whether a local law school runs a clinic in which students provide free legal counseling. Check whether a nearby college or university has an extension program providing financial, legal, and other assistance.

 Don't make a long-term decision that seems to be the perfect solution. For example, you may hear about an overseas job that pays an enormous salary. Ask yourself whether you would seriously consider the position if your finances were more secure. Don't make a rash decision just to fix the problem. The solution has to be reasonable for you and your family.

Here are the steps you should take to get your finances back on track:

TAKE CARE OF YOUR HEALTH

Your physical well-being is more important than your finances. If you're overwhelmed with medical bills, and even are considering stopping treatment because you can't pay your medical expenses, get help immediately. First, talk to your doctor or health-care provider. Be honest about your circumstances. Do a net worth statement or a cash flow statement. Even if these sheets show $0, let your health-care provider see them. Explain that whatever money you get—whether it's Social Security disability, SSI, unemployment—is all your income. Spell out your dilemma. Explain that you're in a severe financial crunch but you need medical care. You should not be turned down for medical care simply because you're unable to pay. If you're in a hospital, talk to a social services liaison. If you're not being treated in a hospital, call your city's social services agency. It's likely that there are programs that will provide you with financial and medical help.

REPLACE LOST INCOME AND SAVINGS

If you've been unemployed for an extended period of time or out of work because of illness, it's important that you start to reestablish your identity as someone who works and has an income. You may want to take a part-time or an hourly position to get back into the workplace, no matter how small your salary is initially. The old adage about how getting a job is easier when you're working is still true. It makes sense, after all: When you're working, you feel better about yourself, and therefore, you'll make a better impression on others.

CONSIDER LIQUIDATING ASSETS TO PAY OFF DEBTS

Hopefully, you'll never have to sell off your assets. But if you've exhausted all your alternatives, this may be a way for you to raise some cash. It's important, however, that you sell off your assets carefully so that you not only raise the maximum amount of cash but avoid tax problems. You may not be able to achieve both objectives with each sale. If there's a conflict, don't let the tax implication "tail" wag the investment decision "dog." (Incidentally, this guideline is always true, even when you're not considering "distress" sales.)

If liquidation of your assets is the only solution, liquidate them in this order:

▶ **Your emergency fund, checking accounts, investment accounts, Christmas club accounts, or assets held in your children's names.** Obviously, any money in bank accounts should be used first to pay off bills. Although, you may be reluctant to use money that is supposed to go to your children in the future, you may not have any choice. Using this accounts for legitimate purposes such as providing a home or food is allowed. For example, if you're a single parent with two kids, you could use money from your children's accounts to pay for two-thirds of your mortgage and two-thirds of the utilities—the proportional cost of supporting your children.

▶ **Stocks or mutual funds.** Once you have used any available cash, you should consider selling off your investments. You should sell or use assets in descending order of liquidity: The more liquid the asset, the least amount of penalties. Also, you should delay selling highly appreciative assets; you want to get your cash as swiftly as possible. Start by selling investments that are always valued at "par"— those whose value does not fluctuate, such as a money-market mutual fund always priced at $1 per share.

If you own stock, bonds, or a mutual fund whose value is well below its cost, and your expectation is that its value won't recover swiftly, you should probably sell it now. The capital loss may offset capital gains or reduce your overall tax bill.

If you own bonds, remember that bond prices react to interest rates. If interest rates are falling, your bonds' values should increase, and vice versa. Historically, bond values have generally been less volatile than stock prices. When interest rates move sharply, bond prices follow suit—in the opposite direction. The farther in the future the bond's maturity date, the more volatile its price. If interest rates are rising, your bonds' values are declining, so you can limit losses (or perhaps lock in a gain) by selling now.

▶ **Personal valuables such as furnishings, jewelry, and real estate.** You may think that selling off an engagement ring or a leather couch is an easy way to raise money, but you won't get much for these items. It's a better idea to downsize your home, especially if you can still get a good price for your house. Remember, you'll have 24 months in which to buy another home, to shelter any gain from the sale. Selling your home and renting a smaller house or an apartment may be a better option. If you can't sell your home, consider renting it as a way to cover your costs and make some money. If you have collections such as coins or stamps, you should have them appraised. You may be pleasantly surprised at how much money you can get from these collections—now is not the time to be sentimental about the time you spent putting the collection together with your grandparents when you were a child.

▶ **Assets not in pensions or annuities.** Don't liquidate any distributions from your 401(k) plan, tax-deferred annuities, or IRAs because you'll have to pay federal tax, probably a state tax and, if you're under age 59$\frac{1}{2}$, a 10 percent penalty on the money you've withdrawn. Sorry, but just because you're having a tough time, the IRS will not waive these penalties, which can be very steep. More importantly, if you sell off your retirement assets, you may deprive yourself of your safety net for your retirement. Unless you're very young, you probably will not be able to rebuild these accounts to povide money for your retirement.

Negotiate Overdue Bills

If your back is up against the wall, tell your creditors your situation and explain that you may be headed for bankruptcy. Some creditors will work with you, perhaps settling for fifty cents on the dollar, rather than wait for you to declare bankruptcy. Some creditors will let you pay a certain amount immediately and forgo the remainder of the debt. If possible, see whether you can borrow from friends or family and sell some assets to get a debt wiped off the slate.

Seek Financial Assistance

Now is not the time to say, "I can't afford to hire someone to help me." There are valuable low-cost counseling services, cooperative extensions at universities, and other services that will help you. Here are two:

Debtor's Anonymous General Service Board
P.O. Box 400
Grand Central Station
New York City NY 10163-0400
(212) 642-8220

National Foundation for Consumer Credit
For an affiliated consumer credit counseling
service in your area, call (800) 388-2227.

Also, don't hesitate to investigate public or private sources for financial assistance. Many of these programs are especially helpful in a short-term emergency. Public programs include unemployment compensation, Medicare and Medicaid, food stamps and assistance for the dependent elderly, rent subsidies, fuel deliveries, low-cost banking, utility and phone services, and charitable and social services programs. To locate such programs, begin by checking the government and social services listings in your phone book. The Federal Emergency Management Agency (FEMA) administers government grants and loans for geographic areas that the President has declared a disaster area.

CUT SPENDING

To save on health, accident, or life insurance coverage, you might consider competitively priced group policies offered by your employer, a membership organization, or a private provider. Be sure you are aware of waiting periods and meet preexisting-condition requirements before you cancel old policies.

USE UNSECURED CREDIT

With careful management, credit can be a very valuable tool in a temporary financial emergency. If you think you may be late making a payment, call the lender in advance and try to make special arrangements to lengthen payments. If you're already overextended, contact the lender and ask to work out a repayment plan, which may reduce the risk of a negative credit report, repossession of assets, or court action.

USE SECURED CREDIT

Borrow against your assets. If you own a home, consider borrowing against a portion of the equity through refinancing, a second mortgage, or a home equity line of credit. Generally, interest paid on home-related debt is tax-deductible. Remember, though, that these loans put your home at risk, so check all terms and conditions, such as balloon payments and title-search or appraisal fees. You also may be able to borrow on favorable terms against your equity in an employer pension plan, 401(k) plan, or whole life insurance policy. If you work for a nonprofit group, your 403(b) plan may not have a loan provision. If so, you should consider rolling over your money into an account that does provide loan privileges.

CONSIDER BANKRUPTCY

If you have no hope of repaying your debts, declaring bankruptcy is a last resort (see Chapter 13).

WINDFALLS

Congratulations! The prize van has just pulled into your driveway. Or you've scratched off the winning number on a lottery ticket. Or your long-lost great Aunt Sadie has left her fortune to you.

Think optimistically. Assume that at some point you will suddenly have a large unexpected financial windfall. Whether you win the lottery or inherit an estate, you'll definitely need advice and guidance to prevent the windfall from turning into a disaster.

Don't laugh . . . all too many lottery winners run through their money and end up in worse financial shape than they started in. Some lottery winners confess that they wish they had never won the money; for them, the headaches were worse than the benefits.

But you're not going to let a fortune go to waste! Right? You've got to learn how to protect your windfall, invest it for the future, and figure out what impact you want the money to make in your life.

WHAT TO DO WHEN YOU COME INTO MONEY

After the initial shock wears off, you'll want to make sure the money is really yours. Although it may be tempting to tell your boss what he or she can do with your job, you should exercise some self-control. Don't announce your good fortune to the immediate world, especially if a substantial sum of money is involved. Get a third party—a trusted friend or attorney—to verify your winnings or your inheritance. Once you know that you're really a "winner," you need to make some careful decisions.

1. **Get a professional adviser—a financial planner, accountant, or attorney.**
   Obviously, you want to consult someone whom you trust and whose advice you value. If you choose to consult a planner, you should talk to someone who is paid on a fee basis rather than commission. You want advice, not someone whose objective is to sell you financial products in order to make higher commissions.

2. **Don't disrupt your life or dramatically change your spending habits.** Don't alter your lifestyle, if you can help it. Give yourself a period of time, preferably six months, to adjust to your new situation. Don't make any major decisions about

what you should do with your windfall. After all, you don't come up to bat with the bases loaded too often, so take your time in the batter's box.

3. **Deposit payment checks immediately in a bank account, in your name only or in a joint account for you and your spouse.** Don't give anyone power of attorney with regards to your money. From these accounts, put your money into short-term certificates of deposit (CDs) at local banks. If you have more than $100,000, you will have to split the money at several banks since the Federal Deposit Insurance Corporation (FDIC) will insure your money up to only $100,000 per financial institution. An alternative is to deposit the funds in a money-market mutual fund, which is protected by the Securities Investors Protection Corporation (SIPC). SIPC protects $100,000 of cash and $400,000 of securities against default or liquidation by the holder of the account. In addition, most brokerages have insurance guaranteeing $9.5 million of protection, so your brokerage accounts are generally protected up to $10 million. Other places to put your cash are Treasury bills or a mutual fund that invests in Treasury bills. Again, always check to see whether your money is protected and what the limits of this protection are.

4. **Get tax advice immediately.** Mistakes made with any large amounts of money can be extremely expensive. If the money you receive is taxable, you should probably set aside a portion of the money to cover your taxes for the year. If the money is not taxable (as with certain gifts, inheritances, and life insurance proceeds), you probably should seek advice on how this increased wealth may change your future tax situation. Remember, you want to make decisions about the net proceeds from a windfall, not the gross amount. You want advice from an experienced tax professional who is familiar with your kind of situation. If you have any doubts about the advice, get a second opinion. When it comes to the IRS, you can't be too careful.

5. **Make financial arrangements for special situations.** For example, if the money is a judgment resulting from an accident claim and you or a child is disabled, establish specific arrangements with care providers so that you or your family member will be taken care of in the future. You will have to estimate the future cost of medical care. The worst thing you can do is spend a windfall that came from a disaster—leaving you or a loved one with no resources for the future.

6. **Redefine your financial goals.** Think about what changes in your life you would like to make. Get specific estimates of what it will cost to make these changes. Before you make investment decisions, think about where you want to be in the next year or two. Review the chapters in this book on buying a home or relocating. In short, evaluate your finances.

7. **Establish a new estate plan.** You don't want your heirs wrestling with probate or paying excessive estate and income taxes on your windfall. Talk with an attorney and find out exactly which of your assets are taxable. You may, for example, want to establish a trust for your insurance policies. You may also want to establish other trusts for your family members.

8. **Prepare a new net worth statement.** Include a schedule of your windfall assets, especially if you will be receiving money for a period of time.

9. **Determine how much income, if any, you will need from this windfall.** If you're still working and intend to continue working, you probably don't need income and can then invest entirely for growth.

10. **Look at your debt.** Pay down your debts, first paying off your nondeductible debts such as credit cards, student loans, and any others loans not secured by any property. Typically, debt costs you more in interest than you can earn on it with a safe investment. You can calculate how much a given debt is costing you:

   ▶ Nondeductible debt costs you the annual percentage rate (APR) of the loan. For example, if you have a 12 percent credit card, the outstanding balance costs you 12 percent.

   ▶ Deductible debt, such as home equity lines of credit, costs less *if you itemize*. See worksheet 15-1 to find the cost of this type of debt. Keep in mind that if you're in a new tax bracket, so you may not want to pay this down.

You should do an income tax projection of your tax liability for the year, taking into account capital gains if you've had any profitable investments. Then you can decide whether repaying a debt or selecting an investment is the best option. If you're now in the 31 percent or 36 percent tax bracket, your after-tax cost of a debt may be half of the interest rate.

Worksheet 15-1: Figuring the after-tax cost of debt

Assumptions: ❖ 9% home equity loan
            ❖ 28% federal tax bracket
            ❖ 7% state tax bracket

	Example	You
1. Your top federal bracket	.28	_____
2. 1 – Line 1 (1 – .28 = .72)	.72	_____
3. State and local tax bracket	.07	_____
4. Multiply Line 2 by Line 3 (.72 X .07 = .0504)	.0504	_____
5. Add Line 1 and Line 4 (.28 + .0504 = .3304)	.3304	_____
6. 1– Line 5 (1 – .3304 = .6696)	.6696	_____
7. Multiply deductible loan rate by Line 6 (.09 home equity loan X .6696 = .0603)	.0603	_____
8. Multiply Line 7 by 100 (100 x .0603 = 6.03)	6.03%	_____

This is the after-tax cost of your loan.

ACT PRUDENTLY WITH YOUR NEW FINANCES

Who wouldn't like to go into a store and make a purchase without looking at the price? Inevitably, a dramatic change in your income will allow you to make changes in your life-style. But you should aim to make financial decisions as carefully as you did before the windfall. Doing this is not going to be easy. You'll be hearing from every long-lost relative and friend and lots of people you don't even know, all offering advice or asking for money.

In fact, if you've already been working with a financial planner, you may have to switch planners if your current planner isn't experienced in handling assets over a certain value.

CAUTION Don't think you have to stay with your current planner because he or she helped you when your income was relatively modest. Suddenly, you're in a new federal, and probably state and local, tax bracket and you may need a new expert to help you as well.

Even a relatively modest sum of money—$10,000 or $20,000—may be a windfall for you. Obviously, this amount won't be enough to alter your lifestyle dramatically; that's why you should make some simple but smart decisions about the money. Usually, the best move you can make is to reduce your debt, especially your high-interest credit card balances. "Invest" the money by putting an additional $100 every month toward repaying your debts. Then, when you have repaid your debts, you will have money left to set aside for an investment.

If you don't have many debts, use the windfall to establish an emergency fund if you don't already have one. Put the money into an interest-bearing account or an account that provides you with free checks.

THE PITFALLS TO AVOID

This can be an exciting chance for you. After all, people rarely get a chance to make a fresh start with their finances. In addition to possibilities, however, a windfall also creates greater responsibilities. It's up to you to handle your new money wisely. It's all too easy to rely too much on an adviser or listen to your friends who urge you to relax and enjoy the money. The bigger the windfall, the more careful you must be. You should take your time making decisions and get as as much advice as you need. But beware of the following:

▶ **Advisers who want control of your money.** It doesn't matter whether your lawyer or accountant is your brother-in-law or your best friend whom you've known since kindergarten. It's your money. *Don't give up control of your money, under any circumstances.* Even if you're feeling overwhelmed by the responsibility, never get into a position in which you make someone else responsible for your money.

▶ **Friends and relatives who ask or beg for money.** While it's tempting to help out friends and loan them money, it can become difficult to turn someone down. You should listen politely to your friends and then use a stalling tactic. Explain that your adviser has told you not to make any decisions until you've done some personal financial planning. If the person is persistent, asking for a particular sum of money, tell the person to call your adviser. Generally, this will stop most people looking for money.

▶ **Charitable requests or suggestions that you start your own charity.** If you genuinely want to contribute to a good cause, that's fine. However, if you're thinking of making a charitable donation in order to get a tax deduction, you will first have to do some tax planning. You will have to determine the benefit from a tax standpoint of making the contribution. Get tax advice before you make any substantial charity donations. Remember, too, that you should have all your own finances in order before giving to charities.

A windfall used properly can provide a great jumpstart to your financial planning. With the money, you may be able to buy a new home (see Chapter 6) or help pay for your kids' college education (see Chapter 7). Most importantly, remember that the money will impact your entire life. That's why it's imperative that you learn to be a good steward of your money—it will do what you want without talking back to you!

YOUR ACTION PLAN

Financial Disasters

▶ Get help from friends, family, professionals, social services.

▶ Start to replace lost income and savings.

▶ Liquidate assets if necessary.

▶ Negotiate with creditors.

▶ Cut your spending.

▶ Borrow against assets.

▶ File for bankruptcy if you've exhausted all other options.

Windfall

▶ Get an advisor.

▶ Maintain your current lifestyle.

▶ Put the money in an insured bank account or other insured investment.

▶ Consult a tax expert to make plans for your new tax bracket.

▶ Review your estate plans and make changes, such as establishing trusts.

▶ Update your insurance policies.

▶ Pay down debts, depending on their after-tax cost.

▶ Develop an investment strategy.

GLOSSARY

A. M. Best Company   A company that publishes a rating of insurance companies, assessing financial strength and ability to pay claims.

Accelerated Cost Recovery System (ACRS)   Method of cost recovery that provides for a higher charge in the earlier years and a declining periodic charge thereafter.

Accelerated Depreciation   Writing off an asset so that the cost is recovered in the early years of the asset's life.

Accrued Interest   Interest that has been earned on a bond since the last interest payment was made.

Accumulated Dividend   Dividends paid each year by an insurance company and left with the company to earn interest.

Active Participation   If you make the decisions regarding the management of a rental property you own, you are said to actively manage it.

Adjusted Gross Estate   An individual's gross estate less allowable deductions for mortgages, bank loans, etc.

Adjusted Gross Income (AGI)   All income subject to tax, less certain deductions permitted by law, such as in unreimbursed business expenses, alimony, contributions to IRAs, etc. It is used as a basis for determining the amounts deductible for miscellaneous deductions, casualty or theft losses, and medical expenses.

Administrator   A person appointed by the court to supervise the handling of an individual's estate in the event no will has been executed.

Alternative Minimum Tax   The additional tax that applies to individuals, trusts, and estates with certain tax preference items.

Annuitant   The person who is covered by an annuity and who will normally receive the benefits of the annuity.

Annuity   A contract that provides a series of payments for life or a specified period.

Assignee   The person to whom the rights under a policy are transferred by means of an assignment.

Assignment   A transfer of the ownership rights of an insurance contract. In order to be valid when the claim is paid, any assignment must be filed in writing with the insurance company.

Assignor   The person who transfers rights under an insurance policy.

Automatic Premium Load   A provision that allows the company to use the policy's cash value automatically to meet premium payments.

Basis   For tax purposes, the value used as the starting point in figuring gain or loss, depreciation, or depletion.

Bearer Bond   A bond that does not have the owner's name registered with the issuer and that is payable to the owner.

Beneficiary   The party who receives proceeds under an insurance policy, trust, or will.

Callable Bond   A bond that may be redeemed under stated conditions by the issuing municipality or corporation prior to maturity. The term also applies to preferred shares that may be redeemed by the issuing municipality or corporation.

Capital Asset   This term refers to any property, whether or not it is connected with a trade or business. A taxpayer's household furnishings, personal residence, and automobile are capital assets. Although gain on the sale of this kind of property is treated as capital gain, no loss is recognized for income tax purposes unless the property was held for the production of income.

Capital Gain or Loss   Gains and losses resulting from the sale of capital assets. They are classified as long-term or short-term, depending on the length of the time the asset was held.

Cash Value   The "savings element" in a permanent life insurance policy, which is the legal property of the policy owner.

Certificate of Deposit   A time deposit with a specified maturity date.

Community Property   Property owned in "common" (both persons owning it all) by a husband and wife that is acquired while they are residing in a community property state.

Concealment   The willful withholding of information that might materially affect insurability.

Cost Recovery   Systematic method of spreading the cost of an asset over its expected useful life.

Coupon Bond   A bond with interest coupons attached. Coupons are clipped as they come due and are presented to the issuer for payment.

Coupon Rate   The specified interest rate or amount of interest paid on a bond.

Death Benefit   The proceeds of the policy that will be paid after the death of the insured.

Debenture   A promissory note backed by the general credit of a company. Debentures are usually not backed by a mortgage or lien on any specific property.

Decedent   A person who has recently died.

Decreasing Term Insurance   Term insurance coverage that decreases over the period of the contract, until the policy expires (for example, mortgage redemption insurance).

Dependent   For 1995, a person is a dependent if the following conditions are met:

1. His or her gross income is less than $2,500. However, if the individual is a child of the taxpayer and is either a student or under 19, the $2,500 gross income rule is waived.

2. Taxpayer supplies over one-half of the support of the dependent; and

3. The dependent is either a close relative of the taxpayer or has his principal place of abode with the taxpayer.

Depreciation   The allocation of the cost of a fixed asset over a period of time.

Disclaimer   The refusal, rejection, or renunciation of a claim, power, or property.

Discount Bond   A bond that is sold for less than its face amount of principal.

Diversification   Accumulation of different securities to reduce the risk of loss.

Dividend Reinvestment Plan   A plan that permits stockholders to have cash dividends reinvested in the corporation's stock.

Dividend   Return of premium, on a participating policy.

Domicile   An individual's permanent home.

Endowment Insurance   A permanent life insurance policy that offers death protection for a specified period of time. If the insured lives past the period specified, the contract pays the face amount of the policy to the insured.

Estate Tax Balance Sheet   A summary of all property that an individual has an interest in at his or her death (our term for the Federal Estate Tax Return, *Form 706*).

Estate Tax   A tax paid on property that is owned at an individual's death. The tax is paid on the property as a whole before it is distributed.

Executor   An individual appointed through a will to administer and distribute property upon the testator's death.

Face Amount   The amount indicated on the face of the policy that will be paid at death or when the policy matures.

Fiduciary   An individual who manages property or acts for another individual and is placed in a position of trust.

Gift Tax   A tax imposed on the transfer of money or property through gifts made by an individual.

Gift   Any willing transfer of money or property without payment. There must be a showing of "detached and disinterested generosity."

Grantor   A person who makes a gift.

Gross Death Benefit   The face value of an insurance policy before the reduction for policy loans.

Gross Income   All income received by the taxpayer from any source, unless exempt from tax. It includes gains, salaries, bonuses, fees, profits, interest, rents, dividends, etc.

Guaranteed Insurability Rider   A rider that permits the policyholder to purchase additional amounts of insurance at stated intervals without proof of insurability.

Guaranteed Renewable   A contract provision that permits the insured to keep a policy in force. With the exception of premium increases, no changes in the contract may be made.

Guardian   An individual who has the legal right and duty to take care of another person or his or her property because that person cannot legally take care of himself or herself.

Incompetency   Refers to individuals who lack the ability or legal right to manage their own affairs.

Incontestable Clause   A provision that states that after a policy has been in force for a certain length of time (generally two years), the insurer cannot deny a claim unless the premium has not been paid.

Indemnify   To compensate or reimburse an individual for possible losses of a particular type.

Inflation Guard Endorsement   A provision in a homeowner's contract that allows for periodic increases in the amount of coverage.

Inheritance Tax   A tax on money or property that an individual inherits.

Insurability   The condition of the proposed insured—age, occupation, health, and so on—that makes him or her an acceptable risk.

Intangible Drilling Costs   An operator's expense for wages, fuel, repairs, hauling, and supplies that are incurred in the preparation and drilling of wells for the production of oil and gas.

Inter Vivos   Between the living; from one living person to another.

Intestate   Dying without having made a valid will.

Investment Company   A company or trust that uses its capital to invest in other companies. There are two types of investment companies: closed-end and open-end.

Irrevocable Trust   A trust that cannot be changed, altered, or revoked.

Itemized Deductions   Deductions from adjusted gross income for various taxes, interest paid, charitable contributions, and miscellaneous. If taxpayer's deductions are less than the standard deductions, taxpayer uses the standard deductions; otherwise, taxpayer uses total itemized deductions.

Joint Life and Survivorship Annuity   Periodic payments that are made to two beneficiaries. At the death of the first beneficiary, the survivor will continue to receive payments.

Joint Ownership   Ownership of property by more than one person.

Joint Tenancy   A form of joint ownership in which, if one of the owners dies, his or her interest in the property automatically passes to the other joint owner(s).

Keogh Plan   Retirement plan available for self-employed individuals.

Legal Age   The age at which an individual becomes old enough to make a contract, generally 18 to 21 in most states.

Legatee   A person who inherits property by will.

Life Estate   A property right, the duration of which is limited to the life of a person holding it.

Load Fund   A mutual fund that charges a sales fee for buying or selling shares.

Loan Value   The amount of cash value that may be borrowed by the insured.

Margin   The amount paid by the customer when the broker's credit is used to purchase securities.

Marital Deduction   A deduction allowed under certain conditions for federal estate tax purposes, for property left to a surviving spouse.

Maturity Date   The date on which a loan or bond comes due and is to be paid off.

Money Manager   A professional who manages investments according to clients' investment objective.

Mutual Company   An insurance company owned by the policyholders.

Net Asset Value   The value of a mutual fund share.

Net Death Benefit   The insurance proceeds payable after adding accumulated dividends and deducting policy loans.

Net Payment Index   A method of comparing the cost of term life insurance policies, developed and formalized by the National Association of Insurance Commissioners.

No-Load Fund   A mutual fund that does not charge a sales fee for buying or selling shares.

Nonprobate Property   Property that passes without reference to a will.

Paid-up Additions   A dividend option that permits the policyholder to use dividends to purchase additional life insurance.

Policyowner   The person who may exercise the rights and privileges in the policy contract. The policyowner may or may not be the insured.

Power of Appointment   A part of an individual's will, deed or trust document that gives someone the right to decide who will receive property or how the property will be used.

Power of Attorney   A document that authorizes an individual to act on another individual's behalf.

Preference Items   Certain income and deduction items that receive preferential tax treatment, for example, accelerated depreciation. Some of these preferred items are subject to the alternative minimum tax in addition to regular income tax.

Preferred Stock   A class of stock with a claim to the company's earnings before payment to common stockholders can be made.

Principal   The face value of the debt.

Probate   1) The process of proving that a will is genuine; 2) Distributing property that passes according to the terms of a will.

Proxy   Written authorization given by a shareholder to represent and vote his or her shares at a shareholder meeting.

Recapture   Additions to income for deductions or credits against tax taken in prior years.

Registered Bond   A bond whose ownership is recorded with the bank that distributes the interest and principal payments.

Return   An investor's profits, whether through interest, dividends, or capital appreciation.

Revocable   Susceptible to being altered, modified, or canceled.

Rider   A form attached to an insurance contract that modifies the benefits and conditions of coverage.

Self-Proving Will   A will requiring witnesses to sign an affidavit indicating that you were of sound mind and so on, at the time the will was signed and witnessed.

Stock Company   An insurance company owned by the stockholders.

Straight-Line Method of Cost Recovery   Provides equal periodic changes to expenses over the estimated life of an asset.

Tenancy by the Entirety   A form of joint ownership between husband and wife that includes a right of survivorship; at the death of the husband or wife, his or her interest in the property will pass to the surviving spouse.

Tenancy-in-Common   A form of joint ownership between two or more individuals that does not include a survivorship element; at the death of one of the owners, his or her interest in the property may be designated to a future owner.

Term Insurance   Life insurance that does not have cash accumulation and provides pure insurance protection for a specified period of time.

Testamentary   Having to do with a will.

Testator   A person who makes a will.

Treasury Bills   Short-term debt issued by the U.S. government.

Treasury Bond   Long-term debt issued by the U.S. government.

Treasury Note   Medium-term debt issued by the U.S. government.

Trust   A property interest held by one person for the benefit of another.

Trustee   A person who holds money or property for the benefit of another.

Unified Credit   A credit used to offset estate and/or gift taxes up to stated limits. The amount of the credit for 1987 and thereafter is equal to $192,800. This will offset $600,000 of estate and/or gift taxes.

W-4 Form   Employee's withholding allowance certificate. Form filed with employer so that employer can withhold federal income tax from pay. *Form W-4* remains in effect until employee changes it. By correctly completing this form, employee can match the amount of tax withheld from wages to his or her tax liability.

Waiver of Premium   A rider which provides that, if the insured becomes totally disabled, premiums on the life insurance policy will be waived and the policy will remain in force.

Whole-Life Insurance   A level amount of permanent life insurance, with increasing cash values; premiums are paid for the entire life of the insured.

Will   A legal document in which a person declares how his or her possessions will pass after his or her death.

Wrap Account   An account with an all-inclusive annual fee paid to the brokerage firm. The fee includes the services of a money manager and all the trading costs associated with the account.

Yield to Call   The rate of return on a bond from the date acquired to its call date.

Yield to Maturity   The rate of return on a bond from the date acquired to its maturity date.

Yield   The interest rate paid to investors.

Zero Coupon Bond   A bond that is sold at a deep discount to its face value and does not pay interest. It can be redeemed for its face value at maturity.

APPENDICES

APPENDIX 1

Will You Have Enough to Retire?

Will you be financially independent at retirement? Everyone looks forward to retirement with their health intact and the financial resources to enjoy their post-employment years. Retirement *must* be planned for! Planning early for retirement will improve your chances of attaining your retirement goals. To determine if and when you can afford to retire, there are two essential elements — *how much* you need and *when* you will need it.

Retirement planning involves an analysis of the money that will be available to you from *all* sources when you retire. According to mortality studies, most people will need retirement income for *more than* 15 years — often to age 85. Most of us understand that Social Security was not meant to replace our salary. That is also true of our pensions.

You should think of retirement income as a three-legged stool. Your retirement income should come from your company benefit plans, Social Security and your own savings and investments. Just as the three-legged stool will not stand unless it has all three legs intact, your retirement income will not be as secure unless you have *all three* components. Accordingly, you must start planning for your financial security today.

At retirement, you will have income available from several sources. These may include some or all of the following:

- ❖ Pension/Retirement Plan
- ❖ Savings/Thrift Plan
- ❖ Social Security
- ❖ Other Investments (including IRAs)

Follow the next seven steps and use *Your Retirement Worksheet* to help determine how much income will be available from each of these sources to replace *your* salary at some given date in the future. Remember, retirement planning is not an *exact* science and the *Worksheet* reflects many assumptions. Gather together the following documents to help you through the *Worksheet*:

❖ Your most recent company benefits statements

❖ Your most recent investment account statements

Follow Chris Down the Road to His Retirement

The *Worksheet* includes an example of one employee planning for his retirement.

❖ Chris is 40 years old and earns $40,000 per year.

❖ He wants to retire in 15 years at age 55.

❖ He has $50,000 in his company Savings Plan and contributes 6% of his salary (his company also matches his contributions).

❖ Chris also has $10,000 in a mutual fund, earmarked for retirement, to which he adds $1,000 each year.

❖ Chris is married but his wife does not have any retirement benefits of her own.

Follow Chris through the process and then do your own projection. You should plan on updating these worksheets once every year. This way, as your needs and ability to save change, you will recognize these changes and be able to act upon them.

It's never too early. Get started now — *tomorrow may be too late!*

Retirement Worksheet Instructions

Step 1: *Estimate Your Retirement Living Expenses*

Use the **Worksheet** to estimate the income you will need during retirement. This method uses the retirement income "rule of thumb." You should assume that you must replace approximately 60% – 80% of your pre-retirement income during retirement.

Step 2: *Estimate Your Pension Plan Income*

Check your most recent benefits statement or ask your benefits representative for an estimate of your pension plan benefit at some date of your choice in the future. To plan adequately for retirement, you *must* account for the effects of inflation. Use the **Worksheet** and **Table A** (following the *Worksheet*) to reflect the effects of inflation on your pension.

Chris requested an estimate of his pension at age 55 — in 15 years. He can receive $1,000 per month for his lifetime beginning at age 55. Chris has also assumed he will live to age 85 and, therefore, be retired for 30 years. Chris assumed that inflation would average 4% per year and that he could earn 7% on his investments.

Step 3: *Estimate the Income from Your Savings Plan*

❖ Chris' current Savings Plan balance is $50,000.

❖ He also saves 6% of his $40,000 salary or $2,400 per year.

❖ Chris has a 50% company match on his 6% contribution or $1,200.

❖ A total of $3,600 ($2,400 + $1,200) is added to his account each year.

To account for inflation, we have assumed that Chris' salary will increase with inflation each year. Chris assumed he could earn a 3% "real" rate of return — said differently, he expects to earn 3% more than inflation. Using the **Worksheet** and **Tables B and C,** see how much your savings plan will contribute to your three-legged stool.

Step 4: Estimate Your Income from Social Security

To get the best estimate possible of your Social Security benefit payable at age 62:

❖ Call Social Security at 1-800-772-1213

❖ Request Form SSA-7004, *Request for Earnings and Benefit Estimate Statement*

❖ Complete the form, entering your desired age at retirement *(Hint: fill out more than one form to see the effect of different retirement dates)*

❖ Receive an estimate of your benefit in approximately six weeks

Use the **Retirement Worksheet** and **Tables D and E** while you wait for your estimate from the Social Security Administration. **Table D** provides approximate monthly benefits for you and your eligible dependents once you reach age 65. These figures are based on the assumption that you have worked steadily, received pay raises at a rate equal to the U.S. average throughout your working career and retired at the normal retirement age — currently age 65. **Table E** will adjust the benefit if you are retiring before age 65.

Chris, while waiting for his estimate, used **Table D** and found that if he worked until age 65, he and his wife would collect $1,547 each month when they turn age 65. Although his salary is $40,000, he used the $36,000 column for the estimate. Since Chris is planning to retire at age 55, he will not receive as much as the chart indicates. Also, Chris must remember, since he is retiring at age 55, he will not receive *any* Social Security for seven years until age 62.

Step 5: Estimate Income from Your Outside Investments

❖ Chris has $10,000 in a mutual fund earmarked for retirement.

❖ He adds $1,000 per year to this account.

Chris assumed he could earn a 3% "real" rate of return. Use the **Worksheet** and **Tables B and C** to see how much your outside investments will contribute to that three-legged stool.

Step 6: Will Your Income Satisfy Your Retirement Needs?

Use this worksheet to put together all the pieces. If you have more income than expenses, then the future looks bright. If your income falls short, don't despair. You have the power to *change* the outcome!

Step 7: How to Satisfy Your Deficit

If you found that you have a deficit in *Step 6*, you will not be able to meet your retirement goals, if you continue on your current path. You *can* change the outcome using these four alternatives:

❖ Save more.

❖ Work longer and retire later.

❖ Spend less during retirement.

❖ Invest differently — to earn a higher rate of return.

You may want to go through the *Steps 1 – 6* again to play what if? What if I worked longer? What if I spend less? What if my investments earn a higher rate of return? Perhaps, some of these changes will allow you to meet your retirement goals. You may find that your only alternative — or at least the one that will make the greatest impact — is to save more. To determine how *much* more you will have to save to reach your goals, use *Worksheet* and *Tables F, G and H.*

Your Retirement Worksheet

Step 1: Use the Retirement Income "Rule of Thumb"

		Chris	You
Line 1:	Current Annual Salary	$40,000	$ _____
Line 2:	Rule of Thumb Percentage (choose between 60 – 80%)	x 75 %	x _____ %
Line 3:	Retirement Needs (multiply *Line 1* by *Line 2* and round to the nearest $100)	$30,000	$ _____

Step 2: Calculating Your Spendable Pension

		Chris	You
Line 1:	Annual Pension/Retirement Estimate:	$12,000	$ _____
Line 2:	Inflation/Earnings Factor from *Table A*	x 65 %	x _____ %
Line 3:	Annual Spendable Pension/Retirement (multiply *Line 1* by *Line 2* and round to the nearest $100	$7,800	$ _____

Step 3: Calculating Annual Income from Your Savings Plan

		Chris	You
Line 1:	Current Savings Plan Balance:	$50,000	$ _____
Line 2:	Income Factor from *Table B*	x 0.08	x _____
Line 3:	Income from Current Savings Plan Balance (multiply *Line 1* by *Line 2*)	$4,000	$ _____
Line 4:	Future Savings Including Company Match	$3,600	$ _____
Line 5:	Income Factor from *Table C*	x 0.95	x _____
Line 6:	Income from Future Savings (multiply *Line 4* by *Line 5*)	$3,420	$ _____
Line 7:	Annual Savings Plan Income (add *Line 3* to *Line 6* and round to the nearest $100)	$7,400	$ _____

Step 4: Calculating Income from Your Social Security Benefit

		Chris	You
Line 1:	Annual Social Security Benefit	$20,868	$ _____
Line 2:	Early Retirement Adjustment Factor from *Table E*	x 36 %	_____ %
Line 3:	Income from Social Security (multiply *Line 1* by *Line 2* and round to the nearest $100)	$7,500	$ _____

Step 5: Calculating Annual Income from Your Outside Investments

		Chris	You
Line 1:	Current Outside Investment Balance:	$10,000	$ _____
Line 2:	Income Factor from *Table B*	x .08	x _____
Line 3:	Income from Current Outside Investments Balance (multiply *Line 1* by *Line 2*)	$ 800	$ _____
Line 4:	Future Annual Savings	$1,000	$ _____
Line 5:	Income Factor from *Table C*	x 0.95	x _____
Line 6:	Income from Future Savings (multiply *Line 4* by *Line 5*)	$ 950	$ _____
Line 7:	Annual Outside Investments Income (add *Line 3* to *Line 6* and round to the nearest $100)	$1,800	$ _____

Step 6: Calculating Annual Surplus or Deficit

		Chris	You
	Expenses:		
Line 1:	Total from *Step 1*	$30,000	$ _____
	Income:		
Line 2:	Pension/Retirement Plan from *Step 2*	$ 7,800	$ _____
Line 3:	Income from Savings Plan from *Step 3*	7,400	_____
Line 4:	Social Security from *Step 4*	6,700	_____
Line 5:	Income from Outside Investments from *Step 5*	1,800	_____
Line 6:	Total Income (Add *Lines 2 – 5* and round to the nearest $100)	$23,700	$ _____
	Annual Surplus/Deficit:		
Line 7:	Subtract *Line 6* from *Line 1*, if positive, you have a deficit and should complete *Step 7* If negative, you have a surplus — congratulations!	$6,300	$ _____

Step 7: Calculating the Required Additional Savings

		Chris	You
Line 1:	Annual Deficit from *Step 6*:	$ 6,300	$ _____
Line 2:	Annuity Factor from *Table F*	x 19.60	x _____
Line 3:	Multiply *Line 1* by *Line 2*	$123,480	_____
Line 4:	Annual Savings Factor from *Table G*	x 0.054	x _____
Line 5:	Required Annual Savings (multiply *Line 1* by *Line 2*)	$ 6,668	$ _____
Line 6:	Current Salary	$40,000	$ _____
Line 7:	Divide *Line 5* by *Line 6*	0.167	_____
Line 8:	Multiply *Line 7* by 100	x 100	x _____
Line 9:	Required Additional % of Annual Salary Savings (round to the nearest whole %)	17 %	_____ %
	OR		
Line 10:	Amount from *Line 3*	$123,480	$ _____
Line 11:	Fixed Dollar Savings Factor from *Table H*	x 0.097	x _____
Line 12:	Required Additional Annual Savings (Multiply *Line 10* by *Line 11* and round to the nearest $100)	$12,000	$ _____

Table A: What Percentage of Your Pension Can You Afford to Spend?

Duration of Retirement in Years	Inflation Rate/Earnings Rate			
	3%/7%	3%/8%	4%/7%	4%/8%
5	95%	95%	93%	93%
10	89%	89%	85%	85%
15	84%	84%	79%	79%
20	79%	80%	74%	74%
25	76%	77%	69%	70%
30	73%	74%	65%	66%
35	70%	72%	62%	64%
40	68%	70%	59%	61%

Table B: How Much Income Will Your Current Balance Generate?

Years to Retirement	Real Rate of Return			
	2%	3%	4%	5%
1	.05	.05	.06	.07
3	.05	.06	.07	.08
5	.05	.06	.07	.08
10	.05	.07	.09	.11
15	.06	.08	.10	.14
20	.07	.09	.13	.17
25	.07	.11	.15	.22
30	.08	.12	.19	.28
35	.09	.14	.23	.36
40	.10	.17	.28	.46

Note: The *Tables B and C*, "real" rates of return reflect your earning after taxes and inflation. Use the 2% column if the money is growing outside of a tax-sheltered account. Use 3% for investments in an IRA or company savings plan and a portion of your money is invested in stock funds. Use 4% if most of your money is invested in stocks. Use the 5% factors only if investments are tax-sheltered and invested almost entirely in stock funds, including small company and international stock.

The income above assumes interest and principal are distributed over a 30 year period of time.

Table C: How Much Income Will Your Future Contributions Generate?

Years to Retirement	Real Rate of Return			
	2%	3%	4%	5%
1	.04	.05	.06	.07
3	.14	.16	.18	.21
5	.23	.27	.31	.36
10	.49	.58	.69	.82
15	.77	.95	1.16	1.40
20	1.08	1.37	1.72	2.15
25	1.43	1.86	2.41	3.10
30	1.81	2.43	3.24	4.32
35	2.23	3.08	4.26	5.88
40	2.70	3.85	5.50	7.86

Table D: Monthly Social Security Benefits at Age 65

Your Age in 1996	Who Receives Benefits	Your Present Annual Earnings				
		$15,000	$24,000	$36,000	$48,000	$62,700
65	You	$622	$845	$1,100	$1,179	$1,248
	Spouse* or Child	311	422	550	589	624
64	You	637	865	1,128	1,213	1,289
	Spouse* or Child	318	432	564	606	644
63	You	626	850	1,110	1,197	1,277
	Spouse* or Child	313	425	555	598	638
62	You	626	850	1,111	1,203	1,287
	Spouse* or Child	313	425	555	601	643
61	You	627	851	1,114	1,210	1,299
	Spouse* or Child	313	425	557	605	649
55	You	604**	821**	1,077**	1,193	1,308**
	Spouse* or Child	298	406	532	589	646
50	You	594**	809**	1,057**	1,186**	1,323**
	Spouse or Child***	291	397	519	582	650
45	You	598**	815**	1,061**	1,197**	1,356**
	Spouse or Child***	293	400	521	587	666
40	You	587**	802**	1,040**	1,174**	1,338**
	Spouse or Child***	286	391	507	572	652
35	You	562**	768**	994**	1,122**	1,281**
	Spouse or Child***	270	369	477	539	616
30	You	566**	774**	997**	1,127**	1,287**
	Spouse or Child***	272	372	479	542	618

* Benefit at age 65 or at any age with eligible child in care who is under age 16 or disabled.

** These amounts are reduced for retirement at age 65 because the Normal Retirement Age (NRA) is higher for these persons; the reduction factors are different for the worker and the spouse.

***The amount shown is for the spouse at NRA or caring for an eligible child (under age 16 or disabled), or for the child; the benefit for a spouse younger than NRA who does not care for an eligible child would be reduced for early retirement.

Source: William M. Mercer Inc.

Table E: Adjustments to Social Security for Retirement Before Age 65

Age at Retirement	Factor
64	89%
63	83%
62	76%
61	54%
60	50%
59	47%
58	44%
57	41%
56	38%
55	36%

Table F: Annuity Factor

Years in Retirement	Real Rate of Return			
	2%	3%	4%	5%
20	16.35	14.88	13.59	12.46
25	19.52	17.41	15.62	14.09
30	22.40	19.60	17.29	15.37
35	25.00	21.49	18.66	16.37
40	27.36	23.11	19.79	17.16

Table G: Annual Savings Factor

Years to Retirement	Real Rate of Return			
	2%	3%	4%	5%
1	.495	.493	.490	.488
3	.327	.324	.320	.317
5	.192	.188	.185	.181
10	.091	.087	.083	.080
15	.058	.054	.050	.046
20	.041	.037	.034	.030
25	.031	.027	.024	.021
30	.025	.021	.018	.015
35	.020	.017	.014	.011
40	.017	.013	.011	.008

Table H: Fixed Dollar Savings Factor*

Years to Retirement	Rate of Return			
	2%	3%	4%	5%
1	.334	.329	.325	.320
3	.284	.279	.275	.270
5	.234	.229	.225	.220
10	.135	.129	.123	.118
15	.104	.097	.090	.083
20	.090	.082	.074	.066
25	.083	.073	.064	.056
30	.080	.068	.058	.049
35	.079	.065	.054	.044
40	.079	.064	.051	.040

*Assumes a 4% rate of inflation

Over ⟹

And finally, use this sheet to determine how much of your Social Security benefit is taxable.

Worksheet: Taxation of Social Security benefits in 1995

		Example	You
Line 1:	Enter your Social Security benefit (if you are married, use your combined benefits)	$12,000	_____
Line 2:	Enter 1/2 of Line 1	6,000	_____
Line 3:	Add up all components of AGI from your federal income tax return, but leave out your Social Security benefit	43,000	_____
Line 4:	Enter any tax-exempt interest (you'll find this figure also on your tax return)	2,000	_____
Line 5:	Add Lines 2, 3 and 4	51,000	_____

If the amount on Line 5 is less than $32,000 and you are married (or less than $25,000 and you are single), STOP! None of your Social Security benefit is taxable!

If the amount on Line 5 is greater than $32,000 and less than $44,000 and you are married (or greater than $25,000 and less than $34,000 if you are single) complete Lines 6 through 9 and then STOP. The figure on Line 9 is the taxable amount of your Social Security benefit.

If the amount on Line 5 is greater than $44,000 and you are married (or $34,000 if you are single) complete Lines 6 through 16. The figure on Line 16 is the taxable amount of your Social Security benefit.

		Example	You
Line 6:	**Social Security income tax Base Amount** ($32,000 if you are married; $25,000 if you are single)	32,000	_____
Line 7:	Subtract Line 6 from Line 5 ($51,000 - $32,000)	19,000	_____
Line 8:	Line 7 times .5	9,500	_____
Line 9:	Enter the lesser of Line 2 or Line 8.	6,000	_____
	If Line 5 is less than $44,000 and you are married ($34,000 if you are single), STOP. This Line 9 figure is the taxable amount of your Social Security benefit. If Line 5 is more than $44,000 and you are married (or $34,000 if you are single), complete Lines 10 through 16.		
Line 10:	**Social Security income tax Adjusted Base Amount** ($44,000 if married; $34,000 if single)	44,000	_____
Line 11:	Subtract Line 10 from Line 5 ($51,000 - $44,000)	7,000	_____
Line 12:	Multiply Line 11 times .85	5,950	_____
Line 13:	If married, enter $6,000; if single, enter $4,500	6,000	_____
Line 14:	Add Lines 12 and 13	11,950	_____
Line 15:	Multiply Line 1 times .85	10,200	_____
Line 16:	Enter the lesser of Lines 14 or 15. This is the taxable amount of your Social Security benefit.	10,200	_____

The Road Less Traveled ...

By completing this exercise, you are already far ahead of most of us. Unfortunately, most of us believe that we will be able to retire whenever we want. As you are now aware, it takes a great deal of planning. Make a commitment to revisit this exercise once each year — perhaps when you receive your annual benefits statement.

A couple of final notes to remember ...

We made a number of assumptions in these worksheets. For example, we assumed that you will live to age 85. That sounds conservative, but 5% of men live past age 90 and 5% of women live past age 94. Inflation — in Chris' example, was 4% — it may be more or it may be less. Chris' pension could change. Social Security will likely be cut back in some way. Tax laws will change. Chris could lose his job, become disabled or suffer a pay cut.

You get the idea. There are no guarantees! It is our judgment that you should always be investing 15% of your total gross pay for retirement. We think that represents a reasonable tradeoff between a comfortable retirement tomorrow and a happy life today.

APPENDIX 2

HOW TO USE THE *PERSONAL DOCUMENT LOCATOR*

Each adult should *individually* complete the questions on the next page. In addition, please complete all applicable items on the remaining pages. Please note that all items are alphabetized by category.

Leave blank any item that does not apply to you. Include the *location* and a brief *description* of those items that apply to you.

If you are married, this record should be kept in a secure location known to husband or wife. If you are not married, keep it in a location known to a close friend or relative.

You should complete the information now and update it each year.

Your name: _____ Date: _____

Note the following *important* information in the event of your death:

   1. I have written a personal letter to _____
      This letter is located _____

   2. I have a living will: ❑ Yes ❑ No
      The following people have copies of this will:
      name: _____ phone: ( ) _____
      name: _____ phone: ( ) _____

   3. I have made arrangements to donate the following organs
      for transplant:
      organ: _____ donate to: _____
      organ: _____ donate to: _____

      Please call _____ immediately in the event of death.

Spouse's Name: _____ Date: _____

Note the following *important* information in the event of your death:

   1. I have written a personal letter to _____
      This letter is located _____

   2. I have a living will: ❑ Yes ❑ No
      The following people have copies of this will:
      name: _____ phone: ( ) _____
      name: _____ phone: ( ) _____

   3. I have made arrangements to donate the following organs
      for transplant:
      organ: _____ donate to: _____
      organ: _____ donate to: _____

      Please call _____ immediately in the event of death.

	Description/value	**Location**	**Date of valuation**
Accounts payable			
Accounts receivable			
Appraisals			

Automobile documents

Location of document

Vehicle #1

Make/Model/Year: _____

❖ Registration _____

❖ Bill of sale _____

❖ Finance agreement/lease _____

Location of document

Vehicle #2

Make/Model/Year: _____

❖ Registration _____

❖ Bill of sale _____

❖ Finance agreement/lease _____

Location of document

Vehicle #3

Make/Model/Year: _____

❖ Registration _____

❖ Bill of sale _____

❖ Finance agreement/lease _____

Bank accounts	Bank name and address	Account number	Other signatures
Checking			
Savings			
Certificate of deposit			

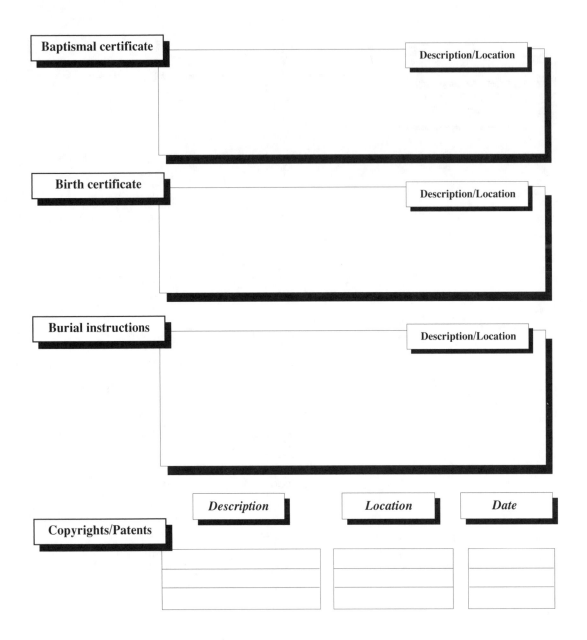

Baptismal certificate | Description/Location

Birth certificate | Description/Location

Burial instructions | Description/Location

Copyrights/Patents | *Description* | *Location* | *Date*

Deeds	Description	Location	Date
Residence(s)			
Mortgage(s)			
Leases			
Cemetery plot			

Diplomas	Description/Location

Divorce papers

Description/Location

	Description	Location	Date
Employment data			
Bonus plan			
Contract			
Deferred compensation			
Group insurance			
Pension plan			
Profit-sharing			
Stock options			
Other employee benefits			

	Description	Location	Date

Income tax returns

Federal

State

Other

Innoculation certificates

Description/Location

Insurance policies	Description	Location	Date
Life*			
Accident/Health			
Disability			
Property/Casualty			
Major medical			
Other			

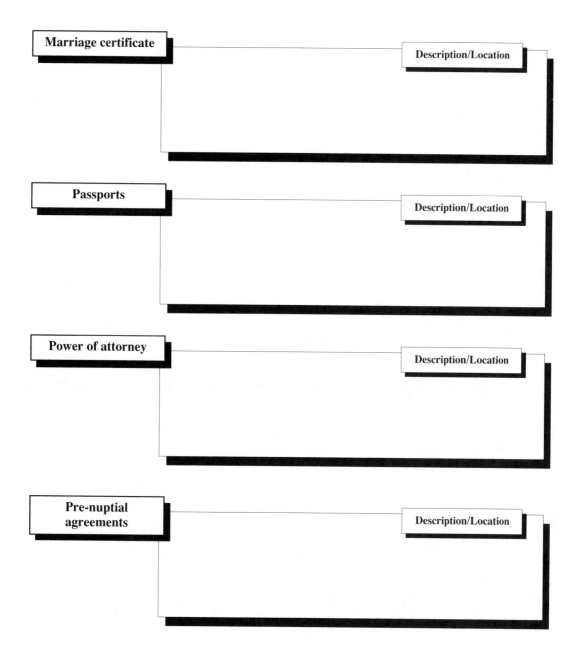

Safe deposit boxes

Primary box

❖ Location _____

❖ Box number _____

❖ Individuals with
access to box

name _____ phone: (   ) _____

name _____ phone: (   ) _____

name _____ phone: (   ) _____

❖ Location of keys _____

❖ Contents _____

_____

_____

_____

Secondary box

❖ Location _____

❖ Box number _____

❖ Individuals with
access to box

name _____ phone: (   ) _____

name _____ phone: (   ) _____

name _____ phone: (   ) _____

❖ Location of keys _____

❖ Contents _____

_____

_____

_____

Securities certificates*	Description	Location	Date
Stocks			
Bonds			
Money market funds			
Other			

*Attach schedule if necessary

Social security cards

Description/Location

Trust agreements

Location of document

Agreement #1

❖ Original _____

❖ Conformed copy _____

Agreement #2

❖ Original _____

❖ Conformed copy _____

U.S. savings bonds

Location of document

❖ List of bonds _____

❖ Bonds _____

Wills

Location of document

❖ Original _____

❖ Conformed copies _____

Miscellaneous documents

Document	Description	Location	Date

Personal contacts	Name/Address	Telephone
Financial consultant		
Attorney		
Primary bank		
Secondary bank		
S & L		
Trust officer		
Trustee		
Employee benefits officer		
Insurance agent		
Executor		
Income tax preparer		

The following individuals should be notified in the event of my death:

Name	Telephone

I belong to the following organizations which I would like notified in the event of my death:

Organization	Contact	Telephone

INDEX

▼